M000205901

Foreword

Tommy Casanova is arguably one of the greatest college football players of all time. As an all-around athlete for the LSU Bengal Tigers from 1969-1971, Casanova was a three-time All-American. Unable to play as a freshman due to NCAA rules, Casanova was perhaps precluded from becoming an unheard of, four-time college All-American. Casanova appeared on the cover of the September 13, 1971, edition of *Sports Illustrated*, where he was touted as "The Best Player in the Nation." A consummate leader on and off the field, Casanova went on to earn a medical degree and to serve in the Louisiana Legislature as a Senator. Today, Dr. Casanova maintains a medical practice in his hometown of Crowley, Louisiana.

May 29, 2000

I am not and do not pretend to be a football expert. I am not particularly good at preparing or analyzing a game plan – X's and O's were never my forté. My college football experience was instinct and reaction–if you stopped for a split second to think you got beat for a touchdown, missed a block, or dropped a pass. What looked exciting from the stands was really just mud, blood and sweat. It was line up each play and try to beat the guy across from you. It didn't matter if he was big or small, fast or slow, All-American or second team–my job was to beat him, and beat him soundly.

I did not care who he was, who he knew, how nice of a guy he was or what his mother thought of him. My teammates, each facing similar battles, were counting on me, just like I was counting on them. Individually and as a team we played for a school that we each had chosen, and that we each wanted to represent to the best of our abilities.

I think it is safe to say that my college football experience mirrors that of thousands of other young men so blessed. Young men who are better people today because of college football. For many, college football was the means to get an education, yet beyond the classroom an education of less formality was becoming part of our nature without us realizing it. While focusing on an upcoming opponent, we learned that preparation is important, and that it pays off; that practice and repetition make difficult things second nature; that discipline and self-sacrifice are essential components when working as a team; that eleven players of average ability working together can accomplish more than eleven "stars" playing without a common cause; that people do not demand that you always win, but that you always give your best; that you never stop to look at the size of the mountain, you just start climbing, then scratch and climb as hard as you can until time runs out and more often than not you get to the top.

That for me is college football. It would be interesting to know what the experience of other college players has been in regard to the value of their formal education symbolized by it's diploma versus the informal education the practice fields symbolized by arthritic joints. I know in my case the formal education opened many doors for me, but it's the informal education that helped me once inside.

Thomas H. Casanova III, M.D.
LSU Tigers 1969, 1970, 1971

Preface

The Southern way of life is as endearing as the people that live it. In the South, people's customs, their speech, and their very actions depict a unique existence; thereby distinctly distancing them from their isolated, Northern counterparts. However, there is perhaps no other defining trait of Southerners that best describes the way they approach and enjoy life than the manner in which they avidly ascribe to the Saturday fall phenomenon known as Southeastern Conference Football.

As a youngster, I can remember vividly my father's unbridled autumn anticipation for college football season to finally arrive, and the many games that followed on television—especially games involving the teams of the SEC. Even during my earliest years I was transfixed by the unflappable, intrepid images of Alabama's Paul "Bear" Bryant, clad in his checkered white and crimson fedora and matching coat. I can also remember with utmost clarity his unmitigated, commanding scowl that helped him realize more wins than any other coach in college football's colorful and proud history. I can further recall the visions of SEC stalwarts Bo Jackson of Auburn, and Herschel Walker of Georgia, rolling through hapless defenses like runaway trains. These fledgling impressions have remained with me through the years, like etchings in the stone tablet of my mind.

As I grew older, during my teenage years, I learned to love and long for the excitement of watching the purple and gold Fighting Tigers of L.S.U. pour exuberantly out of the tunnel in Death Valley in Baton Rouge. I found, after my first game in the old dugout arena, that Tiger football was Louisiana's Saturday night main event. It was infinitely intoxicating. The pure exhilaration that came from being inundated by the near-deafening, ubiquitous roar emanating from the lungs of a throng of eighty thousand, bourbon-frenzied, Mediterranean-blooded fans, was nothing less than awe-inspiring to a young Cajun from a small, southwestern Louisiana town. I was hooked immediately.

However, it was not until later, as a college boy at the Ole War Skule, that I would fully recognize and respect the many proud traditions that all the member institutions of the SEC so proudly embody. It was during my college days at LSU that I witnessed my first SEC road game and saw first-hand the indomitable spirit and fanfare of the other conference schools. After being weaned and brought up on these indelible football experiences, I came to fully realize after graduation, in my early adulthood, that college football is indeed the king of spectator sports, and that the Southeastern Conference, without question, is its most beloved, and storied domain.

This book is a dedication to the glory and accomplishment of the educators, coaches and athletes that have been associated with the Southeastern Conference–in its past and present form. Spawned by my fondness for the American game of football and ultimately by my undying love for the Southeastern Conference and all that it represents, I embarked on the task of writing about the total college football experience in the SEC. In doing so, I wanted to write a history of the conference itself, its earliest beginnings, and how the game and the league–much like our country, evolved and changed over time. I wanted to write about each school and all of their proud traditions–their mascots and alma maters; their fight songs; their greatest coaches and players; and even their stadiums. I also wanted to include information on what to do while you were visiting each college town–like where to eat and where one can enjoy an adult beverage, or two, if they are so inclined.

However, after compiling this short list of topics to be covered, I realized that there was still more to be written. Eventually, my experience as an overzealous college football fan forced me to recognize the one most-important element that I was so callously overlooking–the fans themselves–and their most honored and favored pastime–the "art" of tailgating.

Good food and football games in the South go together like white and rice. Whether it be barbecue in Birmingham, or a bowl of spicy Cajun gumbo in Baton Rouge, a feast is always present before game time in the fun-loving SEC. Some SEC fans might say that the pregame warmup is as big a part of the game day experience as the contest itself. I know this well having grown up in south Louisiana, where my family always enjoyed well-prepared food. Food is such an important part of my family's composition, that my younger brother Jeffrey is a bona fide Cajun chef. Inspired by my grandmother's love for bringing people together with good food, Jeff's culinary insight and penchant for producing mouth-watering delicacies on game day are legendary in Baton Rouge, where he can be found prior to kickoff at most home games cooking up his seasonal favorites.

To my delight, and for the benefit of your most untested taste buds, Jeff has graciously added to this tribute to the Southeastern Conference schools by penning twelve of his most treasured recipes. I hope you all will enjoy the recipes as much as our family and friends in Louisiana have over the years. Each of the recipes are easy to read and to follow and all are sure to please. Enjoy this book and use it to teach and pass on the many proud and interesting traditions of the Southeastern Conference. Having said that, I bid you adieu. "Bon appetit' et Laissez les bon temps roulez" SEC fans!

This second edition of the ultimate tome on Southeastern Conference football history and tradition contains a few subtle changes. The new volume builds on the copious feedback we received regarding the first edition related to where to go in each SEC college town. Furthermore, this new version contains dozens of new coach and player profiles as well as updated records and statistics through the end of the 2003 season. There are even new features on the SEC Championship Game and the Sugar Bowl, including a brand new authentic Cajun recipe for you devout tailgating aficionados.

~ *Chris Warner*
July, 2004

5

Table of Contents

Introduction

The Southeastern Conference:
A Tradition of Excellence

Legendary college football commentator Keith Jackson, in describing the SEC football experience, once aptly stated that "...there are few instances of alleged entertainment and relaxation that can match a college football game in stirring the deepest flames of partisanship and outright provincialism. And down South you can color that partisanship passionate!"

The irreplaceable "Voice of the Volunteers" on radio during the 1950's, George Mooney, once stated, "...No matter where I was broadcasting from, I found the fans in the South to be knowledgeable, fair–and yes, loud and frenzied. They are very proud of their rich football heritage. And they are very proud of their schools, their teams–and the deep pride that goes with being from the South." Dan Jenkins simply summed up the popularity of the game of football in the South with the following statement: "To Southerners, football is as essential as air conditioning."

Long before the advent of the lucrative, media-driven, professional sports franchises, and television, there was simply college football. Prior to the onslaught of professional football in America after World War II, college football was the main outdoor spectator sport in the United States for nearly a century. Given this, it is no wonder then why the largest football-playing venues in the country are college football stadiums.

7

Introduction

Back in the days prior to television, hundreds of thousands of college football fans across the South listened to their favorite SEC football teams via radio. In those days, each school had its very own announcer with his own distinctive voice that all of their fans could readily identify with. With the advent of television, college football has grown even larger in popularity. Furthermore, the competitive level of football played each fall in the SEC, and the millions of people who tune in each week to watch its marvelous display, are prime examples of this burgeoning American phenomenon.

The familiar ties of regional loyalty, along with the pomp and pageantry accompanying the game itself and all of its youthful trappings, have made the SEC football experience like no other in the United States. The beautiful, often coquettish Southern belles dressed in their gameday garb; the alma maters and the fight songs; the lively mascots; the rivalries; the reunion of lasting friendships; and the enjoyment of good southern cuisine all make SEC football a very special, and cherished ritual in the South. In fact, Southern Division I football is perhaps rivaled only by tailgating, and the beauty of it all is that the two pastimes go hand in hand in the tradition-rich Southeastern Conference.

Southeastern Conference football is the paragon of the college athletic experience. During its storied, seventy-one year existence, the SEC has evolved into the most impressive league of organized, intercollegiate gridiron competition in the history of the United States. No other Division I football-playing conference can boast of the many accolades and attendance records that the SEC currently holds. Furthermore, the Southeastern Conference has produced more All-American football players than any other conference.

Each of the Southeastern Conference schools, at some point during their existence, has enjoyed success on either a conference or national level. In fact, some of the schools have been so fortunate as to enjoy continued success at both levels. Alabama, Tennessee, Auburn, LSU, Ole Miss, Georgia and Florida have all

8

held, at least one time or another, their lofty place atop the national polls at the end of the football season. Altogether, the SEC has won a total of 15 national championships since the conference was formed in 1933.

Since the expansion of the Southeastern Conference and the beginning of the practice of playing a championship game in 1992, the SEC has four times won the national championship—Alabama in 1992, Florida in 1996, Tennessee in 1998 and LSU in 2003.

Since 1992 the SEC and the Big 12 have won more national championships than any other conference. The SEC has won 4 titles with three different schools while the Big 12 has equaled the mark with two different schools.

During the 2003 college bowl season the SEC and Atlantic Coast Conference each won five bowl games, earning the most bowl game victories among the conferences. The SEC won five of seven games while the ACC won five of six of their bowl games.

Louisiana State University's number one ranking in the USA Today/ESPN Coaches Poll led a slate of five SEC teams ranked in the final 2003 college football rankings. The Associated Press gave LSU a final ranking of 2nd. Georgia finished the season ranked 7th in the AP and 6th in the coaches' poll, while Ole Miss finished 14th in the coaches' poll and 13th in the AP poll. Tennessee finished the season ranked 16th in the coaches and 15th in the AP while Florida finished 25th in the coaches poll and 24th in the AP poll. Since the SEC expanded its membership in 1992 it has had 59 teams ranked in the final USA Today/ESPN Coaches and AP polls, an average of nearly five SEC teams per season.

SEC During the Last Decade (1994-2003)
(School, record, winning percentage, bowl games played)

1. Florida – 99-23-1, (.809), 10
2. Tennessee – 99-26, (.792), 10
3. Georgia – 84-37-1, (.693), 8
4. Auburn – 76-43-1, (.638), 7
5. LSU – 76-44-1, (.632), 7
6. Alabama – 75-47 (.615) 5
7. Ole Miss – 69-49 (.585) 6
8. Arkansas – 68-53 (.562) 7
9. Miss. State – 57-60 (.487) 4
10. South Carolina – 50-64-1 (.439) 3
11. Kentucky – 42-72 (.368) 2
12. Vanderbilt – 28-44 (.250) 0

SEC During the Last Five Years (1999-2003)
(School, record, winning percentage, bowl games played)

1. Georgia – 48-16, (.750), 5
2. Tennessee – 46-17, (.730), 5
3. Florida – 45-19 (.703), 5
4. LSU – 42-21 (.667), 4
5. Ole Miss – 39-22 (.639), 4
6. Auburn – 38-23 (.623), 4
7. Arkansas – 39-24 (.619), 5
8. Alabama – 34-27 (.557), 2
9. South Carolina – 27-32 (.458), 2
10. Miss. State – 26-33 (.441), 2
11. Kentucky – 21-37 (.362), 1
12. Vanderbilt – 14-43 (.246), 0

Since the beginning of divisional play in 1992, the Western Division has a slight 111-102 lead in head-to-head competition against the teams of the Eastern Division.

SOUTHEASTERN CONFERENCE
COLLEGE FOOTBALL NATIONAL CHAMPIONS
(Year, Team, Poll(s))

1951 – Tennessee, AP, UPI
1957 – Auburn, AP
1958 – LSU, AP, UPI
1960 – Ole Miss, FWAA
1961 – Alabama, AP, UPI
1964 – Alabama, AP, UPI
1965 – Alabama, AP, FWAA
1973 – Alabama, UPI
1978 – Alabama, AP, FWAA
1979 – Alabama, AP, UPI, FWAA
1980 – Georgia, AP, UPI, FWAA
1992 – Alabama, AP, UPI, USA Today, FWAA
1996 – Florida, AP, USA Today, FWAA
1998 – Tennessee, AP, USA Today, FWAA
2003 – LSU, USA Today/ESPN

Note: Arkansas was the 1964 FWAA National Champion as a member of the now-defunct Southwest Conference.

SOUTHEASTERN CONFERENCE TOPS IN NUMBER
OF ALL-TIME BOWL APPEARANCES, WINS

The schools making up the SEC have appeared in 331 bowls through the 2003-04 bowl season. The SEC has appeared in (331) and won (165) more bowl games than any other conference in the nation. Here is the breakdown of the various leading conferences and how they've performed in bowl games through the years.

(Conference, bowl games appeared, record, bowl winning percentage)
1. Southeastern ....331, (165-153-13), .518
2. Big Twelve ....281, (132-145-4), .477
3. Big Ten......................................205, (102-100-3), .505
4. PAC Ten ....199, (100-93-6), .518
5. Atlantic Coast ....185, (97-83-5), .538
6. Big East ....130, (63-66-1), .488

*During the 2003-2004 bowl season, the SEC went 5-2 in bowl play. Only one other conference, the ACC, won five games during the post-season. The ACC went 5-1 in bowl games during the 2003-2004 bowl season.

SEC COMPOSITE BOWL RECORD
(School, bowl record, bowl winning percentage)

Alabama ....29-19-3 (.598)
Arkansas ....11-20-3 (.368)
Auburn ....16-12-2 (.567)
Florida................................14-17 (.452)
Georgia...............................21-15-3 (.577)
Kentucky.............................5-5 (.500)
LSU ....17-17-1 (.500)
Ole Miss ....19-12 (.613)
Mississippi State ....6-6 (.500)
South Carolina ....3-8 (.273)
Tennessee..............................23-21 (.523)
Vanderbilt..............................1-1-1 (.500)

Overall.................................165-153-13 (.518)

SEC on a Recent Bowl Run

The SEC has claimed three straight Sugar Bowls. LSU defeated Illinois 47-34 in 2002, Georgia defeated Florida State 26-13 in 2003 and LSU defeated Oklahoma 21-14 in 2004 to claim the BCS National Championship. The SEC has won three consecutive Capital One Bowls with Tennessee defeating Michigan 45-17 in the 2002 game while Auburn beat Penn State 13-7 in the 2003 game. In 2004 Georgia won its first Capital One Bowl since 1993. In 2004 the SEC won the Cotton Bowl for the first time since the 2000 Cotton Bowl when Arkansas defeated Texas, 27-6. Ole Miss won its first Cotton Bowl since 1956. The SEC has won eight straight Independence Bowls with Arkansas winning its first in Shreveport in December, 2003. During the 2003-04 bowl season the SEC also won its first Music City Bowl since the bowl game's inception in 1998.

SEC Leads The Nation in NFL Players On Rosters

At the beginning of the 2003 NFL football season, the SEC led the country with 263 former players on professional rosters. The Big Ten was second with 207, followed by the PAC-10 with 191, the Big 12 with 187 and the Atlantic Coast Conference with 144. Furthermore, the SEC had 9 of its 12 teams rank in the Top 40 among all NCAA institutions with former players on NFL rosters. Florida led the SEC and the country (tied with Notre Dame) with 40 former players on NFL rosters.

2003 Opening Day NFL Rosters – SEC Players Only

Alabama (20)
Arkansas (9)
Auburn (25)

Florida (40)
Georgia (36)
Kentucky (10)
LSU (24)
Ole Miss (17)
Mississippi State (18)
South Carolina (18)
Tennessee (36)
Vanderbilt (10)

SEC Football Records

TOTAL OFFENSE

PLAYS

GAME:
1. 78- Whit Taylor, Vanderbilt vs. Georgia (20 rushes, 58 passes) 1982
2. 74- Tim Couch, Kentucky vs. LSU (8 rushes, 66 passes) 1997
   74- Dusty Bonner, Kentucky vs. Louisville (12 rushes, 62 passes) 1999

SEASON:
1. 635- Jared Lorenzen, Kentucky (76 rushes, 559 passes) 2000
2. 617- Tim Couch, Kentucky (64 rushes, 553 passees) 1998
3. 613- Tim Couch, Kentucky (66 rushes, 547 passes) 1997

CAREER:
1. 1,560- Eric Zeier, Georgia (158 rushes, 1,402 passes) 1991-94
2. 1,534- Peyton Manning, Tennessee (153 rushes, 1,381 passes) 1994-97
3. 1,481- Stan White, Auburn (250 rushes, 1,231 passes) 1990-93

YARDS GAINED

14

GAME:

1. 540- Archie Manning, Ole Miss vs. Alabama (104 rushing, 436 passing) 1969

    540- Rohan Davey, LSU vs. Alabama (12 rushing, 528 passing) 2001

3. 527- Eric Zeier, Georgia vs. Southern Miss (-17 rushing, 544 passing) 1993

SEASON:

1. 4,151- Tim Couch, Kentucky (-124 rushing, 4,275 passing) 1998
2. 3,904- Rex Grossman, Florida (8 rushing, 3,896 passing) 2001
3. 3,827- Jared Lorenzen, Kentucky (140 rushing, 3,687 passing) 2000

CAREER:

1. 11,020-Peyton Manning, Tennessee (-181 rushing, 11,201 passing) 1994-97
2. 10,841-Eric Zeier, Georgia (-312 rushing, 11,153 passing) 1991-94
3. 10,500-Danny Wuerffel, Florida (-375 rushing, 10,875 passing) 1993-96

YARDS PER GAME

SEASON:

1. 377.4- Tim Couch, Kentucky (-124 rush, 4,275 pass, 11 games) 1998
2. 354.2- Rex Grossman, Florida (8 rush, 3,896 pass, 11 games) 2001
3. 347.9- Jared Lorenzen, Kentucky (140 rush, 3,687 pass, 11 games) 2000

YARDS PER GAME

YARDS PER PLAY

GAME: (Min. 10 plays)
1. 21.4- Eagle Day, Ole Miss vs. Villanova (10 for 214) 1954
2. 19.9- Parker Hall, Ole Miss vs. Sewanee (10 for 199) 1938

GAME: *(Min. 20 plays)*
1. 14.18- Derrick Taite, Mississippi State vs. Tulane (33 for 468) 1994
2. 13.2- Eric Zeier, Georgia vs. Texas Tech (23 for 303) 1993
3. 13.0- Peyton Manning, Tennessee vs. Kentucky (39 for 508) 1997

GAME: *(Min. 40 plays)*
1. 11.9- Tim Couch, Kentucky vs.Louisville (42 for 498) 1998
2. 11.5- Jared Lorenzen, Kentucky vs. Vanderbilt (42 for 485) 2001
   11.5- Rohan Davey, LSU vs. Alabama (47 for 540) 2001

GAME: *(Min. 50 plays)*
1. 10.04- Steve Taneyhill, South Carolina vs. Miss. State (51 for 512) 1995
2. 9.15- Eric Zeier, Georgia vs. South Carolina (54 for 494) 1994
3. 8.63- Tim Couch, Kentucky vs. Vanderbilt (57 for 492) 1998

SEASON: *(Min. 300 plays)*
1. 9.10- Rex Grossman, Florida (429 for 3,904) 2001
2. 8.57- Pat Sullivan, Auburn (333 for 2,856) 1970
3. 8.42- Danny Wuerffel, Florida (371 for 3,125) 1995

CAREER: *(Min. 900 plays)*
1. 7.75- Danny Wuerffel, Florida (1,355 for 10,500) 1993-96
2. 7.18- Peyton Manning, Tennessee (1,534 for 11,020) 1994-97
3. 7.03- Pat Sullivan, Auburn (974 for 6,844) 1969-71

TOUCHDOWN RESPONSIBILITY

GAME:
1. 7- Tim Couch, Kentucky vs. Louisville (all passing) 1998
   7- Danny Wuerffel, Florida vs. Tennessee (1 rushing, 6 passing) 1995

16

7- Tim Couch, Kentucky vs. Indiana (all passing) 1997

7- Showboat Boykin, Ole Miss vs. Miss. State (all rushing) 1951

7- Terry Dean, Florida vs. New Mexico State (all passing) 1994

7- Tim Couch, Kentucky vs. Northeast Louisiana (1 rushing, 6 passing) 1997

7- Doug Johnson, Florida vs. Central Michigan (all passing) 1997

SEASON:

1. 41- Danny Wuerffel, Florida (2 rushing, 39 passing) 1996
2. 40- Tim Couch, Kentucky (3 rushing, 37 passing) 1997
3. 39- Peyton Manning, Tennessee (3 rushing, 36 passing) 1997

CAREER:

1. 122- Danny Wuerffel, Florida (8 rushing, 114 passing) 1993-96
2. 101- Peyton Manning, Tennessee (12 rushing, 89 passing) 1994-97
3. 82- Shane Matthews, Florida (7 rushing, 74 passing, 1 receiving) 1989-92

RUSHING

MOST RUSHES

GAME:

1. 47- Herschel Walker, Georgia vs. Florida (192 yards) 1981
2. 45- Madre Hill, Arkansas vs. Auburn (186 yards) 1995
3. 43- Charles Alexander, LSU vs. Wyoming (231 yards) 1977

SEASON:

1. 385- Herschel Walker, Georgia (1,891 yards) 1981
2. 335- Herschel Walker, Georgia (1,752 yards) 1982
3. 324- Rudi Johnson, Auburn (1,567 yards) 2000

CAREER:

1. 994-Herschel Walker, Georgia (5,259 yards) 1980-82
2. 882- Dalton Hilliard, LSU (4,050 yards) 1982-85
3. 873- Errict Rhett, Florida (4,163 yards) 1990-93

RUSHES PER GAME

SEASON:

1. 35.0- Herschel Walker, (385 in 11 games) 1981
2. 30.4- Herschel Walker, Georgia (335 in 11 games) 1982
3. 28.3- Charles Alexander, LSU (311 in 11 games) 1977

CAREER:

1. 30.1- Herschel Walker, Georgia (994 in 33 games) 1980-82
2 22.5- Emmitt Smith, Florida (700 in 31 games) 1987-89
3. 20.9- Kevin Faulk, LSU (856 in 41 games) 1995-98

YARDS GAINED

GAME:

1. 321- Frank Mordica, Vanderbilt vs. Air Force (22 rushes) 1978
2. 316- Emmitt Smith, Florida vs. New Mexico (31 rushes) 1989
3. 307- Curtis Kuykendall, Auburn vs. Miami (33 rushes) 1944

SEASON:

1. 1,891-Herschel Walker, Georgia (385 rushes) 1981
2. 1,786-Bo Jackson, Auburn (278 rushes) 1985
3. 1,752-Herschel Walker, Georgia (335 rushes) 1982

CAREER:

1. *5,259-Herschel Walker, Georgia (33 games) 1980-82
2. 4,557-Kevin Faulk, LSU (41 games) 1995-98
3. 4,303-Bo Jackson, Auburn (38 games) 1982-85

YARDS PER GAME

SEASON:

1. 171.9-Herschel Walker, Georgia (1,891 in 11 games) 1981
2. 162.4-Bo Jackson, Auburn (1,786 in 11 games) 1985
3. 159.3-Herschel Walker, Georgia (1,752 in 11 games) 1982

CAREER:

1. 159.4-Herschel Walker, Georgia (5,259 in 33 games) 1980-82
2. 126.7-Emmitt Smith, Florida (3,928 in 31 games) 1987-89

3. 113.2-Bo Jackson, Auburn (4,303 in 38 games) 1982-85
YARDS PER RUSH

GAME: *(Min. 40 rushes)*
1. 7.5- Moe Williams, Kentucky vs. South Carolina (299 on 40) 1995
2. 6.8- Moe Williams, Kentucky vs. Cincinnati (272 on 40) 1995
3. 6.5- Herschel Walker, Georgia vs. Ole Miss (265 on 41) 1981
SEASON: *(Min. 200 rushes)*
1. 6.8- Garrison Hearst, Georgia (1,547 on 228) 1992
2. 6.4- Bo Jackson, Auburn (1,786 on 278) 1985
3. 6.3- Johnny Dottley, Ole Miss (1,312 on 208) 1949
TOUCHDOWNS RUSHING

SEASON:
1. 19- Garrison Hearst, Georgia 1992
   19- Shaun Alexander, Alabama 1999
   19- LaBrandon Toefield, LSU 2001
CAREER:
1. 49- Herschel Walker, Georgia 1980-82
2. 46- Kevin Faulk, LSU 1995-98
3. 44- Dalton Hilliard, LSU 1982-85

ALL-PURPOSE YARDS

GAME:
1. 429- Moe Williams, Kentucky vs. South Carolina (299 rush, 57 rec., 73 KOR 1995
2. 376- Kevin Faulk, LSU vs. Houston (246 rush, 8 rec., 16 KOR, 106 PR) 1996
3. 338- Josh Reed, LSU vs. Alabama (293 rec., 5 PR, 40 KOR) 2001
SEASON:
1. 2,109- Kevin Faulk, LSU (1,279 rush, 287 rec., 265 PR, 278 KOR) 1998

2. 2,104- Kevin Faulk, LSU (1,282 rush, 134 rec., 375 PR, 313 KOR) 1996
3. 2,067- Herschel Walker, Georgia (1,891 rush, 84 rec., 92 KOR) 1981

SEASON AVERAGE:

1. 191.7- Kevin Faulk, LSU (1,279 rush, 287 rec., 265 PR, 278 KOR in 11 games) 1998
2. 191.3- Kevin Faulk, LSU (1,282 rush, 134 rec., 375 PR, 313 KOR in 11 games) 1996
3. 187.9- Herschel Walker, Georgia (1,891 rush, 84 rec., 92 KOR in 11 games) 1981

CAREER:

1. 6,833- Kevin Faulk, LSU (4,557 rush, 600 rec., 832 PR, 844 KOR) 1995-98
2. 5,749- Herschel Walker, Georgia (5,249 rush, 243 rec., 247 KOR) 1980-82
3. 5,596- James Brooks, Auburn (3,523 rush, 347 rec., 1,726 KOR) 1977-80

CAREER YARDS PER GAME AVERAGE:

1. 174.2- Herschel Walker, Georgia (5,749 yards in 33 games) 1980-82
2. 166.7- Kevin Faulk, LSU (6,833 yards in 41 games) 1995-98
3. 147.3- James Brooks, Auburn (5,596 yards in 38 games) 1977-80

This book is the story of the evolution of the organized game of football in the southeastern region of the United States from its earliest beginnings in the nineteenth century. Additionally, it is a tribute to the Southeastern Conference itself, in all of its past and present glory. Leading to the inevitable formation of the Southeastern Conference in 1933 and beyond, the text begins with a brief history of college football's inauspicious inception

north of the Mason-Dixon line. From there, the narrative chroni-
cles the gridiron pastime's expansion to the Southern region,
while simultaneously paying tribute to the many cultural and
human interests that propelled the college game during its formative years.

Close attention is payed to the manner in which the game
itself evolved and changed tumultuously over time, and how the
Southeastern Conference was conceived in an effort to bring
order, fairness and continuity to the game. The unique histories
and traditions of each of the member schools of the Southeastern
Conference are included, along with other interesting, lesser-
known campus-related facts and trivia. Additionally, twelve
authentic Cajun tailgating recipes can be found inside–one for
each of the conference's member institutions. The information
contained within these pages should serve as a practical guide
and reference source for the most avid Southeastern Conference
Football fan as well as a conversation piece and keepsake for the
more sedentary enthusiast.

Most importantly, this book is dedicated to all the Southern
people who live for Saturdays in the fall, for those individuals who
plan their business and personal engagements around their
favorite team's football schedule; for those who always experience
a rise in their body temperature when they enter the stadium; for
those who shed a tear during the singing of their alma mater; and
especially, for those who know all the words to their school's fight
song. It is for the people who wake up early on Sunday morning
after a win so they can read each and every one of the sports
columns about the game they witnessed the day before. It is for
all those who enjoy good company and good food in the parking lot
before the game, as much, and if not more, than the food and company at a fancy restaurant. These things that we hold dear–all

true SEC fans know and love, and look forward to each autumn. It's that time of year when the heated summer temperatures begin to fade and yield to colder days, when the leaves begin to change color, and when the youthful partisan spirit within us all crackles like the kindling of a well-planned winter fire.

tradition Tradition is defined as the
handing down of beliefs,
legends, and customs from
generation to generation.

~ University of Georgia
Football Media Guide

A Brief History of Football in the South

Origins of the Game of Football in America

In 1820, students at the College of New Jersey (now Princeton) participated in a soccer-like game, called ballown, in which they advanced the ball by punching it with their fists. Eastern colleges shortly thereafter began competing in the game, which resembled soccer more than it did the modern games of rugby or football.

Other early forms of the modern game of football, derived from the rules of rugby, were played by college students during the late 1860's. Eventually, representatives of Harvard, Yale, Columbia, Rutgers and Princeton Universities met at Springfield, Massachusetts, in 1876, and formed a new set of football rules and the Intercollegiate Football Association. The resulting combination of rugby and soccer became popular, and as time progressed, the new game of American football slowly evolved.

Prior to 1885, when the number of football players on the field was reduced to 11, the game was noticeably different. For instance, prior to the rule changes of 1885, there were 25 members on each side. Furthermore, the field of play was 300 feet by 500 feet and each goal post was 25 feet apart, connected by a crossbar ten feet above the ground. In this version of the game, the ball was moved primarily by "scrummaging" (both sides massed together around the ball shoulder to shoulder, with their heads down, trying to push

24

their opponents off the ball). During these earliest exhibitions, several thousand spectators were known to show up to watch the burgeoning spectacle.

Football – A Diversion from War

While the Ivy League's Rutgers and Princeton were playing the first collegiate football game in November of 1869, East Tennessee University, predecessor of the University of Tennessee, was still busy clearing the monument of debris left behind by the Southern and Northern armies–which had both utilized its campus buildings as hospitals during the war. Since East Tennessee had been somewhat sympathetic to the Union during the war it was rewarded among the first universities in the old confederacy to acquire land grant institution status (Morrill Act of 1862).

In the early 1890's in the South, most noteworthy colleges and universities were small, and many still were recovering from the vast devastation and disheartenment of the Civil War some twenty five years before. The epic conflict had deeply divided the two separate populations of North and South, and the South–humbled mightily in defeat, had lost most, if not all of its former wealth and status.

College football in America emerged amidst the painful aftermath of this most debilitating Civil War. Our young country, once divided by its differences, was arduously and miraculously reunited by a bloody, and costly ordeal. In many cases, the struggle had even split families. In fact, in some situations during the war it was common to find cousins and even brothers fighting against one another.

The South, subsequent to the capitulation of Lee's Army at Appomattox, was humiliated in defeat. War-torn and tattered, the region of Southern states was faced with the realization that its self-proclaimed sovereignty had been usurped by the Union and replaced with a bevy of corrupt, and sometimes black, carpetbagger governments.

The emergence of the game of football allowed these sectional differences between the North and South–ones that remained long after the war was over, to be momentarily forgotten, and in some cases reconciled, on the playing field. In light of this, football was one of the few ties that quickly and successfully bound otherwise highly divergent national institutions with a common experience and point of reference.

Through organized competition on the gridiron, young men–especially those of the South, were able to once again, albeit in a different manner, prove their worth and their manhood; thereby regaining the self-pride and sense of purpose that the war between the states had stripped them of. In the South, football emerged as a much-needed outlet of frustration and despair for both the players–and the spectators. Each game presented a definitive opportunity to achieve victory and vindication–two things Southerners greatly longed for in the wake of the Civil War. Furthermore, winning football games allowed Southern boys to erase many of the stinging transgressions they endured during the war and it provided much-needed hope for a successful, enjoyable life in the new South.

The Proliferation of the Game

The University of Kentucky was the first to play football in the South. Florida was the last. On April 9, 1880, football in the Southeast made its debut at Old Stoll Field on the University of Kentucky, then known as Kentucky A&M. Kentucky served as host to two visiting teams–Transylvania College and Centre College. Transylvania prevailed in that contest 13 3/4 to 0.

The Lexington Daily Transcript reported on the event:

"An estimated 500 ladies and gentlemen watched the game. The head-on collisions between the players were equal to the explosion of Spanish bulls crashing into one another."

Kentucky A&M was enthralled by the game of football. They formed their own squad and issued a challenge to Transylvania for a best-of-three series slated for November 1881. Kentucky won the first game, but dropped the second two. The *Knoxville Journal*, in 1891 reported, "The game of football is beginning to gain a foothold in Knoxville." By 1895, nine colleges from today's SEC were playing intercollegiate football.

As the number of colleges playing football spread like wildfire across the country and the South, new formations and plays were slowly introduced. In 1888, tackling below the waist was legalized. This particular rule change resulted in a significant increase in injuries. As other rule changes and new formations were added, the game became even more violent, and dangerous to the players. Player safety in the early years was further jeopardized due to the lack of adequate protective equipment such as helmets, shoulder pads, etc.–items that had not yet been conceived and introduced. During the early years, players were known to grow their hair long and bushy to cushion the fierce bodily contact that was experienced during play.

A game characterized by rough play from the onset, football appealed to the basic qualities of combat. Much like warfare, football effectively challenged each team to gain ground on the playing field through various and sundry methods. Brute force, daring sleight of hand, and tactical maneuvers are techniques that are still employed by each side today. Because of this, football early on was a game of fierce bodily contact. Undoubtedly, the game's enormous past and current spectator appeal remains linked to its thrilling exhibition of strength, skill, speed and deception.

In addition to its rugged nature, a distinctive element of the game of football, even in its earliest years, was the social aspect of the event that made it especially enjoyable. In the beginning, it was customary that each game was preceded by an extravagant luncheon and then followed by a wild game and fish supper, in which both teams participated together. This practice marked the beginning of the beloved modern American college football pastime of "tailgating."

Originally developed as a game to promote physical fitness and to foment competition between colleges after the Civil War, the gridiron found favor among players and spectators quickly. From the beginning, the game was a physical sport, played by only the toughest young men on college campuses. It was the large number of football-related injuries and fatalities that nearly resulted in the abolition of football and eventually led to the forming of the NCAA in 1905.

The early development of football in America occurred during the period of time subsequent to the Civil War known as the "Gilded Age," a term coined by famous American author Mark Twain. This era in American history is often referred to as America's joyous time of rebirth and renewal. During this time, an astounding post-Civil War industrial boom created unprecedented opportunities for wealth and prosperity for all young men in America. The emergence of football was simply another by-product of this innovative time that saw many technological advancements that changed the way Americans worked and lived. Football players during this era grew up in the world view of Horatio Alger. They believed that hard work and thrift would be rewarded with great success.

The SIAA

As football's popularity grew, so did the increasing need for an organizing body to help ensure fairness and consistency in the game. In 1894, William L. Dudley of Vanderbilt University promoted the establishment of the SIAA (Southern Intercollegiate Athletic Association) to "develop and purify" athletics among participating colleges and universities. The formation of the SIAA was welcomed by the schools since there was no existing organizing body at the time. Furthermore, the SIAA was the first major athletic conference in the United States.

The crowning achievement of the SIAA was that it successfully wrestled control of college athletics from the students, placing it instead firmly in the hands of the school's administrators. Prior to the inception of the SIAA, football was a game that was controlled by underclassmen on college campuses. As a result of this lack of organized leadership, the early game of football was rife with unfairness and inconsistencies.

At the time the SIAA was forming, a good many of the colleges in the South were already on their way to becoming million-dollar athletic programs. In an effort to combat this alarming trend, a constitution for the SIAA was drafted that drew heavily on the definition of "amateur" and "professional" athletes. Purification of the game of football was to be established through concise, delineated rules of player eligibility–an all-important aspect of the college game that has remained a fountain of controversy through the years. During the progressive years leading to World War I, the SIAA quickly grew into a large conference that included both big and small institutions.

A "professional athlete" was strictly defined by the governing body (SIAA) as "...somebody that used his athletic knowledge and skill for personal gain." The league's constitution clearly stated that professionals were strictly forbidden from participating in the sport. Additionally, football players in the SIAA were required to have been students at the college or university he represented. They had to register within 30 days of the beginning of school so as to prevent the proliferation of "ringers"–talented football players who would often earn money illegally by playing for several Southern football-playing schools. These "tramp athletes" were commonplace at the time among the south's football-playing institutions.

The hiring of star athletes by coaches, trainers and alumni of larger schools in search of a winning team was practiced due to the ease with which student athletes could transfer from one school to another without the loss of playing eligibility. Tramp athletes were known to have played for three or four schools simultaneously without ever attending classes. During the earliest years of football in the South it was even common to find coaches, such as LSU's A.P. Simmonds, a Yale graduate, in the school's lineup. During an 1894 game in Baton Rouge, Coach Simmonds scored the Bayou Bengals only touchdown in a lopsided 26-6 defeat. In fact, it was not uncommon to witness a player compete for as many as eight years for the same school. This blatant practice was rampant in the Southeastern Conference at the time.

Football's Brush With Death

By the turn of the century, in spite of the game's enormous popularity, concerns nevertheless materialized over the future of football in America. Brutality and foul play had so tainted the sport that President Theodore "Teddy" Roosevelt felt it necessary to prompt a serious national discussion about the debilitative nature of the game. Roosevelt's remarks were completely justified.

During the 1905 football season, the game's brutal nature, typified by mass formations such as the flying wedge and gang tackling, resulted in 18 fatalities and 159 serious injuries on college football playing fields; as was reported by the influential football mind of Yale's Amos Alonzo Stagg in the *Chicago Tribune* that same year. President Roosevelt issued a statement to the representatives of Harvard, Yale and Princeton that it was "...up to them to save the sport of football by removing every objectionable feature." Roosevelt added that "Brutality and foul play should reserve the same summary punishment given to a man who cheats at cards."

Brutality and related fatalities had become a major concern among the playing institutions. Prior to President Roosevelt's landmark statements in 1905, the game of football had become a barbaric, and often deadly, game. According to John F. Stegeman, just a few years earlier, in 1897, the football season had proved to be a particularly rough one for the University of Georgia. One of

Georgia's better-known football players, Vonalbade Gammon, was rendered unconscious by a blow he endured during the Bulldogs' gridiron contest with Virginia. Interest in the game was so great among spectators and players that young Vonalbade was quickly carried to the sideline and forgotten by his teammates, who were consumed with the task at hand–beating the Cavaliers. A doctor in the crowd who worried about Gammon's poor condition, ordered him taken to a nearby hospital in an ambulance drawn by a horse. The Samaritan doctor's actions were in vain that day, however, for Gammon later died from his injuries early the next day.

In light of this debacle, the Georgia legislature, via special session, voted to ban football within the state. However, before the bill ending football forever could be signed into law by the Governor, the mother of the fallen boy pleaded in a last-minute letter to Georgia's chief executive to refrain from doing so (signing the bill), saying that, "It would be inexpressibly sad, to have the cause he (Vonalbade) held so dear injured by his sacrifice. Grant me the right to request that my boy's death should not be used to defeat the most cherished object of his life." The Governor of Georgia, consequently, did not sign the bill into law.

Following the 1905 season that saw an alarming number of fatalities and crippling injuries, a number of schools banned football altogether. Fearing additional unnecessary deaths, the Universities of Columbia, Northwestern and Stanford all ceased playing until rule changes could be implemented that would make the game safer for its participants.

The NCAA

Compelled by Roosevelt's comments, Chancellor Henry M. McCracken of New York University called a conference of college representatives to the White House in Washington in 1905 to consider whether or not college football should be reformed, or abolished completely. This initial meeting of delegates from 13 college football playing schools in early December of 1905, spurred the creation of the organization that we today know as the NCAA. Rule changes were debated at the initial meeting and during a subsequent meeting on December 28th in New York City, the Intercollegiate Athletic Association of the United States was formed. The IAAUS was formally constituted in March of 1906, and took its current name, the NCAA, (National Collegiate Athletic Association) in 1910.

The formation of the NCAA marked the beginning of a series of rule changes that would forever alter and rescue the game of football in America. The major focus of the deliberations in Washington and New York centered on ending the typically rough, mass-formation plays, as well as the large amount of on-the-field fighting that regularly occurred.

The rule changes of 1906 eliminated the less civilized aspects of the early game, such as making punches to the face of the ball carrier–a common tackling practice, illegal. Other rule changes agreed upon by the fledgling NCAA related to legalizing the forward pass, establishing the current definition of an offensive line of scrimmage, making football look a lot less like rugby, and establishing the ten-yards-for-a-first-down rule.

The Forward Pass

"Fear not thy rivals, though for swiftness known;
Compare thy rivals' judgement and thy own;
It is not strength, but art, that obtains the prize,
And to be swift is less than to be wise.

~Homer, *The Iliad*

The biggest rule change in football occurred when the forward pass was legalized in 1906. Although it was not immediately used to its fullest extent, the pass would forever change the complexion of the game. The forward pass opened up the game of football from its former heavy-handed, smash-mouthed approach of deliberate brute force, making room for further innovation and change. Specifically, the pass allowed for a natural progression toward a more open, quick-striking offense that was much more appealing to both participant and spectator. Being oblong in shape, and possessing an inherent tendency to spiral when lofted, the football was obviously meant to be thrown.

The first team to use the forward pass was Wesleyen in a game against Yale in 1906. In spite of their innovative courage, Wesleyen still lost the game 21-0. However, St. Louis University's head coach Eddie Cochem used the forward pass extensively from 1906 to 1907. In 1907, St. Louis won all 11 of their games and led the Nation in scoring by using the forward pass. Although Cochem demonstrated that the forward pass was an effective tactic for moving the football, it was nevertheless not universally embraced by college football coaches until later. "Three yards and a cloud of dust" would continue to be the favored method of moving the football for offensive coaches, in spite of the rule change, since there were penalties involved with incomplete passes.

In the beginning, there were restrictions placed on the passing game. For example, if the ball touched the ground, the ball became the other team's at the point where the pass was thrown. Put more simply, an incomplete pass was a turnover. Also, a pass completed in the end zone was a touchback for the defending team, and furthermore, if the pass wasn't thrown within the hash marks, or if it hit an ineligible receiver, the ball went to the defending team.

Following the implementation of the forward pass and the slough of other rule changes, teams invented new offensive and defensive strategies. Tactics employing the pushing and pulling of the ball carrier, as well as the flying tackle evolved. In spite of the rule changes of 1906, the number of fatalities from football continued to rise, reaching a tragic total of 33 deaths in 1908. The NCAA, prompted by this unsettling news, again convened to make further rule changes. The subsequent rule changes of 1908 by the NCAA resulted in a much safer game of football.

The rule changes of 1908 stipulated that seven men were required on the offensive line of scrimmage, thereby limiting the team's ability to assemble in mass formation. Additionally, pulling and pushing the ball carrier, interlocked interference, crawling on the ground, and the "flying tackle" were subsequently barred from play. Additionally, in 1909, the NCAA ordered even more changes. New rules stated that the points awarded for a field goal be reduced from 4 points to 3 points; and during the following year, in 1910, the game was divided into four separate quarters instead of two halves.

During this progressive first decade of the twentieth century the game of football underwent significant changes. These major changes, culminating with the most prominent ones in 1912, forever changed the game of football and the manner in which it was played. This was so because the new rules promulgated during that year truly opened up the passing game for all football teams.

The sweeping rule changes in 1912 stated that teams had four downs to make a first down, and that the length of the field would be 100 yards, instead of the previous 110. Also, it was decided that the value of a touchdown would change from five to six points. Regarding the passing game, the new rules stipulated that all distance restrictions were to be removed from the game. Furthermore, a completed pass in the end zone thereafter was a touchdown and no longer a turnover like it had been before; and finally, an incomplete pass was a loss of down and no longer a turnover.

These rule changes allowing for a more progressive passing game were the most significant in bringing the college game of football to its current level of play. The forward pass was implemented primarily to remove the premium on weight and size and to develop greater possibility for speed, agility and cunning in the game of football. As a result of the innovation of the pass, injuries were reduced considerably, thereby creating a safer game for its participants.

Subsequent to the additional 1912 rule changes, in the South, football continued to grow in popularity among colleges and universities. However, as time passed and competition increased, the rules of eligibility did not fit the diverging circumstances of both groups, (big and small schools) resulting in a loss of the cohesion that had made the SIAA a former success. This turbulence ultimately led to the creation of the Southern Conference.

The Southern Conference

The Southern Conference was born on February 25, 1921 at a meeting in Atlanta, Georgia. After a short hiatus spawned by the critical years of World War I, fourteen of the larger institutions from the 30-member Southern Intercollegiate Athletic Association (SIAA) reorganized to form the Southern Conference. Those charter members included Alabama, Auburn, Clemson, Georgia, Georgia Tech, Kentucky, Maryland, Mississippi State, North Carolina, North Carolina State, Tennessee, Virginia, Virginia Tech and Washington & Lee. Athletic competition began in the fall of 1921. In 1922, seven more schools – Florida, Louisiana State, Mississippi, South Carolina, the University of the South, Tulane and Vanderbilt – joined the fold.

The stated purpose of the Southern Conference was "...to promote intercollegiate athletics in every form, and to keep them in proper bounds by making them incidental and not a principal feature of university life."

The Southern Conference was promoted by the larger state universities and land-grant colleges, who were pushing for a new sanctioning organization. Although the SIAA was successful in wrestling the reins of college football from the players to the faculty, it had failed miserably in its attempts to control and restrict player eligibility to constitutionally defined student athletes. Members of the newly formed Southern Conference wanted to increase control over player eligibility by disallowing freshmen from playing sports and by instituting a one-year residency rule and a migrant rule. Additionally, the leaders of the conference schools wanted to definitively establish succinct measures to confine athletic activity strictly to amateurs.

The Southern Conference was comprised of both larger state universities and land grant colleges, as well as smaller liberal arts colleges. Again, the diverging interests of the varying institutions within the conference caused dissension among the ranks. The larger schools wanted to push for a new sanctioning organization, and to preclude freshmen from playing. Additionally, the bigger schools wanted to institute a one-year residency rule and a migrant rule in order to increase eligibility requirements and to once and for all eliminate the proliferation of "ringers" and "tramp athletes."

The major downfall of the Southern Conference was that it covered such a large geographical area. The conference's 23 members inhabited nearly the entire southeastern area of the United States from Maryland to Louisiana. This massive territory made management and travel difficult for the conference leaders and school members. Furthermore, many of the schools held varying educational objectives. Some of the smaller, private liberal arts colleges were at a serious disadvantage from a resources standpoint, since the larger state universities and land grant institutions possessed more funding and support in their respective areas.

As a result of these inherent differences, regulations regarding the size of athletic squads, the number of scholarships, expenses of travel, or the number of coaches employed could not be imposed on all conference members. Most important related to this was the implementation of a rule regarding the number of grants-in-aid a school was allowed to support.

Although there were a number of considerations that ultimately led the group of larger Southern universities to form a more compact, homogenous organization, it was mainly geographic concerns that prompted the shakeup of the Southern Conference. As a result, all 13 schools west of the Appalachians became charter members of the new Southeastern Conference.

Former sportswriter O.B. Keeler wrote in the *1933 Illustrated Football Annual* the following statement regarding the eventual breakup of the Southern Conference and the forming of the Southeastern Conference:

"Since the conclusion of the last football season there has been secession in Dixie. Rebellion, no less. One bright and sparkling day in December the old Southern Conference blew up with a detonation that shocked the natives as much as would the explosion of an under-nourished and water-logged firecracker...The old conference was too big and the geographical range too great for unity of thought and purpose. It stretched from the terrapin-infested shores of the Chesapeake and the bonded-bourbon depositories of Kentucky to the moss-hung oaks of Florida and Louisiana, and included twenty-three institutions of widely different scholastic and athletic standards. It was too unwieldy, everybody admitted."

The Southeastern Conference

"The Southeastern Conference is organized to form a more compact group of institutions with similar educational ideals and regulations in order that they, by joint action, increase their ability to render the services for which they were founded and for which they are maintained, by making athletics a part of the educational plan and by making them subservient to the great aims and objects of education and placing them under the same administrative control."
~ Article II, *Southeastern Conference Constitution*, 1933

By the end of the roaring twenties, several members of the Southern Conference had decided that a real change was necessary.

37

However, the leadership of the 13 member institutions that chose to secede and form the Southeastern Conference agreed that one thing needed to stay the same, and that was the ideal that athletics was part of the overall educational plan for colleges and universities. The Southern Conference had experimented with mild change during the early 1920's, but no positive results were ever realized from its actions. The leaders of the new conference felt that a more compact organization of institutions of "similar ideals" might make a difference in their operations and therefore bring about improvement in the fairness and consistency of the rules regulating athletic competition.

In February of 1933, Dr. Frank L. McVey, President of the University of Kentucky, and one of the South's leading educators, was elected first president of the Southeastern Conference.

The Southern Conference's 13 members west and south of the Appalachian Mountains all became charter members of the conference. These founding member institutions were Alabama, Alabama Polytechnic Institute (now Auburn University), University of Florida, Georgia Institute of Technology, University of Georgia, University of Kentucky, Louisiana State University, Mississippi State University, University of Mississippi, University of the South, University of Tennessee, Tulane University, and Vanderbilt University.

The Sanity Code

Prior to the onset of World War II, the NCAA wanted badly to do something about the ongoing problem of universities recruiting athletes to specifically play football. However, the war rightfully captivated the attention and energy of the nation and funneled it to the most important goal of defeating the Axis powers of Germany, Italy and Japan. As a result, the war effort considerably slowed the attempts of the NCAA to form a Sanity Code that would bring some semblance of order and fairness to the process in which universities garnered collegiate football players.

Subsequent to the war, the fact remained that any grant-in-aid for an athlete was still considered a violation of the amateur rule. In short, scholarships for athletes were illegal. In spite of this distinction, the practice of recruiting athletes to play football continued unabated–especially in the competitive Southeastern Conference. In 1935, prior to the start of World War II, the SEC had begun the practice of doling out athletic scholarships. Initially, each SEC institution was allowed to grant up to 125 athletic grant-in-aid scholarships for students who played football.

The NCAA took an immediate stand against this practice by the SEC, stating: "...the business of the colleges is education and not the entertainment of the multitude." The NCAA admitted that athletics contributed to the educational establishment, and that there was a need for athletics on college campuses. However, they also feared that the evolution of television and its revenue-generating capacity was going to make football a big business for colleges and universities. The Sanity Code made a futile last attempt at staying this imminent development.

In spite of the NCAA's objections, the SEC continued its rule of granting scholarships based on athletic ability, and that such grants did not make the recipients ineligible for competition. However, the early fifties did witness the beginning of an attempt by the SEC to curtail the number of grants-in-aid a university could extend to football players. In 1953, 40 football grants were allowed by each school. In 1954, the number was increased to 55. In 1962 it was scaled back to 45, and in 1964 back to 40.

In 1953, following a confluence of conferences in the adoption of the practice of granting athletic scholarships, the NCAA finally capitulated. During that watershed year, the NCAA formally adopted the rule allowing the giving of athletic scholarships by universities. The following paragraph concerning financial aid was added to the NCAA's working papers:

"Any college athlete who receives financial assistance other than that administered by his institution shall not be eligible for intercollegiate competition. However, this principle shall have no application to assistance received from anyone whom the athlete is naturally or legally dependent."

The NCAA, in 1953, by dropping the prohibition against aid to student athletes, went on official record in support of the idea that athletic participation had educational value comparable of any other course of study on a college campus. This measure marked the burgeoning movement of college football as a big business. The arrival of television further solidified college football's financial prowess, and the SEC was no exception. College football on television in the South became immensely popular, since so many more fans were able to follow their respective state school teams. The advent of television brought the excitement and pageantry of college football into the comfort of every Southern home. College football, throughout its proud and storied history, quite frankly, had never been bigger.

Tulane University, Georgia Tech and the University of the South eventually vacated the SEC, leaving the ten remaining founding member institutions. Tulane was a charter member of the SEC and left the league at the end of the 1965-66 academic year. The Green Wave football team competed as an independent from 1966 until 1996 when it joined Conference USA. Incidentally, in all sports besides football, Tulane was a member of the Metro Conference from 1975 to 1995.

Georgia Tech, like Tulane, was one of the charter members of the Southeastern Conference in 1933, joining from its predecessor, the Southern Conference. Tech eventually left the SEC after the 1963 season and became an independent. Georgia Tech then later joined the Metro Conference in 1975 for all sports but football for three years, 1975 to 1978. Tech would later leave the Metro to join the Atlantic Coast Conference in May of 1978.

Today, the Southeastern Conference is comprised of twelve schools representing ten separate Southern states. Six member institutions–Alabama, Arkansas, Auburn, LSU, Ole Miss, and Mississippi State, comprise the Western Division of the conference. Another six schools form the Eastern Division–Florida, Georgia, Kentucky, South Carolina, Tennessee and Vanderbilt.

The conference received a facelift in 1990 when Arkansas and South Carolina were added to the mix of schools. This landmark addition boosted the member enrollment to twelve schools, six within each separate division. Furthermore, a championship game pitting the top two teams from each division was implemented in 1992 in order to decide, on the playing field, a true conference champion for the first time during the league's history. Since these recent changes, the "new and improved" SEC has outshined many of college football's preeminent conferences.

In the East, college football
is a cultural exercise.
On the West coast,
it is a tourist attraction.
In the Midwest,
it is cannibalism.
But in the Deep South,
it is religion,
and Saturday is the Sabbath.

~ Marino Casem, Alcorn State University

West

Alabama

At the University of Alabama there is no other tradition that surpasses winning football games. The Crimson Tide of Alabama is historically the SEC's most successful football team. The thundering red elephants have attended more bowl games and have amassed more championships than any other Southeastern Conference school. The indomitable pride of Alabama's great football tradition was indelibly forged by the game's greatest Division I coach, the legendary, Paul "Bear" Bryant–a man whose noble legacy will outlive countless future generations of Alabama football fans.

Name: University of Alabama
Nickname: Crimson Tide

In its earliest days, the Alabama football team was referred to as "The Varsity" or the "Crimson and White" after the school's colors. From this moniker, the players were then also nicknamed "The Thin Red Line" by sportswriters. "Thin Red Line" was used regularly until 1906, when the term "Crimson Tide" was coined by Hugh Roberts, former Sports Editor of the *Birmingham Age-Herald*. Roberts utilized "Crimson Tide" in his description of an Alabama-Auburn game played in Birmingham in 1907, (Auburn and Alabama began playing football in 1892 and met for the first time on Feb. 22, 1893, in Birmingham) the last football contest between the two schools until 1948 when the series was resumed. The game transpired upon a field of red mud; against a heavily-favored Auburn team; and in the end, the "Thin Red Line" of Alabama forced a 6-6 tie. From that day on, "Crimson Tide" became the favored reference of Alabama fans. Former Birmingham sportswriter Zipp Newman popularized the oft-used moniker more than any other journalist.

Founded: 1831.

The State of Alabama was admitted to the Union in 1819. In 1827, Tuscaloosa, the state's capital, was chosen as birthplace of the University of Alabama. On April 18, 1831, the University enrolled fifty-two students. At the time, the campus consisted of only seven buildings; two faculty houses, two dormitories, the laboratory, the hotel (now Gorgas House), and the Rotunda.

By 1852, the enrollment at the University of Alabama had more than doubled to 126. In 1860, Alabama became a military university, replete with military department and discipline systems established. In 1865, during the Civil War, Union Troops burned all but four of U of A's 14 buildings–the carnage included the President's Mansion, the Gorgas House, the Roundhouse, and the Observatory as well.

Location: Tuscaloosa, Alabama.

The name "Tuscaloosa" is an Indian term meaning "black warrior." Antebellum mansions and Southern hospitality give the West Alabama city of Tuscaloosa the refined shine of a classic Southern community. Though Union Troops ravaged the city along the banks of the Black Warrior River, Tuscaloosa remains a Deep South antebellum antiquity. Another surviving landmark, the President's House, built in 1841, is a highlight of the University of Alabama campus. University life dominates Tuscaloosa's culture, especially during college football season, when Alabama fans young and old cheer on the famed Crimson Tide.

Alabama began playing football in the early 1890's like most other southern schools. The Athletic Department was officially formed in 1915.

Population: 85,000
Enrollment: 20,000
Colors: Crimson and White.

As early as 1892, Alabama uniforms were described as being white, with crimson stockings, accompanied by large crimson letters "U. Of A." on their sweaters. Also, football players were known to wear crimson sweaters adorned with a white "A."

Mascot: (Elephant)

Mascot name:

The Alabama Football Team became associated with the "elephant" in 1930, when sportswriter Everett Strupper of the *Atlanta Journal* reported on a fan's exclamation "Hold your horses, the elephants are coming" as the eleven huge players rumbled on to the field. Strupper and other writers continued to refer to the Alabama linemen as "Red Elephants," the color of their crimson jerseys. That 1930 team, under the leadership of Coach Wallace Wade, posted a 10-0 overall record. The "Red Elephants" rolled over Washington State 24-0 in the Rose Bowl and were subsequently declared National Champions.

Band Name: "Million Dollar Band"

The name was bestowed upon Alabama's band by W.C. "Camp" Pickens, an Alabama alumnus and football manager in 1896. Accounts of the story vary somewhat, but due to their fundraising prowess, the group was known as "The Million Dollar Band" by Pickens. Pickens, after a 33-7 loss to Georgia Tech, was asked by an Atlanta reporter, "You don't have much of a team, what do you have at Alabama?" Pickens replied, "A Million Dollar Band."

Stadium: Bryant-Denny Stadium

Named for former Head Coach, Paul "Bear" Bryant and former University President, George Denny. Amidst homecoming festivities on October 4, 1929, Alabama's football stadium was originally presented by Gov. Bibb Graves to then University of Alabama President George Denny. Seating capacity at the time of the original presentation was an impressive 12,000. During the early years prior to the construction of Bryant-Denny, the Crimson Tide played on the quadrangle in Tuscaloosa until games were transplanted to University Field in 1915. The Alabama Legislature enacted a resolution to officially name the stadium Bryant-Denny Stadium at the annual A-Day game on April 10, 1976. In 1998 seating capacity at Bryant-Denny was increased when the East Stand upper deck was completed along with 81 luxury skyboxes. George Hutcheson Denny (1870-1955) served as President of the University of Alabama for nearly a quarter of a century. Denny Chimes and Bryant-Denny Stadium serve as a reminder of Denny's legacy at the University of Alabama. Bryant-Denny Stadium today holds 83,818.

Alabama's other football-playing venue, Legion Field in Birmingham, was built in 1926, with a capacity of 21,000. The stadium's moniker commemorates the American Legion and America's war heroes. Today, after several renovations, Legion Field has a capacity of 83,091, placing it among the nation's largest stadiums. However, in 1999 it was announced that Alabama would no longer play the "Iron Bowl" (annual game with Auburn) at Legion Field.

First game: Alabama's first football game was played against Birmingham High School on November 11, 1892 at Old Lakeview Park in Birmingham. Alabama won 56-0. The very next day,

November 12, 1892, Alabama lost to the Birmingham Athletic Club, 5-4. According to James B. Sellers, Intercollegiate play started for the Tide on February 22, 1893, in Birmingham, when Alabama was thwarted by Auburn, 32-22.

First game in stadium: October 4, 1929 - Alabama 22, Ole Miss 7
First night game: Alabama's season-opener against Spring Hill in Mobile in 1940 was the Tide's first game under the lights.
Directions: Coming from I-20/59, take either the McFarland Blvd. (U.S. 82) exit and go North to University Blvd. or take 1-359 into downtown Tuscaloosa.

Where to go:
A must-see in Tuscaloosa is the Paul "Bear" Bryant Museum, located at 300 Bryant Drive on campus. A mecca of Southern college football centered around the SEC's most successful coach. The place is so revered by Alabama natives that suitors have been known to propose marriage to their girlfriends there. Open daily.
Denny Chimes – The "Walk of Fame" at Denny Chimes has been an Alabama tradition since the spring of 1948. Etched into the base of Denny Chimes are the names of the 139 men that have captained the Crimson Tide football team. Located on the south side of the quadrangle adjacent to University Boulevard, the popular campus landmark is named in honor of George H. Denny, who served as President of Alabama from 1912-1936 and in 1941. Alabama is the only SEC school that honors its former gridiron captains in this way, and some consider the ceremony at Denny Chimes one of the most important Crimson Tide traditions.

Eating:
Dreamland - They say the best barbecue ribs in the world are served here. You decide. 5535 15th Avenue East in Tuscaloosa.
Eating and Drinking:
The Ivory Tusk - A great gathering place for football fans.

Within walking distance of the campus. 1215 University Boulevard. (205) 752-3435.

The Hound's Tooth - Considered one of the best sports bars in America. Plenty of TVs, games, pool tables and its characteristic wraparound bar make it a fun stop. On the Strip. 1300 University Blvd. Phone: (205) 752-8444.

All-Time Record: 758-293-43 (.721)
SEC Record: 329-142-20 (.670)
SEC Championships: 21 (1933, 34t, 37, 45, 53, 61t, 64, 65, 66t, 71, 72, 73, 74, 75, 77, 78, 79, 81t, 89t, 92, 99).

National Championships: (12) 1925, 26, 30, 34, 41, 61, 64, 65, 73, 78, 79, 93

Undefeated Seasons: Alabama has posted nine unblemished records with the most victories coming in 1992, when the Tide celebrated its football centennial with an astounding 13-0 record including the inaugural SEC Championship game and the Sugar Bowl.

Alabama Greats:
Coaches:

From 1892 to 1922, the University of Alabama went through a series of coaches...Eugene B. Beaumont, Eli Abbott, Otto Wagonhurst, Allen McCants, W.A. Martin, M. Griffin, M.S. Harvey, James Heyworth, W.B. Blount, Wallace Leavenworth, J.W.H. Pollard, Guy Bowman, D.V. Graves, Thomas Kelly and Xen C. Scott.

Wallace Wade - (1923-1930) Alabama's football program finally settled down with the arrival of Wallace Wade, who coached the team to a 61-13-3 record through 1930. Under the direction of Coach Wallace Wade, for whom the road next to Bryant-Denny Stadium is named, Alabama became a national power in football. He led the team to its first bowl game, the Rose in

49

Pasadena, and to its national championship in 1925, and to others in 1926 and 1930. Subsequent to Alabama's defeat of Washington State 24-0 on January 1, 1931, Wade left the Capstone for Duke University. Wade was inducted to the National Football Foundation Hall of Fame in 1955. He died on October 6, 1986.

"Tradition is a rich asset for any team. Tradition and success are traveling companions." ~ Wallace Wade

Frank Thomas - (1931-1946) A graduate of Notre Dame and a protégé of Irish legend Knute Rockne, Coach Frank Thomas' Crimson Tide teams from 1931 to 1946 amassed a record of 115-24-7(81.2%), including the first Southeastern Conference title in 1933 and national championships in 1934 and 1941. Six of his teams appeared in major bowl games, including three Rose Bowls. Four of Thomas' teams enjoyed undefeated seasons, including his 1934 and 1945 teams, which won Rose Bowl Championships. A young man named Paul "Bear" Bryant played end for Thomas from 1933 through 1935.

Harold Drew - (1947-1954) The next coach was Harold D. "Red" Drew from 1947 to 1954, whose teams went 55-29-7. Under Coach Drew, Alabama was led to the 1953 SEC Championship.

Between 1955 and 1957, the Crimson Tide faltered to 4-24-2 under the leadership of J.B. Whitworth. The glory days of Coach Bryant followed.

Paul "Bear" Bryant – Undeniably the biggest cult icon to ever come out of the State of Alabama. The "Bear" was a simple man who knew the game of football like no other. Bryant died within months of retiring in 1983 at the age of 69. His lifetime record is 323-85-17 (.824). Bear had an unbelievable 72-2 record in Tuscaloosa and an unblemished 25-0 record in Homecoming games. The Bear also served as Alabama Athletic Director for a short while during his long career at the Capstone. As a player for

Alabama, Bryant lost only three games. The "Bear" began his remarkable coaching career at Maryland in 1945. A year later he went to Kentucky, where he coached for eight years. Kentucky had Adolph Rupp so he moved on to Texas A&M for four years. In 1958, Bryant began his 25 year legacy at the University of Alabama.  During that time Bryant won an amazing 232 games and six national championships (1961, 1964, 1965, 1973, 1978, 1979).

Coach Bryant Versus His Protégés

Coach Bryant's career record against his pupils was 43-6. The games were against head coaches who either played for him or coached on his staff previously. Coach Bryant won 31 straight games against his pupils before losing to Pat Dye of Auburn 23-22 his last season.

Georgia Head Coach Wally Butts, once remarked on Paul "Bear" Bryant, "The definition of an atheist in Alabama is someone who doesn't believe in Bear Bryant." According to John D. McCallum, George Blanda, who played for Coach Bryant at Kentucky, remarked, "When Coach Bryant walked into the locker room I always had the urge to stand up and cheer. Seeing that face for the first time—granite firm, grim, full of grit—I thought, 'This must be what God looks like.'"

"Paul Bryant, the "great rehabilitator" at Maryland, Kentucky, and most recently at Texas A&M, now faces his stiffest challenge in 14 years as a head coach. He inherits an Alabama squad that has

won only four of 30 games in the past three years."—*Sports Illustrated*, September 22, 1958.

The Words of Paul "Bear" Bryant:

"*In business, life, or sports—these principles apply. There is no easy shortcut to success. Success is made from planning, hard work, dedication, determination, helping others, some luck, and a good relationship with God.*"

"*Football changes and so do people. The successful coach is the one who sets the trend, not the one who follows it.*"

"*If you don't have discipline, you can't have a successful program.*"

"*If you believe in yourself and have dedication and pride–and never quit, you'll be a winner.*"

"*I can reach a kid who doesn't have any ability as long as he doesn't know it.*"

"*Sacrifice. Work. Self-discipline. I teach these things, and my boys don't forget them when they leave.*"

"*Mama called.*" – Coach Bryant's explanation for leaving a championship team at Texas A&M to return to his struggling alma mater.

"*When you're number one, you don't play for the tie.*"

"*I don't hire anybody not brighter than I am. If they're not smarter than me, I don't need them.*"

Bear Bryant's three rules for coaching:

1. Surround yourself with people who can't live without football.
2. Recognize winners. They come in all forms.
3. Have a plan for everything.

"I'm known as a recruiter. Well, you've got to have chicken to make chicken salad."

"You must learn to hold a team together. You lift some men up, calm others down, until finally they've got one heartbeat. Then, you've got yourself a team."

"It's only a little bone." ~Coach Bryant after suiting up for the Crimson Tide against Arkansas in 1936, despite having a broken leg.

"Boys, I'd like to introduce you to Coach Wallace Wade. He's the man responsible for the great tradition of Alabama football." ~Bear Bryant, introducing Wade at a practice in 1980.

When the melancholy word of Bear Bryant's unsuspecting death reached the mainstream media in January, 1983, as to be expected, there was an overwhelming outpouring of emotion by his countless fans. The words spoken shortly after Bryant's death by former Huntsville High quarterback Robby Rowan, who played under Bryant in the early 1970's, summed up well the purpose of Bryant's existence as the molder of young men.

"He (Bryant) always planned to win but he also taught you to have a plan if you lose," Rowan said. "Now, I can relate to what he was saying better than when I was in school.

"All my days aren't winning national championships, and all my days aren't on top of the world," Rowan said. "Life has its peaks, but it also has its valleys, and he (Bryant) was preparing us for

those valleys, educating us on striving to win but also having a plan for when you don't win."

Gene Stallings - (1990-1996) After losing his first three games at Alabama, Coach Stallings won 70 games in seven seasons to average 10 wins a year during his tenure as head man at the Capstone. A former player for Coach Bryant, Stallings finished

his career at Alabama with a respectable (70-16-1) record and a unanimous 1992 undefeated, National Championship Season, Alabama's most recent to date.
"The expectation level is high at the University of Alabama and it should be. What's wrong with people expecting excellence?"
~ Former Alabama Coach, Gene Stallings

Players:

Joe Namath - (1962-1964) 6' 2" - 190 lbs - Quarterback, hailing from Beaver Falls, Pennsylvania. Even though a knee injury severely limited his playing time in his senior year, Joe Namath was still instrumental in leading the Crimson Tide to a national title.

The venerable number 12 came off the bench in the 1965 Orange Bowl to complete 18 passes for 255 yards and two touchdowns to earn Most Valuable Player honors in the Tide's 21-17 loss to Texas. An All-American and All-SEC choice at Alabama, Namath went on to an NFL Hall of Fame career with the New York Jets, highlighted by a Super Bowl III MVP performance in 1969. He tied with Ken Stabler, a later

NFL MVP, for Alabama's quarterback of the decade for the 1960's. In 1985, Namath was inducted to the Pro Football Hall of Fame.

In three years as quarterback at the University of Alabama, Namath led the Crimson Tide to a 29-4 record, including three bowl appearances. He set Alabama records for pass attempts (428), completions (230), yards (3,055), and touchdowns (29). Despite the fact that Alabama lost the 1965 Orange Bowl to Texas, 21-17, Namath was voted the game's Most Valuable Player. While at Alabama (including bowl appearances), Joe ran for 15 touchdowns and gained 628 yards on the ground for a combined total of 44 touchdowns and 3,652 yards.

"No, man, I majored in journalism. It was easier."~Joe Namath responding to a reporter who asked him if he majored in bas-ketweaving at Alabama (from *Talk of the Tide*).

Ozzie Newsome - (1974-77) Split End. Ozzie Newsome was voted Alabama's "Player of the Decade" for the 1970's. Newsome collected 102 receptions for 2,070 yards and 16 TD's during his Alabama career. Amazingly, he averaged 20.3 yards per catch, still the SEC's best mark on a minimum of 100 catches. During his time at the Capstone, the Tide went 42-6, and won three SEC Championships. Newsome also returned punts for Alabama aver-aging 7.5 yards on 40 returns. Newsome went on to enjoy a 13-year NFL career, where he started 176 of 182 games for the Cleveland Browns, where he was the Browns' first round draft pick in 1978. Nicknamed the "Wizard of Oz" by his professional contemporaries, Newsome was named All-Pro in 1979 and 1984. In 1999, Newsome was enshrined to the NFL Hall of Fame in Canton, Ohio. Newsome was born March 16, 1956, in Muscle Shoals, Alabama.

Cornelius Bennett - (1983-1986) (#97) won the nation's Vince Lombardi Trophy (making him the first LB to ever win an award designed for linemen). A three-time All-American from 1984-1985, Bennett was chosen as Alabama's Player of the Decade for the 1980's and a member of the all-decade team of the

SEC for the 1980's. Indianapolis made him the second player picked in the '87 draft after a senior year that included 10 QB sacks, 6 forced fumbles, 21 total tackles for loss, and two passes tipped, despite missing the first two games of season. He was a three-time All-SEC pick with 287 tackles, 16 sacks, 15 passes defensed, and three fumbles recovered. Bennett is a native of Birmingham, Alabama.

Lee Roy Jordan - (1960-62) A former two-time All-American, Jordan is considered the greatest inside linebacker in Crimson Tide history. Voted Alabama's Player of the Decade for the 1960s and to ESPN's all-time college football team in 1989, Jordan was also enshrined into the NFL Hall of Fame in 1983. During his career at the Capstone Jordan helped Alabama compile a 29-2-2 record. Jordan will perhaps best be remembered for his greatest single game–his unforgettable 1963 New Year's Day Orange Bowl performance against Oklahoma. In that 17-0 Alabama triumph, Jordan was credited with an amazing 31 tackles.

Derrick Thomas - (1985-1988) A four-time All-SEC and All-American, Butkus Award winner and NFL All-Pro linebacker.

Thomas is remembered for his outstanding linebacker play while at Alabama. His quick feet and nose for the ball helped Thomas become Alabama's all-time game (5), season (27) and career (52) sack leader. During the 1988 season, Thomas led Alabama with 12 tackles for loss totaling minus 46 yards. He was undoubtedly one of the most feared defenders in the SEC and NFL during his playing years. A nine-time

Pro Bowl player, Thomas died less than a month after being paralyzed in a car crash on an icy road. Thomas was 33 at the time of his death in January, 2000.

"I just want to thank God for blessing me with some athletic talent and letting me play for the University of Alabama."~Derrick Thomas

John Hannah - (1970-72) Hannah is widely-considered to be the finest lineman to ever play the game of football. An All-American selection during his senior year of 1972, Hannah was also an All-SEC pick in 1971 and 1972. A member of Alabama's Team of the Century, he was selected to ESPN's all-time college football squad in 1989 and was also a member of Alabama's  Team of the Decade in the 1970s. The recipient of the 1972 Jacobs Award, granted annually to the conference's best blocker, Hannah went on to a fabulous professional career where he was an All-Pro for several seasons. In 1991, he was named to the Pro Football Hall of Fame. He is also a member of the Alabama Sports Hall of Fame. Hannah is a native of Albertville, Alabama.

Bob Bell once said of Hannah, "I've seen a lot of great college offensive linemen. The greatest was John Hannah."

Johnny Mac Brown – A two-time All-Southern Conference player (the SEC wasn't formed until 1933) Brown is best remembered for his role in Alabama's 20-19 win over Washington in the 1926 Rose Bowl. In that contest Brown was on the receiving end of what were at the time two extremely long passes of 58 and 62 yards. The 58-yarder was thrown by Grant Gillis and the 62-yarder was lofted by Pooley Hubert. Brown's catches helped Bama to victory in that historic Southern college football conquest. Inducted into the College Football Hall of Fame in 1957, Brown is also a member of the All-Rose Bowl Team. The Dothan, Alabama native was known as the "Dothan Antelope" during his playing days and he was the first of four brothers to eventually play for the Tide. He died on November 15, 1974 in Beverly Hills, California.

Johnny Musso – An All-American in 1970 and 1971, Musso was named the "SEC Player of the Year" in 1971, the same year he served as team captain. Remembered for his toughness, the Birmingham native is a member of Alabama's Team of the 20th Century, the All-Decade Team of the 1970s, and the Alabama Sports Hall of Fame. A former Academic All-American, Musso accounted for 2,741 rushing yards and 495 receiving yards and 38 total touchdowns during his illustrious college football career. Musso is a member of the College Football Hall of Fame in South Bend, Indiana.

Harry Gilmer – A native of Birmingham, Alabama, Gilmer is recognized and remembered as an early legend of Alabama football. Gilmer's talents at passing, running, tackling, returning kicks and kicking forged a remarkable college football career at the Capstone. As an All-America and All-SEC player in 1945, Gilmer was voted MVP of the Rose Bowl after leading Bama to a 34-14 win over USC. His 16 career interceptions rate as second best in Alabama history, while his 436 punt return yards earned during the 1946 season remain the best in Alabama football history. In addition to interceptions and punt returns, in 1946 Gilmer also led the team in passing, rushing, and kickoff returns. Gilmer is a member of the College Football Hall of Fame.

Shaun Alexander – The former 1999 "SEC Player of the Year," Alexander notched three conference and 15 Alabama rushing records in addition to earning All-America honors his senior year. The Florence, Kentucky native broke Bobby Humphrey's rushing record, becoming Alabama's all-time leading rusher with 3,565 yards (4.9 yards per carry) in four seasons. Alexander reached

1,000 yards faster than any other player in school history (after his 7th game) and he set 15 school records during his career, notching 15 100-yard games, 41 rushing touchdowns and 50 total touchdowns. During his senior year Alexander finished 7th in Heisman Trophy balloting. In 2000, Alexander was drafted nineteenth overall in the first round of the NFL draft.

Kenny Stabler – Known affection-
ately as "The Snake," Kenny Stabler is one of the most popular Tide stars to ever wear the Crimson and white. As colorful off the field as he was on, Stabler played on Alabama teams that combined a 28-3-2 record. In 1956 he led Bama to a perfect 11-0 season, including a 34-7 win over Nebraska in the Orange Bowl. In that victory over the Cornhuskers Stabler completed 12 of 17 passes for 218 yards and rushed for 40 more while earning MVP honors. The SEC Player of the Year during his senior season, Stabler, along with Broadway Joe Namath, is a member of the Tide's All-Century team. After college Stabler was a first-round draft choice of the Houston Astros in the Major League Baseball draft, but he turned down that offer to instead play football with the Oakland Raiders.

Jay Barker – The Trussville, Alabama native was a sophomore when he led the Crimson Tide to a national championship in 1992. The winner of the Johnny Unitas Golden Award in 1994, Barker finished fifth in Heisman Trophy balloting the same year. Barker finished his four-year career at the Capstone the winningest quarterback in school history, posting a 34-2-1 record as the Tide's starting quarterback, completing 402 of 706 passes (.569) for 5,689 yards and 24 touchdowns. An All-America and All-SEC selection his senior year, Barker was the Birmingham News' SEC Offensive Player of the Year and was a finalist for the Davey O'Brien Award, given each year to the top quarterback in college football.

Sylvester Croom – An All-America and All-SEC selection in 1974, Croom, a native of Tuscaloosa, Alabama, was presented the Jacobs Trophy, given annually to the SEC's best blocker. A two-year starter for the Tide, Croom played on Alabama squads that went a collective 32-4. Alabama won the SEC Championship all three of his playing years and he won a national championship in 1973. In 2003, Croom became the SEC's first black head football coach when he was hired by Mississippi State University to replace the retiring Jackie Sherrill.

Dwight Stephenson – An All-America and All-SEC selection in 1979, Stephenson was voted the Jacobs winner, the award granted to the SEC's best blocker. Selected to Alabama's Team of the Decade for the 1970s, Stephenson, a Hampton, Virginia native, was also picked for the Quarter-Century All-SEC Team (1961-1985). Following his career at Bama, Stephenson played professionally with the Miami Dolphins and was picked NFL Man of the Year.

History:

Football came to the Capstone in 1892 via a youngster named Bill Little, who had attended Phillips Andover Academy in Massachusetts the year prior. Little's presentation of his football uniform, football, and cleated shoes served to warm his newfound Alabama colleagues to the game. In 1892, an Athletic Association and volunteers for a team were assembled and the University's first football team was formed. Subsequently, the "Thin Red Line" evolved into "The Crimson Tide." Money was also collected to hire a coach, and E.B. Beaumont was tapped to be the Tide's first football coach. Beaumont's tenure lasted four games of which Alabama won two. The gridiron sport quickly gained favor among young men at the University of Alabama. In 1896 the University's Board of Trustees passed a rule forbidding athletic teams from traveling off campus. During the 1897 season only one football game was played at Alabama and in 1898 no games were played. Student opposition to this decision was so strong that the trustees lifted the ban on travel for the 1899 season, when regular play resumed. Football at Alabama would continue without interruption until World War I in 1918, which forced the University to cancel all of its scheduled games that year.

Great Bowl Games:

*Alabama has appeared in 51 bowl games through the years. As of January, 2004, their all-time bowl game record is 29-19-3 (.598).

Alabama went to five consecutive Rose Bowls from 1926-1938, posting a 3-1-1 record. Alabama enjoyed its last trip to the Rose Bowl in 1946, with a 34-14 win over Southern California. It was also the last bowl game for Coach Frank Thomas.

1953 Orange Bowl: (Most points scored in a bowl game–61, against Syracuse)

1963 Orange Bowl: Alabama 17 Oklahoma 0 (Tide finished 10-1)

1964 Sugar Bowl: Alabama 12 Ole Miss 7 Tim Davis kicked a bowl record four field goals to seal the win for the Tide.

1975 Sugar Bowl: Alabama 13 Penn State 6 This victory broke the Tide's eight-game post-season losing streak.

1993 Sugar Bowl: Alabama 34 Miami 13 Against a heavily-favored Miami Hurricane squad, Bama posted its 12th National Championship.

It was January 1, 1926, when Alabama upset the University of Washington 20-19 in the Rose Bowl in Pasadena, California. At the time of the contest, Southern football, like most everything else in the South, was regarded as second rate. Most sportswriters laughed at the matchup between the powerful Huskies and the Tide. However, Alabama's Head Coach, Wallace Wade, was not daunted by the formidable task at hand. Wallace prepared his players in the locker room before the game by asking them to play for not just for themselves, or the State of Alabama, but for the South. He stated, "Southern football is not recognized or respected. Boys, here's your chance to change that forever."

"The greatest Southern football victory of all time was Alabama's Rose Bowl victory over Washington. It gained permanent esteem for Southern football." ~ George Leonard

Auburn Historian Wayne Flint aptly explained the magnitude of Alabama's monumental win, "The Tide that went to Pasadena was not just Alabama's team, but the South's team," Flynt said. "They were reliving 100 years of sectionalism between the North and South. Fans were thinking 'this is just like Chancellorsville, just like Gettysburg. Now we've got one more chance for Southerners to show them what we're made of.' Alabama's victory was reported much as a victory at Gettysburg would have been. It was as if Southerners had proven something the South had been trying to prove since the Civil War, that we are as good as anybody else; and that, given a level playing field, and the same number of players on the playing field, we can go out there and beat anybody, even the best the country has possibly produced."

As sports historian Andrew Doyle wrote in an article in *The International Journal of the History of Sport*, that Southerners "regarded the rest of the nation with a complex mixture of assertive pride and defensive hostility, and intersectional football gave full rein to both of these sentiments."

When Alabama defeated Washington, 20-19, in the 1926 Rose Bowl game, Doyle said its display of "masculine strength and virility . . . became proof that the martial prowess and chivalric grandeur of their mythologized ancestors [were] still alive in the modern world."

Additionally, in his interpretation of the event, Wayne Flint asked the compelling question, "Had Alabama lost badly in 1926, by 40 points or more, would football then have become the sort of important, defining experience that it became over the next five decades? Flint then answered his own question, "My answer is no, it would not have. Because the South would have just been proved yet again to be inferior in some other dimension in life, and what would have happened, I think, is the South would have found some other way to excel. It would have invested this kind of emotional energy and physical commitment to something else."

"Alabama, thy name is courage–unyielding valor in all its splendor! Flow on Crimson. Thou hast brought honors aplenty to Dixieland." ~ Zipp Newman, January 1, 1927.

Fight Song: "YEA ALABAMA"
Yea Alabama! Drown' em Tide,
Every Bama man's behind you,
Hit your stride...
Go teach the bulldogs to behave
Send the yellow Jackets to a watery grave,
And if a man starts to weaken,
That's a shame,
Cause Bama's pluck and grit have
Writ her name in Crimson Flame,
Fight on, Fight on, Fight on, men!
Remember the Rose Bowl we'll win then.
Go, roll to victory, Hit your stride!
You're Dixie's football pride,
Crimson Tide!

Alabama Alma Mater

Alabama, listen, Mother,
To our vows of love,
To thyself and to each other
Faithful friends we'll prove.

Faithful, loyal, firm and true
Heart bound to heart will beat
Year by Year, the ages through
Until in Heaven we meet.

College days are swiftly fleeting
Soon we'll leave thy halls
Ne'er to join another meeting
'Neath thy hallowed walls.

Faithful, loyal, firm and true
Heart bound to heart will beat
Year by year, the ages through
Until in Heaven we meet.

So, farewell, dear Alma Mater,
May thy name, we pray,
Be rev'renced ever, pure and stainless
As it is today.

Faithful, loyal, firm and true
Heart bound to heart will beat
Year by year, the ages through
Until in Heaven we meet.
~ Helen Vickers, 1908

Notable Alabama Alumni:
   Sela Ward - actress, (former Alabama cheerleader)
   Jim Nabors - actor (Gomer Pyle), Class of 1951
   Hugo Black - former Supreme Court Justice
   Howell Raines - former *New York Times* Executive Editor
   Mel Allen - broadcast journalist
   Winston Groom - author (Forrest Gump)
   Harper Lee - author
   Dr. E.O. Wilson - Harvard professor, National Medal of Science,
Pulitzer Prize
   Tom Cherones - Director (*Seinfeld*)

Autumn is the best time for those who love sports...because autumn means football. At no other time of the year does one's soul feel so at rest. The brilliant color of the uniforms, the instantaneous deployment of twenty-two men in precise assignment, a spiraling pass, the sound of a punt, the taste of courage and physical aggression–these make the heart pump. Sometimes, I think, my spirit is in limbo from January through August, waiting for the football game to begin again.

~ Michael Novak
Universal Press Syndicate, 1979

Arkansas

Arkansas, the Natural State, was once nicknamed the "Bear State" for a reason. The Ozarks were rife with hungry black bears! In light of this, it is no great mystery why the intrepid Davy Crockett became the area legend and folk hero that he remains today. People born and raised in "Hog Country" tend to stay close to home, and they enjoy passing along folklore about local animals, individuals and events. Razorback football, much like the great outdoors, is a way of life in Arkansas, from the Ozarks to the Delta, and a common rallying point for Arkansans throughout the world. Within the last decade and a half, the Hogs have become members of the Southeastern Conference, reentered national rankings, and regained bowl invitations on their way to re-establishing one of the South's great football powers.

Founded: Established in 1871, the University of Arkansas is the only comprehensive doctoral degree granting institution in Arkansas. During that same year, the Arkansas State Legislature created the Arkansas Industrial Institution at Fayetteville under the conditions of the Federal Land Grant Act of 1862. Students began attending classes in 1872. It is classified as a Carnegie II Research institution. The University of Arkansas in Fayetteville, although recently new to the Southeastern Conference, has enjoyed considerable success since entering the league in 1992. Bringing with them to the SEC a great Southwest Conference tradition, the Razorbacks have represented the conference well during their formative years in the talent-laden SEC.

Nickname: Razorbacks

Athletic squads have not always been referred to as Razorbacks at the University of Arkansas. During the University's earliest years of athletics, the Cardinal was its favored mascot. However, all of that changed in 1909, when Arkansas Football Coach Hugo Bezdek called his players "a wild band of Razorback hogs," after he led his team to a 16-0 thrashing of Louisiana State University on October 30, 1909. This newer, more ferocious, moniker gained favor quickly in Arkansas, and in 1910, the student body voted to officially change the school's mascot from the Cardinals to the Razorbacks.

Location: Fayetteville, Arkansas
The lush green hills of Fayetteville are home to a thriving college town. If Fayetteville's 3,110 acres of parks aren't enough for the most enthusiastic nature-seeker, the northwest Arkansas city of 42,247 rests right below the highest of the Ozark Mountains, and enjoys four distinct seasons. Initially settled in 1828, the city played host to both Union and Confederate soldiers during the Civil War.

Population: 53,300
Enrollment: 16,449

Colors: Cardinal and White.
The use of Cardinal and White as official colors for the athletic squads at Arkansas date back to the earliest days of the athletic program when the school's mascot was the Cardinal bird.

Mascot name: The "Razorbacks"

Stadium(s): As all die-hard Hog fans know, the Razorbacks split their home games between Fayetteville, the site of the main U of A campus, and Little Rock, the capital and largest city of the Natural State. Razorback Stadium in Fayetteville was built in 1938 and currently holds 51,000 people. It is located next to the main university campus. War Memorial Stadium in Little Rock was built in 1948 and holds 53,250 people. It is located in the central part of Little Rock near the Fair Park Blvd. exit from I-630.

The University of Arkansas trustees, citing financial reasons, voted in February of 2000 to move most of the school's home football games to its Fayetteville campus. The Razorbacks will still play in Little Rock, but the vote dimmed hopes for an expanded War Memorial Stadium. The board voted 9-1 to give Little Rock just two games each in 11 of the next 15 seasons.

In every year since 1932, Arkansas has split its home games between its Fayetteville campus and Little Rock. Convenience was a key; until recently, there was no four-lane road into Fayetteville from the rest of the state. Since 1948, Little Rock and Fayetteville each have annually hosted at least three Razorback games, except there were only two at Little Rock in 1954 and at Fayetteville in 1985. In 106 years of Razorback football, at least one game has been played at Little Rock in 83 of those years.

University of Arkansas officials have stated that freshmen retention rates suffered because only three games per year were being played on the campus. In the opinion of the University Trustees, Arkansas should hold more football games on campus if it wishes to sincerely pursue its stated dream of a modern-day national championship in football.

Razorback Stadium

Originally built as a WPA project with a capacity of 13,500, Razorback Stadium was dedicated on October 8, 1938, during a home contest against Baylor. Prior to the 1938 dedication of Razorback Stadium, the Hogs played in a stadium that was constructed in 1901 on land now occupied by the Mullins Library and the Fine Arts Center. The primitive structure had room for 300 spectators along with a fence around the outside. The first of many expansion projects began with the arrival of John Barnhill as Athletic Director in 1947. Barnhill was successful in realizing the construction of another 2,500 seats for the north end of each side of the stadium. In 1950, a new press box was built and 5,200 more seats were added on the west side.

Furthermore, a 5,200-seat east compliment was erected in 1957. Even more construction additions were completed during the years

68

of 1965 and 1969, thereby increasing seating capacity to 42,678 prior to 1985. On September 27, 1969, Arkansas played its first game on Astroturf at Razorback Stadium.

Arkansas took to the change kindly by defeating Tulsa 55-0. On November 11, 1989, the first game with lights was played in Razorback Stadium. Arkansas defeated Balylor that first night under the lights by a score of 19-10.

Stadium capacity: 72,000

Donald W. Reynolds Razorback Stadium recently underwent a major expansion and renovation, which was completed prior to the 2001 season. The $110 million project, which included a $20 million gift from the Donald W. Reynolds Foundation, saw the capacity of the stadium increased from 51,000 to 72,000, but that may not even be the most noticeable improvement. The concrete and steel below the stands has been completely enclosed with a brick and glass façade. The new look rivals that of many of the newer Major League Baseball stadiums. In addition to covering the steel and concrete, the concourses are wider, and concession areas and restrooms have been replaced.

The east concourse is "Championship Alley" with displays of

conference championships, the 1964 national title and every football letterman. The south end zone concourse is "All-American Alley' and is dedicated to Razorback All-Americans. The west concourse is "Bowl Alley" with tributes to each bowl team.

Other than the facade covering, the other most noticeable addition is the enclosure of the south end zone, which features chairback seating and the addition approximately 7,300 total seats with space for an additional upper deck that would push the capacity to 80,000. The enclosure also includes a food court with space for five vendors.

Other major additions include an expanded press box and the addition of luxury suites. Sixty-eight suites/skyboxes were added, bringing the total to 132, and the stadium's capacity includes 8,950 club seats. Other additions include the 15,000 square foot Bob and Marilyn Bogle Academic Center and the 3,800 square foot Wilson Matthews "A" Club, both on the east side where an upper deck, which seats 6,500, was added along with enclosed premium club seating. During the 2000 season, a 30x107-foot SMARTVISION LED video screen, the largest video board at any sports venue in the world, made its debut in the north end zone.

Directions to Donald W. Reynolds Razorback Stadium: Coming from the U.S. 71 Bypass, hit either the Cato Springs Road or the 6th Street exit. If traveling from U.S. 71 North from I-40, hit Exit 43 and continue on 6th Street/Highway 62. Head north on Razorback Road from 6th Street in Fayetteville.

War Memorial Stadium

For over fifty years, War Memorial Stadium has served as the Razorback's venue for games in Little Rock. With a current capacity of 53,737, the stadium was christened in 1948 with a capacity of only 31,500. The stadium's original capacity was expanded from 31,500 to 53,727 and the original grass field replaced during the 1960's. Arkansas went to an artificial surface along with a complete lighting system in 1969.

Subsequent artificial turfs replaced older ones in 1974 and

1984. However, as the impending replacement date for the carpet approached in 1994, Memorial Stadium returned to a natural grass playing field. The press box at War Memorial Stadium was voted tops in the country by the Football Writer's Association in 1974, an honor for both the physical facility and services provided.

Stadium Capacity: 53,727
Record crowd: 55,912 September 19, 1992 Alabama 38, Arkansas 11
First game in stadium: September 18, 1948 Arkansas 40, Abilene Christian 6
Directions to War Memorial Stadium: The stadium is located in War Memorial Park, west of downtown Little Rock. Take Fair Park Boulevard and exit north off of I-630.

Where to go:
Eating:
  B&B Bar-B-Q: 230 East Avenue, Fayetteville, (501) 521-3663
  Dixie Cafe: 501-444-6660 3875 N Shiloh Dr, Fayetteville, AR
  Hog City Diner: 501-443-5588 1 W Center St Fayetteville, AR

Eating and Drinking:
  Hogs Breath Eatery: 501-443-7783 1214 N Garland Ave.

Taverns:
  Beer Keg: 50 East Township Street, (501) 521-3919
  Ozark Brewing Corporation: 501-521-2739 430 W Dickson St.

Total Games Played: 1,072 in 110 seasons
All-Time Record: 619-413-40 (.596)
Southwest Conference All-Time Record: 226-194-15
Bowl Appearances: 34
Bowl Record: 11-20-3 (.368)
SEC Record: 45-50-2 (.473)
SEC Championships: None

Arkansas Greats:

Coaches: Hugo Bezdek (1908-1912) 29-13-1 in five years at Arkansas. Bezdek was the very first full-time paid football coach at the University of Arkansas. Bezdek led the Cardinals (at the time) in 1909 to a breakthrough 7-0 season that included wins over collegiate powerhouses like LSU and Oklahoma. Amazingly, Arkansas scored 186 points in its seven game span that year while allowing only 18 points.

John Barnhill (1946-1950). Barnhill, prior to taking the job at Arkansas, coached for General Bob Neyland at Tennessee. While Neyland served in World War II, Barnhill coached his team in Knoxville. Barnhill's tenure in Fayetteville marked the resurgence of a proud winning tradition at Arkansas. Barnhill won over the football fans in Arkansas by doing something they had not done in nine seasons prior—win! Before Barnhill's hiring, Arkansas painfully endured nine straight losing seasons. Barnhill also was loved by Razorback fans for having successfully recruited Smackover's Clyde Scott, an eventual silver medalist in the Olympic games in 1948.

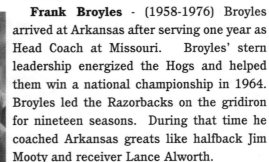

Frank Broyles - (1958-1976) Broyles arrived at Arkansas after serving one year as Head Coach at Missouri. Broyles' stern leadership energized the Hogs and helped them win a national championship in 1964. Broyles led the Razorbacks on the gridiron for nineteen seasons. During that time he coached Arkansas greats like halfback Jim Mooty and receiver Lance Alworth.

While serving as Athletic Director, a position he held at Arkansas after coaching; Broyles once remarked after being asked if he would like football coach Ken Hatfield as much if Arkansas lost half its games, "Sure I would. I'd miss him too."

The words of Frank Broyles:

"Recruiting is and will remain an inexact and highly speculative science."

"No athletic program can ever be better than its recruiting."

"My sales pitch to recruits was simple: At Arkansas, we have great fans, great tradition, and few distractions."

Lou Holtz - Holtz steered the Razorbacks to a seven-year 60-21-2 record from 1977-1983. In 1977, the Razorbacks were ranked no higher than fifth in the Southwest Conference in any of the preseason polls, but none of the sportswriters had factored in the ability of Lou Holtz. During that first year as the head coach of the Razorbacks Holtz shocked the college football world with a brilliant campaign that culminated in the Orange Bowl in Miami in 1978. During that magical season the Hogs finished 11-1-0, defeating Oklahoma in the postseason by the score of 31-6. Adding greatly to the Holtz mystique was the fact that prior to the Orange Bowl, Holtz suspended the Hogs' top two ball carriers and a leading receiver for disciplinary reasons. In spite of the tough decision by their coach, the Hogs went on anyway to roll over the heavily-favored Sooners. As a result, Holtz became a national hero overnight for his strong moral conviction and his unflappable coaching style. Holtz went on to coach at Notre Dame, where he won a national championship in 1988, and at South Carolina in 1999.

Ken Hatfield (1984-89) 55-17-1 in six years for the Hogs. Hatfield returned to Arkansas to coach the Razorbacks and bring much-needed life back to the program. Hatfield did this by winning four games in the fourth quarter, and by winning seven in all during his inaugural campaign. In 1985, Hatfield directed the Hogs to a 10-2 record, edging Arizona State in the Holiday Bowl. Also, in 1986, Hatfield led the Hogs to their first victory over the Texas Longhorns in Austin in over 20 years, in addition to a 14-10 victory over Texas A&M, which led to an Orange Bowl invitation. During Hatfield's last year, he led the Razorbacks to the Cotton Bowl with a stingy defense centered around the determined play of standouts Wayne Martin and Steve Atwater.

Houston Nutt – A Little Rock, Arkansas native, Nutt was recruited by Arkansas and Alabama as a quarterback. After playing two years at Arkansas under Frank Broyles and his successor Lou Holtz, Nutt transferred to Oklahoma State where he finished out his college athletic career and graduated. Nutt took over as head football coach for the Hogs in 1998 and since that time he has elevated the Arkansas football program to unprecedented heights. Prior to coaching at Arkansas Nutt was a head coach at Murray State and Boise State. Known as a powerfully animated motivator, Nutt gets the most out of his players on game day. Nutt's six-year record at Arkansas is a respectable 48-27 (.640), and under his tutelage the Hogs have gone to six straight bowl games, a feat for an Arkansas head football coach that equals only former coach Lou Holtz. Nutt's overall record as a head coach in 11 seasons is 84-49 (.631).

Players:

Lance Alworth - (1959-1961) Alworth is widely considered one of

the greatest athletes in Razorback history. The 1960-61 All-American from Brookhaven, Mississippi is both a College and Pro Football Hall of Fame member. A great all-around player for the Hogs, Alworth led the team in 1961 with 18 receptions for 320 yards and 3 touchdowns to go along with 110 rushes for 516 yards and 5 touchdowns for a 4.7 yard-per-carry average. During the 1961 season, against the University of Tulsa, Alworth returned 7 kicks for 136 yards. On the season, Alworth had a total of 28 returns for 336 total yards. In his brilliant career at Arkansas, he totaled 690 yards on 51 returns.

 **Clyde Scott**-(1946-48) Nicknamed "Smackover" for his hometown namesake, Scott rushed for 1,463 yards during his career, which was a school-best mark at the time. During the 1948 season, Scott rushed 95 times for 670 yards, for an impressive 7.0 yard per-carry average. Scott was also the first Razorback to ever win a medal at the Olympic games. Scott won a silver medal in the hurdles in 1948. Scott's jersey, #12 was retired following his graduation.

 **Joe Ferguson** - Ferguson is arguably the greatest quarterback in Arkansas history. He holds numerous individual Arkansas records. He holds the Hog mark for the most plays in a single game–56 against Texas A&M in 1971, 51 passes, 5 rushes, and one touchdown. He also holds the record for the most pass attempts by a Razorback in a single game–51, also against Texas A&M. On that great outing Ferguson posted 345 yards passing on 31 completions and one interception. During his Razorback career, Ferguson completed 327 of 611 passes for 4,431 yards.

Steve Little - (1974-1977) Little is considered the greatest kicker in school history. A two-time All-American, Little owns school marks for the most points scored by a kicker with 280. Remarkably he still shares the NCAA record for the longest field goal with a 67-yarder against Texas in 1977, during his senior year. Little attempted more field goals than any kicker in school history (89) and made

53, the school's second highest total, and seven of which were over fifty yards.

Brandon Burlsworth - (1994-1998) An All-SEC offensive guard in 1997 and 1998. A First-Team All-American selection by *The Football News*. After redshirting in 1994 after walking on to the Arkansas Razorback football team, Burlsworth earned a scholarship for his outstanding work ethic in the weight room. After providing a backup role on the Hog offensive line during the 1995 SEC Western Division Championship campaign, Burlsworth nabbed a starting job during the spring of 1996 and never again relinquished the guard position he held for the remainder of his career. Burlsworth started 34 consecutive games for the Razorbacks, including the Florida Citrus Bowl on New Year's Day in 1999. Burlsworth's leadership helped the Razorbacks during the 1998-99 season score more points than any other since 1970 and produce more yards than any since 1989. In addition to his many athletic talents, Burlsworth was a good student as well. Burlsworth earned a bachelor's degree in marketing in 1997 and subsequently began his master's studies in business administration. In December, 1998, Brandon Burlsworth became the only Razorback football player in history to ever have a master's degree before he played in his final game. Tragically, just two weeks after being drafted by the Indianapolis Colts organization in the 1999 NFL draft, Brandon Burlsworth's great young life was ended abruptly in an automobile accident.

Cedric Cobbs - A Little Rock, Arkansas native, Cobbs was one of the most highly recruited running backs in the country. A smooth rusher possessing brutish size and speed, Cobbs is remembered by Hog fans as one of the University of Arkansas' brightest football stars. As a true freshman in 1999 Cobbs posted the best rushing performance ever by a Razorback freshman. He rushed for a team-leading 668 yards on just 116 carries despite splitting time with senior Chrys Chukwuma. Cobbs caught

11 passes for 60 yards and returned 12 kickoffs 328 yards. His all-purpose yardage total of 1,056 was the second highest ever by a Hog freshman. A Doak-Walker Award candidate prior to his sophomore season, Cobbs separated his shoulder against Alabama in their third game and missed the remainder of the season. Cobbs returned in 2001 and continued to battle injuries over the next three seasons to lead all Hog rushers, finishing with 3,018 yards in 46 games played.

Shawn Andrews – A unanimous 2003 All-American selection at offensive tackle (Associated Press, Sports Illustrated, Walter Camp, ESPN, American Football Coaches, Football Writers Association, Sporting News), Andrews was one of the most dominant line forces in all of college football during his three years as a starter at Arkansas. Andrews, who wore a size 17 shoe and a size 54 jersey in col-  lege, routinely destroyed opponents at the point of attack with his superior size and strength. Andrews bypassed his senior season after a stellar 2003 campaign to enter into the 2003 NFL draft.

Retired Jerseys: (12 and 77)

Only two jerseys have been retired by the Arkansas Football Program. Interestingly, one of those jerseys was unretired for four years, but neither of the two jerseys will ever be worn by a Razorback football player again. Following the fantastic career of Clyde Scott during the latter portion of the war-torn decade of the 1940's, the Arkansas' Athletic Department chose to retire his number 12. Twenty-five years subsequent to the retiring of Scott's jersey, a young high school kicking phenom by the name of Steve Little was being heavily recruited by Arkansas. Little required Scott's number 12 as his jersey number and the Hogs requested permission from Scott to allow Little to wear his coveted 12. Scott gave his consent and the rest is Arkansas Razorback lore. Little went on to become the greatest Arkansas kicker of all-time as a two-time All-American selection. Once Little's career at Arkansas was completed, number 12 was again retired.

Sadly, in 1999, the Arkansas Athletic Department retired the jersey of former Razorback great Brandon Burlsworth. A former All-American (and All-SEC standout [1997-1998]) offensive guard for the Hogs, Burlsworth was an unbelievable success story. A former walk-on, Burlsworth built himself into a great college offensive lineman through hard work and determination. Drafted in the third round of the 1999 NFL draft by the Indianapolis Colts, Burlsworth was tragically killed in a car crash only two weeks later, stunning the entire Razorback community. Head Coach Houston Nutt immediately recommended to Athletic Director Frank Broyles that Burlsworth's number 77 be retired. Frank Broyles agreed forthwith, and Burlsworths' locker remains intact today as a tribute to his memory as a complete football player and student athlete.

History:
Great Bowl Games:
   Cotton Bowl: January 1, 1976 Arkansas 31 Georgia 10
   Cotton Bowl: January 1, 1965 Arkansas 10 Nebraska 7
   Orange Bowl: January 2, 1968 Arkansas 31 Oklahoma 6
   Hall of Fame Bowl: December 27, 1980 Arkansas 34 Tulane 15
   Holiday Bowl: December 22, 1985 Arkansas 18 Arizona State 17
   2000 Cotton Bowl: Arkansas 27 Texas 6
   2003 Independence Bowl: Arkansas 27 Missouri 14

Early days at the University of Arkansas

In 1884, students at Arkansas petitioned the Board of Trustees to designate 2.5 acres on campus as football and baseball grounds and to provide monies for its upkeep. The students were successful in acquiring the land for their stated purpose, but were unsuccessful in their fundraising attempt to garner money for upkeep of the grounds.

In 1893, an athletic association was formed at the University of Arkansas in order to "...foster and encourage the growing interest in which the student body is manifesting in the development of the physical man." The association comprised of the Athletic Club, the Tennis Club, the Baseball Club and the Football Club. The sole responsibility of the Football Club was to provide one exhibition per fall season.

The first football team at Arkansas was formed in 1894 by John C. Futrall, manager and coach. For the following 19 years Futrall was Chairman of the athletic committee or as manager of the football team—and often both. In those days, the playing field was simply a patch of spriggy dirt and the players were described as "thugs, pug-uglies, and roughnecks" by the local press. The first Arkansas squad abused nearby Fort Smith High School twice before stepping up to legitimate college competition in the form of the University of Texas. The Longhorns ripped the Razorbacks in Austin, 54-0 in their first intercollegiate contest. Over time, the schedule was expanded to include more contestants and the 1902 squad actually finished 6-3. However, until 1908, the Razorbacks' coach was an unpaid volunteer. The first full-time football coach at the University of Arkansas was Hugo Bezdek. Bezdek, you might recall, is responsible for giving the Razorbacks their name.

The Senior Walk

The Senior Walk is the longest tradition at the University of Arkansas—not in years, but in miles.

Started in 1905, the Senior Walk contains over 120,000 graduates names which have been etched in the campus' sidewalks. Unique among American universities, Senior Walk now stretches over five miles.

Old Main

One of the oldest buildings in the state, Old Main is widely considered "the symbol of higher education in Arkansas." Old Main houses the Fulbright College of Arts and Sciences, its honors program and five academic departments.

Razorback Walk

Razorback Walk is a walk lined by Arkansas Razorback fans

that funnels the players to the stadium from where they exit the team bus. The players get off the bus and walk down through the crowd offering high-fives and shaking hands, while the crowd gets them pumped up through their various partisan chants and cheers. The Razorback Walk is the brain-child of head coach Houston Nutt, who started it in 1998. "We want all of the fans to be there in numbers greeting us at the stadium and wearing their red." Nutt said of the now much-anticipated stroll.

In 1999, the Arkansas fans turned out in droves that stretched from the Tyson Poultry Science building, all the way to the front doors of the Broyles athletic center, in Fayetteville, and down the access road from the north end of the stadium in Little Rock.

The newfound tradition has spread quickly at Arkansas, evidenced by the fact that the Razorback Walk is even practiced by fans at away games as well.

A Proper Hog Call

The familiar chant of "Woo Pig Sooie" is known universally as the Hog Call. However, there are various versions of the Hog Call, along with different spellings. A properly executed hog call is composed of three "calls," slowly raising one's arms from the knees to above the head during the "Woo."

Traditionalists argue an eight second "Woo." The fingers should be wiggled and the "Woo" should build in volume and pitch as the arms rise. Upon completion of the "Woo" phase, both arms are brought straight down with fists clinched as if executing a chin-up while yelling, "PIG." The call is finished by thrusting the right arm into the air, fist clinched, all the while exclaiming with great pride, "Sooie!"

Furthermore, a full Hog Call—the kind one will always hear victorious Razorbacks execute after contests—requires two more Hog Calls, followed closely by the "Razor-Backs" yell, in cadence with the pumping motion of the right arm after the third "Sooie" in synch with the break between "Razor" and "Backs." Therefore, in order, the full and proper Hog Call is:

Wooooooooooooooooooo. Pig. Sooie!
Wooooooooooooooooooo. Pig. Sooie!
Wooooooooooooooooooo. Pig. Sooie! Razorbacks!

The Arkansas Alma Mater
Pure as the dawn on the brow of thy beauty,
Watches thy soul from the mountains of god,
Over the fates of thy children departed
Far from the land where their footsteps have trod.
Beacon of hope in the ways dreary lighted;
Pride of our hearts that are loyal and true;
From those who adore unto one who adores you,
Mother of Mothers we sing unto you.

Fight song:
Hit that line, Hit that line, Keep on going, Move that ball right down the field.
Give a cheer, Rah! Rah! Never fear, Rah Rah
Arkansas will never yield. On your toes Razorbacks to the finish.
Carry on with all your might.
For it's A-R-K-A-N-S-A-S for Arkansas, Fight, Fight, Fi-i-ight.

Noteworthy Arkansas Alumni:
   Jerry Jones - Businessman, owner, Dallas Cowboys, member 1964 National Champs
   Meredith Boswell - Hollywood set designer (Apollo 13, The Grinch)
   S. Robson Walton - Chairman, Wal-Mart stores (largest retailer in world)
   Admiral Vernon E. Clark - Chief of U.S. Naval operations
   J. Walter Keller - developer of the human heart pacemaker
   Robert Mauer - developed fiber optic technology
   Thomas "Mack" McLarty, III - former White House Chief of Staff for President Clinton
   Pat Summerall - NFL broadcaster
   Charlie Jones - NBC sportscaster
   Donna Axum Whitworth - former Miss Arkansas and Miss America

"Football is a religion in the Southland, played by boys and relived daily by their families."

~ Zipp Newman

Auburn

Name: Auburn University

Since its inception, Auburn University has been one of the SEC's most successful institutions—in both academics and athletics. Nestled in the north central part of the state of Alabama, deep in the heart of Dixie, Auburn is a leading division one research facility in the United States. Auburn graduates annually rank among the nation's best and brightest in science, engineering and mathematics. Called by poet Oliver Goldsmith "The Loveliest Village on the Plain," Auburn's sprawling, vibrantly landscaped campus makes it an attractive gem among the SEC schools. And whether you consider yourself a War Eagle, a Tiger or a Plainsman—you're still an Auburn fan.

Founded: Chartered in 1856,

The university traces its beginning to the East Alabama Male College, a private liberal arts institution whose doors opened in 1859. From 1861 to 1866 the college was closed because of the Civil War. The college had begun an affiliation with the Methodist Church before the war. Due to financial straits, the church transferred legal control of the institution to the state in 1872, making it the first land-grant college in the South to be established separate from the state university. It thus became the Agricultural and Mechanical College of Alabama. Women were admitted to Auburn for the first time in 1892, and in 1899 the name of the institution was changed to the Alabama Polytechnic Institute. In 1960, the school acquired a more appropriate name, Auburn University, a title more in keeping with its location, size and complexity.

Location: Auburn, Alabama

Judge John J. Harper, of Harris County Georgia, originally founded the town of Auburn in 1836, foreseeing the small village seated in the Piedmont as a potential centerpiece for education, religion, and the arts.

83

Auburn

Population: 42,000
Enrollment: 21,775
Colors: Burnt Orange and Navy Blue
Nickname: "Tigers"

It is often misunderstood that Auburn has three nicknames–Tigers, War Eagles and Plainsmen. However, Auburn actually has only one nickname–The Auburn Tigers. The nickname "Tigers" comes from a passage in Oliver Goldsmith's poem, "The Deserted Village," published in 1770, "where crouching tigers wait their hapless prey..." The term "Plainsmen" comes from a line in the same Goldsmith poem, "Sweet Auburn, loveliest village of the plain..." Since Auburn's earliest athletes were men from the plains of Alabama, it was only natural for newspaper reporters to shorten the expression to "Plainsmen."

"War Eagle!" is Auburn's battle cry. The "War Eagle" cry rings out at sporting events, pep rallies, alumni meetings or any-where Auburn people gather. The legend of the Auburn War Eagle is most interesting. The story goes that an Auburn student who fought in the Civil War was wounded at the Battle of the Wilderness in Virginia, which was regarded as a most gruesome clash. The Auburn student was wounded badly in the fighting and was left forlorn on the battlefield. After mustering the strength to awaken in spite of his injuries, the student discovered that only he and a baby eagle had survived the tumult. The young confederate soldier made his way back to Auburn, with the baby eagle in tow. The soldier eventually became a professor at the university and the eagle would too gain fame. The soldier and the eagle attended Auburn's first football game in Atlanta's Piedmont Park, and as legend has it, subsequent to Auburn's first touchdown the eagle broke from the clutches of its new-found master and soared high above the playing field. Auburn fans saw this and began to chant the now familiar battle cry "War Eagle!" Supposedly, the old bird died at the end of the game, in which Auburn won 10-0.

84

Mascot:

Auburn University has two mascots. One is a golden eagle and the other is a costumed Tiger named "Aubie." Aubie, who has stalked the sidelines for Auburn since 1979, has thrice been named the #1 mascot in the country by the University Cheerleading Association. Aubie originated as a cartoon character drawn by *Birmingham Post-Herald* artist Phil Neel in 1959 for a football game program. Auburn has enjoyed the company of five golden eagles since the first one perished in 1892. Since that time, Auburn has established a modern aviary outside of Jordan-Hare Stadium for its care. Students of Auburn's Veterinarian School donate their time to look after the popular bird while funds for the upkeep of the sacred bird are generated by students and friends of the university. Auburn's current golden eagle, War Eagle VI, which is nicknamed "Tiger," as were her predecessors, weighs 11 pounds and has a wingspan of 7 feet. It is the largest of all of the War Eagle mascots in the history of Auburn University. War Eagle VI has talons that can squeeze down with a grip of 450 pounds per square inch. To put that fact into its proper perspective, the average person has a grip of about 20 pounds per square inch.

Stadium:

Jordan-Hare Stadium is named for Ralph "Shug" Jordan, Auburn's all-time winningest football coach, and Clifford Leroy Hare, a member of Auburn's first football team, president of the old Southern Conference and longtime chairman of Auburn's Faculty Athletic Conference. On Saturdays during the fall football season, when Jordan-Hare Stadium fills to capacity, Auburn becomes the fifth largest town in the State of Alabama. Since the stadium's inception in 1939, Auburn has won over eighty percent of its games played at Jordan-Hare.

Stadium capacity: 86,063, making it the seventh largest on-campus stadium in the country.

Record crowd: The all-time record for a football game in the state of Alabama (85,319) was set in Jordan-Hare stadium on December 2, 1989, when Auburn defeated unbeaten, untied and second-ranked Alabama by the score of 30-20 in the first Auburn-Alabama game played on the Plains.

First game:

What is now Jordan-Hare Stadium was first opened and dedicated on November 30, 1939, at the Auburn-Florida game. That first stadium held 7,500 seats and consisted of what is now the bottom part of the lower west stands. Renamed "Cliff Hare Stadium" in 1949, 14,000 seats–the present lower east stands–were added, raising capacity to 21,500. Shug Jordan became head coach in 1951 and the stadium underwent three major expansions in fifteen years. More than 40,000 seats, nearly half the stadium's current capacity, were added while Jordan was coach. In an impressive demonstration of admiration and respect, Cliff-Hare Stadium became Jordan-Hare Stadium in 1973, making it the first stadium in the country to be named for an active college coach. The later success of the Pat Dye-coached Auburn teams of the eighties brought about the addition of the east side upper deck as well as the luxury suites in 1987.

First game in stadium: November 30, 1939 Auburn 7, Florida 7 Largest margin of victory in stadium: +66 Auburn 76 UT-Chattanooga 10 on September 9, 1995.

Directions: The stadium is located on the campus of Auburn University. It is buffered on the west by Donahue Dr., on the north by Thach Ave. and on the south by Roosevelt Drive.

Coming from Birmingham: Take Hwy 280 East and turn right on Hwy. 29 (College St.), remain on College Street through downtown Auburn and turn right on Magnolia Street. Then turn left on Donahue. Or you may want to take I-65 South to Montgomery, then I-85 North. Get off on exit 51 on Hwy 29 (College Street) and then turn left off the exit ramp, and left at the second light (Donahue).

Where to go:

Toomer's Corner. Situated on the corner of College Street and Magnolia Avenue, Toomer's Corner has long been the gathering place for Auburn athletic celebrations. This legendary locale is in the center of town, where the Auburn University campus meets the City of Auburn. Supposedly the best lemonade in the South is served within Toomer's drug store. Also, after any football win, and after significant victories in other sports, Auburn students and citizens alike join forces and "roll" the trees at Toomer's Corner with toilet paper. Some of the zanier celebrations can leave Toomer's Corner looking like a winter wonderland.

Eating and Drinking:

Auburn Grille: An Auburn Tiger tradition since 1936. Family dining for breakfast, lunch and dinner. 104 N. College St. Auburn, AL 36830 (334)821-6626

Mellow Mushroom: 128 N. College St. Auburn, AL 36830 (334)887-6356 The best pizza and calzones in town. A local favorite. Also serving 18 different beers on tap.

The **Barbecue House:** 345 S. College St. Auburn, AL 36830 (334)826-8277 Specializing in old-fashioned, pit-style barbecue, for over twenty years.

Touchdowns Pub & Eatery: 675 Opelika Rd. Auburn, AL 36830 (334)826-3400

The Bourbon Street Bar – 103 North College Street, Auburn, Alabama, 36830 (334) 887-1166. Great fun and plenty of spirits...just like in the Big Easy.

The War Eagle Supper Club – 2061 South College Street, Auburn, AL 36832 (334) 821-4455. An Auburn tradition with great live music on game nights.

Guthrie's of Auburn – 804 East Glenn Avenue, Auburn, AL 36830 (334) 826-1661. A local favorite for years.

All-Time Record: 634-379-47 (.625)
Bowl Appearances: 30
Bowl Record: 16-12-2 (.567)
SEC Championships: (5) 1957, 1983, 1987, 1988 (tie w/ LSU) 1989 (tie w/Alabama & Tennessee)
SEC Record: 248-201-18 (.552)
National Champions: 1957

Auburn Greats:

Coaches: Ralph "Shug" Jordan. (1951-1975) Auburn's all-time winningest coach, Jordan won 178 games, lost 83 and tied 6 over a 25 year period on the Plains. Jordan led Auburn to 19 winning seasons in 25 years, seven top ten rankings, twelve bowl victories and one SEC Championship. Four times he was named the SEC Coach of the Year. He was also named National Coach of the Year after leading Auburn to its first and only National Championship in football in 1957. To most Auburn fans who knew him, Jordan is remembered as a true sportsman who handled both victory and defeat with uncommon grace.

The Words of Shug Jordan

"Always remember that Goliath was a 40 point favorite over little David."

"There's a closeness that all Auburn people feel. It's the war eagle spirit."

"When we play Alabama, the coaches don't need to prepare pep talks."

"All I ask is that you give everything you've got on every play. That's not asking very much."

"Tucker Frederickson was the most complete football player I've seen in the 40 years I've been connected with the game."

"Men, there is a time for everything. A time to live and a time to die; a time to love and a time to hate; a time for peace and a time for war; And gentleman, there's a time to beat Alabama. That time is now!"
~Shug Jordan, prior to the 1969 Alabama-Auburn contest.

John Heisman. The legendary coach for which college football's top individual accolade is named. Heisman coached at Auburn from 1895-1899, posting a 12-4-2 record. Auburn is the only school where Heisman coached to have a Heisman Trophy winner. Heisman left Auburn for Clemson and then Georgia Tech, where he lost 10 of 15 meetings with Auburn. Heisman once instructed his players, *"Gentlemen, it is better to have died as a small boy than to fumble this football,"* as well as *"Don't cuss. Don't argue with the officials. And don't lose the game...When you find your opponent's weak spot, hammer it! And finally, When in doubt, punt!"*

Auburn

Mike Donahue: "Iron" Mike Donahue, as he was known, won 99 games in two different stints as Auburn's head coach, tying him with Pat Dye for second on the all-time Auburn victories list. Donahue first coached at Auburn from 1904-1906. After a year layoff from football at Auburn, Donahue then coached Auburn from 1908-1922, for a total of 18 years. Donahue's 1913 SIAC Championship team not only went undefeated at 8-0, but they also did not allow a single point.

Patrick Fain Dye: Pat Dye, who coached at Auburn for twelve years from 1981-1992, won 99 games and four SEC Championships in 12 years as head coach. Dye was an even 6-6 against Auburn's arch nemesis Alabama, but he may be most remembered for bringing Auburn's "home" game with Alabama to the Auburn campus on December 2, 1989—which ended up a 30-20 victory for Auburn. Subsequent to Dye bringing the Iron Bowl to Jordan-Hare, Auburn won five straight home games against Alabama, until the 1999 season when the Tide finally beat the Tigers on their home turf for the very first time.

"At Auburn, practice is hell. But when you line up across from the big, fast, smart, angry boys from Florida, and Georgia, and Alabama, where there is no quality of mercy on the ground and no place to hide, you'll know why practice is hell at Auburn." ~Pat Dye

"If you're a football coach, criticism comes with the territory. If it tears you up, you better get into another profession." ~Pat Dye

Terry Bowden – The son of Florida State legend, Bobby Bowden, the enigmatic Terry Bowden was both loved and hated during his coaching days at Auburn. Bowden coached a total of six seasons on the Plains. However, Bowden only coached in six games for Auburn during his final year in 1998. Bowden resigned and was replaced by "Brother" Bill Oliver after notching an unacceptable 1-5 record to start the season. In 1993, the first-year head football coach led Auburn to its first undefeated, 11-win season. Unfortunately for Bowden, that year Auburn was suffering through its first year of NCAA probation that precluded the Tigers from playing on television and in post-season bowl games. Nevertheless, the

11 wins in 1993 were the opening act of a record-setting 20-game winning streak for Auburn, a mark that still stands today. Bowden's opening 20-game win streak at Auburn is also a NCAA record. Bowden's all-time head coaching record at Auburn is an impressive 47-17-1. Today Terry Bowden is a popular TV personality on college gamedays.

Tommy Tuberville – A native of Camden, Arkansas, Tommy Tuberville has revived Auburn's tradition-rich football program by making them a perennial competitor for the conference title. A daring competitor that uses trick plays and various sleights of hand, Tuberville became Auburn's 25th head football coach in November, 1998. Since that time he has led Auburn to three Western Division championships. Prior to coaching at Auburn Tuberville coached at the University of Mississippi from 1995-1998 where he forged a reputation as a "riverboat gambler" for his irresistable penchant for going for it on fourth down. Tuberville's five-year coaching record at Auburn is 38-23 (.623).

Players:

Jimmy Hitchcock – Known as the "Phantom of Union Springs," Jimmy Hitchcock was Auburn's first All-American in 1932. He was an offensive triple threat as a passer, runner and punter who led Auburn to the 1932 Southern Conference Championship. Against Tulane in 1932 Hitchcock returned an interception 60 yards for an Auburn touchdown and later returned an errant punt snap 63 yards for a second score. Duke head coach Wallace Wade said of him, "Hitchcock is the finest all-around back ever to play against any of my teams." Hitchcock also received All-America honors in baseball and played briefly in the Major Leagues after leaving the plains of Auburn.

Tucker Frederickson – A Hollywood, Florida native, Frederickson was a standout fullback and defensive back for Auburn from 1962-64. A consensus All-American, Frederickson was Player of the Year in the South in 1964 while finishing sixth in Heisman Trophy balloting. A two-time winner of the Jacobs blocking trophy, Frederickson ended his stellar gridiron career at Auburn with back-to-back plus-100 yard games against Georgia and Alabama. Frederickson was the first player chosen in the 1965 NFL draft.

Bo Jackson (1982-1985), Heisman Trophy Winner, 1985. All-America, All-SEC in 1983 & 1985. Jackson rushed for more than 4,300 yards with a 6.6 yard per carry average. During his brilliant career on the Plains, Jackson scored 43 touchdowns, and totaled 4,303 career rushing yards, averaging 113 yards per game. Jackson holds the Auburn single-season record for rushing yards with 1,786 in one season. In 1985, Jackson also scored 17 rushing touchdowns. Subsequent to his college career Jackson starred for the Raiders and also was a rare two-sport professional. Jackson played baseball in the major leagues for the Kansas City Royals as well.

Jackson is considered one of the greatest athletes to ever play American college football. In 1982, 1983 and 1985 he was selected to the All-SEC team. In 1983 and 1985 he was named an All-American, and received the Sugar Bowl and Liberty Bowl MVP awards.

92

Pat Sullivan (1969-1971) Heisman Trophy Winner, 1971. All-America, All-SEC and SEC Player of the Year in 1970 and 1971.

Sullivan threw for over 6,000 yards and 53 touchdowns during his career on the Plains. Furthermore, he ran for another 18 touchdowns. Sullivan led Auburn to a 26-7 record from 1969 to 1971, played in three bowl games, and beat Alabama twice. He is well-remembered by Auburn fans for his masterful 351-yard performance in the Gator Bowl over Ole Miss. He is considered Auburn's greatest quarterback, posting an impressive 26-7 record under his direction. Sullivan was the first college player from the State of Alabama to win college football's highest individual honor. After his career on the plains ended, Sullivan played pro ball for five years with the Atlanta Falcons from 1972-1976 and with the Washington Redskins from 1976-1977. In 1986, Sullivan took an assistant coaching position with Auburn under head coach Pat Dye, where he stayed for six seasons before heading to TCU to assume duties as head football coach. Sullivan took the Horned Frogs from a dismal situation of 2-8-1 in 1992 to a record of 7-5 in 1994, earning Southwest Conference Coach of the Year honors in the process.

Terry Beasley (1969-1971) Beasley was a receiver for Pat Sullivan from 1969 to 1971. Largely considered the greatest receiver to ever play at Auburn, he was All-SEC and All-American during his career. Terry Beasley hooked up with Pat Sullivan for over 2500 passing yards and nearly 30 touchdowns. Sullivan and Beasley still hold Auburn's all-time passing and receiving records, respectively.

Retired Jerseys:

Jackson's #34, Sullivan's #7, and Beasley's #88 are all retired Auburn jersey numbers.

Kevin Greene - After being cut once, Greene walked on at Auburn a second time, made the team, and lettered at defensive end during the 1983 and 1984 seasons. Known for his patented, terrorizing "bull rush," Greene went on to become an All-Pro in the NFL, playing for both the Rams organization and the Carolina Panthers.

Takeo Spikes – The Sandersville, Georgia native is one of the greatest linebackers to ever don the Auburn uniform. In 1997, during his last year at Auburn, Spikes led the Auburn Tigers with a scintillating 136 tackles. Extremely athletic for his position, Spikes proved nearly impossible to block during his abbreviated college career. While at Auburn Spikes was rated as one of the top four inside linebackers in the nation. During his junior season Spikes had 18 tackles against Florida—14 of them solo. The 1996 Auburn Defensive Player of the Year and the Mike Kolen Award as Auburn's leading tackler, Spikes passed up his senior year at Auburn to enter the 1998 NFL draft after being named a first-team All-American by the *Sporting News.*

Tracy Rocker – An Atlanta, Georgia native, Rocker made history at Auburn in 1988 when he was the first player from the SEC to win both the Outland Trophy and Lombardi award. Blessed with great size and speed for a down lineman, Rocker was a three-time All-SEC player and two-time All-American. The premier defensive lineman in Auburn football history, from 1985-1988 Rocker logged 199 solo and 155 assisted tackles—totaling a phenomenal 354 total tackles. Rocker led all SEC linemen in tackles as a freshman and his trench talents helped Auburn to a pair of SEC titles in 1988 and 1989.

Stacy Searels – One of the most versatile offensive linemen in Auburn history, Searels repeatedly opened wide running lanes for Auburn backs Bo Jackson and Brent Fullwood from 1984 to 1987. Highly regarded for his run-blocking ability when Auburn preferred running the ball, Searels was equally adept at pass-blocking once Auburn changed its method for gaining real estate. A three-year starter, Searels was All-SEC in 1986 and 1987 and an All-American in 1987. After completing his college eligibility in 1987, Searels was a fourth round draft choice by the San Diego Chargers.

Frank Sanders – A native of Fort Lauderdale, Florida, Sanders was a standout tight end for the Tigers from 1991-94. After leading the SEC in receiving yards per game and breaking Auburn's single-season record for receptions, the incomparable Sanders was named first-team All America by the Associated Press, the Football Writers Association and Scripps Howard. He caught 58 passes for 910 yards and seven touchdowns during his senior year in 1994. Sanders finished his illustrious Auburn career second in total receptions with 121, receiving yardage with 1998 and receiving touchdowns with 15. He was a second-round draft pick by the Arizona Cardinals in 1995.

Terry Daniel – A consensus All-SEC and All-American as a junior, Terry Daniel had the best year ever by an Auburn Tiger punter. He finished the 1993 season with an impressive 46.9 yards per punt average. During that season Daniel booted 16 punts over 50 yards, 3 over 60 yards, and a career-best of 71 yards. However, Daniel was more than just a distance punter. The Valley, Alabama native landed 11 punts dead inside the 20-yard line, including a 49-yard effort against Alabama that was downed at the 6-yard line and led to an eventual safety.

History:

The year 1892 turned out to be an eventful one for the University of Auburn. 1892 was the year that Auburn played its first football game, as well as the year that women first attended the University. The initial gridiron contest in Auburn history was the handiwork of Dr. George Petrie, a faculty member in the Agricultural and Mechanical College in 1892. Petrie organized and coached Auburn's first football team, and is responsible for scheduling

Auburn's first football game, a 10-0 victory over the Georgia Bulldogs in February, 1892. Professor Herty of Georgia and Professor Petrie of Auburn had met each other during graduate school at Johns Hopkins University, so Herty wrote to Petrie with the idea of the game, and the rest is college football history. After the game was played, Auburn publicly the contest as "the first college game in the Deep South." Georgia asserted the same distinction for its contest with Mercer on January 30, 1892.

For years some of Auburn's primary rivals–Georgia, Tennessee, Georgia Tech and Alabama–never made it to The Plains. Auburn's "home" games with those schools were played in Montgomery, Mobile, Columbus and Birmingham. All of that changed in 1960. Prior to 1960, the Auburn-Georgia game was played in Columbus, Athens, Atlanta, Macon or Savannah from 1892 through 1959. However, in 1960, the Bulldogs finally traveled to the Plains and lost, 9-6. From 1906 until 1970 Auburn and Georgia Tech played 53 straight times in Atlanta–before the Yellow Jackets finally gave in and came to Auburn to lose 31-7. In a series that began in 1900, Tennessee finally played at Auburn in 1974, losing 21-0.

Auburn-Georgia: "The Deep South's Oldest Rivalry" Auburn and Georgia began their series on February 20, 1892 at Piedmont Park in Atlanta and has been played almost ever year since. 1996's quadruple-overtime win by Georgia was the 100th meeting in the series which Auburn leads 48-46-8. The Tigers and the Bulldogs have played every year since 1898 with the exception of 1943, when Auburn didn't field a team due to World War II.

Auburn-Alabama - Referred to as the "Iron Bowl" because of the State of Alabama's heritage in the steel business, these two SEC Western Division teams enjoy one of the South's most intense rivalries. The game is such an event among Alabama circles, that family members taking opposite sides have been known to cease communication between one another during the week preceding the game. These two state teams first clashed in February of 1893 at Lakeview Park in Birmingham, Alabama. Auburn won that initial meeting between the two schools and the rivalry was on. However, after the 1907 meeting between the two schools, the annual matchup was abolished due to a petty squabble over travel expenses and who would referee the game. Amazingly, this feud lasted for 41 long years! In 1947, it took a resolution by the House of Representatives to get the two teams to resume playing one another.

Tiger Walk - An Auburn tradition which began in the early 1960's when Auburn players would walk from Sewell Hall to the football stadium and fans would line Donahue Drive to wish them luck. Over the years the Tiger Walk has grown into a major part of game day at Auburn. Tiger Walk is two hours before kickoff of every home game.

The Tiger Trail of Auburn - Representing a bond between the city and the university, this walk of fame is comprised of 26 granite plaques bearing the names of distinguished Auburn men and women recognized for their contributions to the prestige of the institution.

Great Bowl Games:

The 1937 Bacardi Bowl: Sometimes referred to as the Rhumba Bowl or the Cigar Bowl, it was Auburn's first bowl trip and the only bowl game to ever be played outside of the United States. Auburn and Villanova fought to a 7-7 tie in Havana, Cuba on New Year's Day in 1937. Auburn's first All-American, Jimmy Hitchcock, scored the Tigers' only touchdown of the game on a 40-yard run.

1938 Orange Bowl: Auburn 6, Michigan State 0. Ralph O'Gwynne scored the game's only touchdown, a two yard scamper around the left end, to seal the victory over the Spartans for the Tigers.

1954 Gator Bowl: Auburn 33, Baylor 13. Joltin' Joe Childress was the MVP of the game with 134 yards on 20 carries. Auburn finished the season with an 8-3 record under Coach Ralph "Shug" Jordan.

1984 Sugar Bowl: Auburn 9, Michigan 7. Auburn's sophomore sensation Bo Jackson was the game's leading rusher, for 130 yards on 22 carries. However, it was Al Del Greco's three field goals that made the difference in the New Orleans Superdome that day for Auburn. Coach Pat Dye's Tigers finished with an impressive 11-1 record that year, earned the SEC Championship, and a third place national ranking in the API, UPI and USA Today polls.

1998 Peach Bowl: Auburn 21, Clemson 17. Auburn scores 15 fourth-quarter points to secure the win against a tenacious Clemson defense. Auburn's quarterback, Dameyune Craig, threw for 259 yards in the contest.

Band Name: "Auburn Marching Band"
Fight Song: *War Eagle!*

"War Eagle, fly down the field
Ever to conquer, never to yield.
War Eagle, fearless and true,
fight on you orange and blue,
Go, Go, Go...

On to vict'ry, strike up the band.
Give 'em hell, Give 'em hell
Stand up and yell, Hey!
War Eagle, win for Auburn
Power of Dixie Land!

Alma Mater

"On the rolling plains of dixie
'neath the sun-kissed sky,
Proudly stands, our Alma Mater
Banners high.

To thy name we'll sing thy praise,
From hearts that love so true,
And pledge to thee our
Loyalty the ages through.
We hail thee, Auburn, and we vow

To work for thy just fame,
And hold in memory as we do now
Thy cherished name.

Hear thy student voices swelling, Echoes strong and clear,
Adding laurels to they fame Enshrined so dear.

From thy hallowed halls we'll part, And bid thee sad adieu,
Thy sacred trust we'll bear with us The ages through.

We hail thee, auburn, and we vow, To work for thy just fame,
And hold in memory as we do now Thy cherished name.

Composed by Bill Wood, 1942, Revised 1960

Noteworthy Auburn Alumni:

Fob James - A 1957 graduate, James earned All-America honors as a running back for the Tigers. Moreover, James went on to enjoy a successful business career, founding DP Industries, and he was twice elected Governor of Alabama (1979-83,1994-98).

Timothy D. Cook - Senior V.P. of worldwide operations for Apple Computer, Inc.

Don Logan - A 1966 graduate, Logan is CEO and President of Time, Inc.

Carl Mundy - A 1957 graduate, Mundy retired after serving as Commandant of the United States Marine Corps. (More than 100 Auburn graduates have served as generals or admirals in the United States armed forces).

Rowdy Gaines - A 1982 graduate, Gaines is an Olympic gold medalist, world record holder and television sports commentator.

Dr. John Hilburn - President, Microcomputersystems, Inc., Baton Rouge, LA. (microcomputersystems.com)

"A hundred years ago, football in the South was little more than a curiosity. What a difference a century makes. Today, millions of Southerners join the weekly pilgrimage to their stadiums of choice. Tens of millions follow their favorite teams on television or radio. And names like Bryant, Jordan, Gaither and Neyland are spoken with a quiet reverence once reserved for the likes of Robert E. Lee and Stonewall Jackson."

~ Criswell Freeman
The Wisdom of Southern Football, 1995

Louisiana State University

Louisianians have long been known for their uncompromising "joie de vivre" (joy of life). Weekend festivals throughout the state are a common thread within the Louisiana cultural fabric. Each of these annual festivals showcases the food, music and fun that Louisianians enjoy year-round. As a result of their zest for living "the good life" Louisianians live differently from the rest of America and the South. This is due in large part to the fact that the population of Louisiana consists of an amalgam of both French and Spanish influences–two of the three empires that held the territory of Louisiana prior to the Louisiana Purchase in 1803. As a result of its eclectic makeup, Louisiana is much more like its European counterparts than the other 49 states. This cultural diversity comprises a state community that enjoys the best of what each group has to offer within an environment that is definitely conducive to having a good time. After all, "Laissez-les bon temps roulez!" or "Let the good times roll!" is the motto of the fun-loving French Cajuns from south Louisiana. Therefore, it only seems fitting that Louisianians look forward to Saturday nights in Tiger Stadium with unbridled anticipation. Not only is an LSU football game another chance for Louisianians to see their venerable Tigers play–it's also a huge tailgating party, complete with the trappings of a Louisiana festival–good food, friends and fun!

Louisiana State University (LSU): Pronounced "Ellesshoe."

In 1853, the Louisiana General Assembly established the Louisiana State Seminary of Learning and Military Academy near Pineville, Louisiana. The university opened January 2, 1860, with Colonel William Tecumseh Sherman as superintendent. The school closed in 1863 because of the Civil War. The Seminary reopened its doors in October of 1865, only to be burned in October of 1869. In November of 1869 the school resumed its exercises in Baton Rouge, where it has since remained. Land for the current campus was

101

acquired in 1918, and construction started in 1922. Formal dedication of the present campus occurred on April 30, 1926.

Nickname: "Fighting Tigers"

Drawn from the legendary confederate battalion–Robert E. Lee's "Louisiana Tigers"–who distinguished themselves during the Shenandoah Valley Campaign in Virginia. This elite fighting regiment, which was made up of New Orleans "Zouaves" and Donaldsonville "Cannonneers," was so renowned for their ferocity during battle that even fellow Confederate troops were reluctant to fight alongside the licentious lot. During the fall of 1896, Coach A.W. Jeardeau's team posted a perfect 6-0 record, and it was in that fourth gridiron campaign that LSU adopted the Tiger moniker for its team.

Founded: 1860, Pineville, Louisiana

LSU's strong military heritage earned it the nickname "Ole War Skule." "Ole War Skule" was formerly a popular reference to LSU at the turn of the twentieth century, as was the term "Old Lou." Three LSU presidents were generals in the armed forces. Until 1969, ROTC was mandatory for all entering freshmen, and during that time LSU produced as many officers for World War II as West Point, Annapolis or Texas A&M.

William Tecumseh Sherman, who served as a General for the Union army during the Civil War, was the first Superintendent/President of the university. Initially torn between the North and the South, Sherman finally sided with the Constitution of the United States and left the post in Pineville to assume a command in the Union army at the start of the Civil War. However, Sherman's fondness for the Ole War Skule softened his hardline stance toward the Confederacy. Remarkably, at the request of General Sherman, whose troops sacked and burned much of the rest of the deep South, the Louisiana State Seminary, as well as many Louisiana homes and cities, were spared by Union troops during the Civil War. As a fortunate result, many of Louisiana's most beautiful antebellum homes and plantations survive today.

Location: Baton Rouge, Louisiana

Baton Rouge is the heart of plantation country in the South. The bustling industrial city contains the largest concentration of plantation homes in the South along the Mississippi River corridor. And the name, Baton Rouge? It means "red stick," and it refers to the Indian custom of using a red stick, or baton to mark the boundary between two Indian tribes. To most Louisianians Baton Rouge is simply LSU. The state's flagship university calls Baton Rouge its home and its sports teams — especially football—inspire unparalleled loyalty among its most rabid fanbase. Baton Rouge is also a great venue for popular rock bands, such as the area's very own homegrown sound of Better Than Ezra, which got its start in Red Stick in the late 1980's. One Better Than Ezra song, titled "This Time of Year" was reportedly written on the way to an LSU-Ole Miss game in Oxford.

Population: 219,531
Enrollment: 31,582
Colors: Purple & Gold

The inception of LSU's colors of purple and gold are linked to the Louisiana carnival known as Mardi Gras. In 1893, LSU played its first football game against Tulane University of New Orleans. Upon arrival in the Crescent City, LSU coaches realized that LSU's gray uniforms were drab in comparison to Tulane's green uniforms. This prompted the LSU coach to purchase purple and gold ribbons at a nearby store to adorn the Tiger uniforms. Because of Mardi Gras, the store had plenty of purple and gold material (Mardi Gras colors are Purple, Gold and Green).

Mascot: The LSU mascot is a Royal Bengal Tiger.
Mascot Name: "Mike the Tiger"

Named after the original Tiger trainer, Mike Chambers. Tradition dictates that for every growl by Mike before a football game, the Tigers will score a touchdown that night. Mike rides through Tiger Stadium in his cage on wheels before every football game and is cared for by the students at the LSU School of Veterinary Medicine. Mike I was purchased with student contributions in 1936, from a Little Rock, Ark., zoo. Mike V is LSU's current mascot.

Stadium: Tiger Stadium.

"There's a certain tingling sensation which develops over Tiger Stadium when the lights go on to signify another appearance of the Fighting Tigers of LSU under the darkened Louisiana skies. It has been described as a combination of Mardi Gras, the Colosseum, during Rome's halcyon days, an early-day Fourth of July celebration, New Year's Eve in Times Square, and Saturn Three blasting off from its pad at Cape Kennedy." ~ *LSU Media Guide*

Named for the team's mascot, it is also known as "Death Valley" to LSU opponents. East Stadium was constructed in 1926; West in 1932; North in 1937; South in 1957; and an addition was completed above the West side in 1978. In the 2000 football season, Tiger

Stadium's already large capacity was expanded to 92,600 seats, making it the fourth-largest college football playing venue in the country. When Tiger Stadium is filled to capacity on Saturdays in the fall, it is more populous than 50 of the state's 64 parishes (counties).

Coach Paul "Bear" Bryant once remarked on the experience of Tiger Stadium: "Baton Rouge happens to be the worst place in the world to be a visiting team. It's a dugout arena, and you get all of that noise. It's like being inside of a drum."

"Unbelievable, crazy. That place makes Notre Dame look like Romper Room."~Former Southern Cal All-American, Brad Budde on Tiger Stadium in Baton Rouge.

LSU Head Coach Charles McClendon remarked about Tiger Stadium, "The wild excitement inside Tiger Stadium is shattering. It's like an electric wire running from the stands to the field." Bobby Dodd once stated, "I'd rather face the lions in the Coliseum than the Tigers in Baton Rouge."

The Campanile - Often referred to as "the tower" or "the clock or bell tower," it is the memorial granted by the students and the people of Louisiana to those who lost their lives during World War I.

Huey Pierce Long and the Ole War Skule

Huey P. Long, former flamboyant Louisiana governor from 1928-32, is remembered by Louisianians as "LSU's most ardent and vociferous fan" in Professor T. Harry Williams' timeless Pulitzer-Prize winning, biographical tribute titled, "Huey Long." A native Louisianian, Huey wanted badly for LSU to have a bowl football stadium, and a winning

105

program like the other national football powers of the day. However, university officials said what the university really needed at the time was a dormitory. The clever, undeniable Huey soon learned that the federal government would pay for classroom and dormitory buildings through the Works Progress Administration. In light of this, Long sought and discovered an architect who would design a football stadium with dorm rooms in it. The Tiger Stadium dormitory dwellings were still being used into the 1990's.

Long, infamous for wearing wacky purple and gold outfits on game day, was such an LSU fanatic that he would often fill in as drum major and lead the LSU band around campus and onto the football field. Additionally, he was known on occasion, to act as de facto Head Coach and Recruiting Coordinator—much to the chagrin of figurehead Coach Russ Cohen.

Long is credited with creating and funding LSU's first true athletic department. The quintessential demagogue, Long was once quoted as saying, "I don't fool around with losers," and "LSU can't have a losing football team, because that will mean that I am associated with a loser!" If it were not for Huey Long, one could argue forcefully that LSU would not have turned the corner so soon; and become a prominent, modern football school with an impressive stadium, and such a colorful, storied history. Long fell victim to an assassin's bullet at the height of his power in 1935. The then U.S. Senator and de facto Governor of Louisiana is rumored to have spoken these last words while dying in a hospital bed in Baton Rouge, "...My God, my God, I have so much left to do. Who will look after my darling LSU?" Huey Pierce Long was 42 years old at the time of his death.

Tiger Tradition

One of the most important traditions at LSU is when the Tiger Band arrives at the stadium after its normal tour through campus and lines up on the field just minutes prior to kickoff. The band, amidst a stirring drum roll, marches ceremoniously onto the gridiron, playing the fan favorite tune of "Hold that Tiger" and posting a four-corner salute to the fans already seated in the north, south, east and west sections of the stadium. Also among the pre-game activities is the tradition of the Tiger Golden Girls snapping their head to the right to face the flag at the end of the first line of the "Star Spangled Banner." When the pre-game preparations are completed, the crowd buzzes in anxious anticipation of the stadium announcer finally saying, "It's Saturday night in Death Valley, and here come your LSU Tigers!" as the muscle-bound purple and gold Tigers pour out of the tunnel.

Band: "Golden Band from Tigerland"
Stadium Capacity: 79,940 (91,600 as of the 2000 season)
Record Crowd: 82,390 September 24, 1983 LSU-40, Wash St.-14
First Game: 1893 vs. Tulane (0-34) at New Orleans
First Victory: 1894 vs. Natchez AC (36-0) at Natchez, Miss.
First Game played in Tiger Stadium: November 25, 1924
   Tulane-13, LSU-0

Directions:
   Coming from the East-Take I-10 West, exit Dalrymple Drive. Take a right towards the south and follow Dalrymple through campus and then turn right onto North or South Stadium Drive.
   Coming from the West-Take I-10 East, exit Nicholson Drive to the left and follow Nicholson to Tiger Stadium on your left hand side in about four or five minutes.
   Coming from the South-I-10 is the eventual route. Follow signs to Baton Rouge via East or West I-10.
   Coming from the North-Take I-110 South to I-10 East, exit Dalrymple Drive. Take a right towards the south and follow Dalrymple through campus and then turn right onto North or South Stadium Drive.

Where to Geaux in Baton Rouge:

Eating:

Rocco's New Orleans Style Poboys: (Drusilla Lane, 225-344-1999) Let T-Rock and Bert whip you up a New Orleans Style original. The Smokin' Bert's Hot Sausage is to die for.

The Silver Moon Cafe: (Chimes Street, 225-383-1754) Mama's soul food recipes are as wicked as Bourbon Street voodoo. Red beans and rice like you've never had before. Cash only.

Eating and Drinking:

Mike Anderson's Seafood: (1031 West Lee Drive, 225-766-7823) Anderson played for LSU, where he was an All-American linebacker in 1970. If you like good fried and boiled seafood, this is the place. Cold beer and mixed drinks sold inside and on the Side Porch.

Brunet's Cajun Restaurant: (135 S. Flannery Road, 225-272-6226). Bob and his brother Billy have been in the restaurant business for over 25 years. Bob Brunet played for Louisiana Tech and later for the Washington Redskins. Authentic Cajun food served daily and Cajun music and dancing is featured every Wednesday and Saturday nights on the in-house dance floor.

The Chimes: (3357 Highland Road, 225-383-1754). Located right next door to the Varsity at the North Gates of L.S.U., the Chimes has some of the best food in town. The crawfish etouffeé is excellent and there are plenty of beers on tap. Open seven days a week.

Bars & Taverns:

The Varsity Theatre: (Highland Road at the North Gates of L.S.U. 225-383-7018). This refurbished old theatre is a great venue for live music and retro dancing. Get in on the action after Tiger football games.

Ivar's Sport's Bar & Grill: (2954 Perkins Road, 225-388-0021) Sample some of the very best hot wings around and whet your palate with plenty of ice cold beer. Rated the Best Sport's Bar in Baton Rouge.

Zee Zee Gardens: (2904 Perkins Road, 225-346-1291) Within walking distance of Ivar's, Zee Zee's always has a good thirty-something crowd. A local favorite. Located at the foot of the overpass.

Fred's Bar & Grill: (1184 Bob Pettit Dr., 225-766-3543) Enjoy Fred's Sunset Club on the outside deck. Live music on weekends and gamedays. An LSU tradition.

All-Time Record: 649-369-47 (.637)
Bowl Appearances: 35
Bowl Record: 17-17-1 (.500)
SEC Record: 242-187-22 (.564)
SEC Championships: (9) 1935, 36, 58, 61(tie), 70, 86, 88 (tie), 2001, 2003
National Championships: (2) 1958, 2003
62-0: The score that LSU has beaten its arch-rival Tulane—on three separate occasions—1958, 1961, and 1965.

LSU Greats

Coaches:

Charles Coates (1893-Founded Team) Hall in quadrangle bears his name.

Edward Wingar (1907-1908) 17-2 (.850) in two seasons. 10-0 in 1908. SIAA Champions.

Gaynell Tinsley - Tinsley was a two-time All-American end for the Tigers in 1935 and 1936. The Haynesville, Louisiana native led the Tigers to three straight SEC Championships by playing both ways from 1934-1936. The 1936 LSU team finished the year ranked #2 in the country. Tinsley was drafted in the second round of the NFL draft in 1937 by the Chicago Cardinals. Tinsley later returned to LSU to coach the Tigers from 1948-54. Tinsely's 1949 team at LSU finished 8-3, and ended the season ranked #9 overall.

Bernie Moore (1937-47) 89-39-6 (.671) Led LSU to SEC championships in 1935 and 1936. Under Moore's tutelage, the Bengal Tigers did not lose an SEC game until his third year as head coach. Moore led the Tigers to three consecutive Sugar Bowls, an Orange Bowl and a Cotton Bowl berth.

Paul Dietzel (1955-61) 46-24-3 (.651) Dietzel was 31 years old when he began coaching LSU in 1955. His Tigers would eventually become the 1958 National Champs, earning him National Coach of the Year honors in the process. Dietzel was affectionately referred to by Tiger fans as "Pepsodent Paul" for his sparkling white smile. Dietzel is remembered for his coaching genius that produced a platooning system for the Tigers that rotated three teams on and off the field to compensate for the Tiger's lack of depth, and the inhibiting substitution rules of the day. The White Team, the Go Team and the "Chinese Bandits" were all used by Dietzel to win ball games. The platooning system allowed Dietzel to play 35 to 40 players in each game, thereby keeping his players fresh. Dietzel later served as head coach and athletic director at South Carolina, from 1966 to 1974. The Words of Paul Dietzel:

"The athletic field is very democratic. Each person is judged by personal merit rather than personal wealth or prestige."

"We came to win, not to tie. If I had it to do over a hundred times, I would do the same thing." ~Paul Dietzel, after a two-point conversion failed resulting in a 14-13 loss to Tennessee. The loss ended LSU's 19-game winning streak.

"There are no office hours for champions."

Charlie McClendon (1962-1979) 137-59-7 (.692) By posting winning records in 16 of 18 seasons, "Cholly Mac" became the winningest Coach in LSU History. Although McClendon was LSU's most successful coach, he was berated by fans for continually losing to his famous nemesis in Tuscaloosa, Paul "Bear" Bryant. Nevertheless, McClendon led LSU to two Sugar Bowls, two Cotton Bowls, two

Bluebonnet Bowls, two Orange Bowls, two Sun Bowls, a Tangerine Bowl, a Liberty Bowl and a Peach Bowl. Coach McClendon, throughout his long career at LSU, had 14 teams play in bowl games. In addition, 15 of his teams finished in the AP top 15 during his tenure. In 1970, Coach Charles "Cholly Mac" McClendon was honored as National Coach of the Year.

The Words of Coach Charles McClendon:

"The worst mistake any coach can make is not being himself."

"In Baton Rouge, it's not a law to love LSU, but the city fathers could probably get one passed if they needed to."

"Everybody at LSU wants another great team like '58. The only trouble is that our schedule is so tough, we could have a great year and never know it."

Jerry Stovall-1980-83 (22-21-2) Stovall was named National Coach of the Year in 1982 after posting an 8-3-1 record and losing to Nebraska in the Orange Bowl 21-20.

Harry Rabenhorst, who coached the LSU basketball team to the mythical national championship in 1935, played basketball and football at Wake Forest and holds the NCAA record for the longest recorded punt–110 yards.

Mike Archer – In 1987, 31-year old Mike Archer—the youngest Division I head coach in America, took over for Bill Arnsparger and coached four years at LSU, posting a 27-18-1 (.598) record during that span. A Miami, Florida native and 1976 graduate of the University of Miami, Archer was a star defensive back and punter for the Hurricanes. Archer coached seven years as secondary coach at Miami under Coach Howard Schnellenberger. Archer left Miami in 1984 to become the defensive coordinator at LSU. After LSU, Archer coached at Virginia and Kentucky before spending seven years with the Pittsburgh Steelers. Today, Archer is the defensive coordinator for the Kentucky Wildcats.

Gerry DiNardo – In 1995 DiNardo came to LSU during a down time in LSU's storied football history. Following Curley Hudson Hallman's four-year tenure in which he notched a disappointing 16-28 record, DiNardo came to LSU from Vanderbilt to bring respectability to the once-great LSU football program. A graduate of Notre Dame, DiNardo won early on with Hallman's recruits but during his last two seasons in Baton Rouge his luck and his talent ran out. In five seasons DiNardo posted a more than respectable 32-24-1 (.570) record at the helm for the Tigers, with his biggest win coming in October, 1997 when LSU defeated Steve Spurrier's number one-ranked Florida Gators in an unlikely 28-21 upset in Tiger Stadium. After a short and unsuccessful stint as a head coach in the failed XFL pro league, DiNardo took the head coaching job at Indiana University, a post he still holds today.

Nick Saban – In late 1999, prior to the 2000 football season, Nick Saban was named the 12th LSU head football coach during the SEC era that began in 1933, and the school's 31st overall. Saban succeeded interim head coach Hal Hunter, who took over for a fired Gerry DiNardo. A graduate of Kent State where he was a 3-year letterman as a defensive back, Saban paid his dues by assistant coaching (defensive backs) at his alma mater under Don James, briefly at Syracuse, West Virginia, and for Earl Bruce at Ohio State. In 1983 Saban went to Michigan State and served as defensive coordinator under George Perles for five seasons. In 1988 and 1989 Saban coached the secondary for the Houston Oilers. He assumed his first head coaching position at Toledo in 1990, producing a 9-2 record on the season. In 1991, Saban returned to the NFL for four seasons as Cleveland's defensive coordinator, making the Cleveland Browns' defense one of the NFL's best stop units. In 1995, Saban took the head coaching job at Michigan State where he coached for five seasons, ending with a best 9-2 record in 1999. Often described as a "no-nonsense" type coach, Saban is known as a hard worker, a steadfast defensive instructor and a consummate recruiter of talent. In his first year in Baton Rouge Saban went 8-4, culminating with a 28-14 victory over Georgia Tech in the Peach Bowl. In 2001, he built on his earlier success by leading LSU to its first SEC Championship since 1988 with a climactic come-from-behind victory over the Tennessee Volunteers in the SEC Championship Game. In 2002, LSU finished as SEC Western Division Co-Champs and in 2003 LSU repeated as SEC Champions with a 34-13 victory over Georgia and went on to defeat Oklahoma 21-14 in the Sugar Bowl in New Orleans for the BCS National Championship, its first since 1958.

"What's the hardest thing about being great? Overcoming being good." ~Nick Saban

Players:

Y.A. Tittle, Quarterback (1944-47) - The Marshall, Texas native originally committed to play for the Texas Longhorns in Austin. However, after a dorm-room visit in Austin, Texas from LSU Assistant Coach Red Swanson, Tittle packed his bags and left for Baton Rouge. Tittle used his exceptional athletic ability to lead the Tigers to their first win over Alabama in over thirty years in 1948, bringing with that victory national acclaim to LSU. Tittle completed his college eligibility in Baton Rouge as the Tigers' all-time leading passer, a mark that would later be broken as passing offenses became increasingly popular in the college game. Tittle went on to an illustrious pro football career with the New York Giants, where he was eventually named the league's Most Valuable Player on three separate occasions. He is a member of the NFL Hall of Fame.

Billy Cannon, Running Back (1956-1959) Cannon's legs led the Tigers to their only national championship, in 1958. Known for his overall toughness and resolve, Cannon possessed unparalleled rushing skills. Gifted with both size and speed, Billy Cannon was

113

the prototypical running back during an era of college football that had few true sprinters. Cannon, in his prime, could run a sub 4.5 forty-yard dash–a statistic that is simply mind-boggling for that day and age. Cannon's amazing gridiron talents set him apart from his SEC, and national counterparts, and his exploits on the playing field were the stuff of legend. The Baton Rouge native's ephemeral run into Bengal Tiger and college football lore came during the 1959 season when he returned a punt 89 yards against Ole Miss to catapult the Tigers to a 7-3 victory. Mississippi Head Coach John Vaught had this to say about Cannon's magical romp, "Outside the Louisiana Purchase in 1803, many Cajuns consider Billy Cannon's run the greatest event in state history." For his remarkable accomplishments on the football field, Billy Cannon was named the 1959 Heisman Trophy Recipient. During his illustrious career in Tigertown, Cannon scored 19 touchdowns and rushed for 1,867 yards on 359 carries, for an average of 5.2 yards per carry. Following his 1959 Heisman-Trophy-winning season, Cannon's jersey, #20, was retired to the LSU Football Hall of Fame. Athlon Southeastern Football in 1969 proclaimed Cannon "The best Southeastern Conference player in the last 11 years."

Tommy Casanova, Safety (1968-1971) All-American 1969, 1970, 1971. Known for his versatility, Casanova played on both sides of the ball as a running back and kick returner as well as a three-time All-American safety during his career as a Tiger.

114

Fighting Tigers

From 1969-71, he intercepted seven passes, rushed for 302 yards on 72 carries for five touchdowns, returned 44 punts for 517 yards and returned 17 kickoffs for 334 yards. He was renowned as a fearless competitor both on and off the field at LSU.

He remains as one of seven three-time First Team All-Southeastern Conference performers at LSU, joining the likes of David Browndyke (1987-89), Kevin Faulk (1996-98), Dalton Hilliard (1982, 83, 85) and Tommy Hodson (1986-89). Today, Casanova is a medical doctor in his hometown of Crowley, Louisiana. In 1995, Casanova was named to the National Football Foundation & Hall of Fame located in South Bend, Indiana.

Bert Jones, Quarterback (1969-1972) 1972 All-American. Jones, a standout signal-caller for the Bayou Bengals during the early 1970's, had as strong an arm as any quarterback in the history of the college game. Jones' verile right arm led the Tigers to a record of 26-6-1 during his career in Baton Rouge, playing in three bowl games and winning an SEC title during his sophomore campaign. Jones is most notably remembered by Tiger fans for his 28-8 victory over Notre Dame in 1971 and over Ole Miss in 1972 when, with time expired, he threw a touchdown pass to Brad Davis, giving the Tigers an improbable 17-16 victory. The Ruston, Louisiana native was chosen as the first pick in the 1973 NFL draft, by the Baltimore Colts.

Tommy Hodson, Quarterback (1986-89) LSU's All-time Leading passer. An All-SEC performer for four years in Baton Rouge, Hodson was one of LSU's greatest quarterbacks. During his stellar collegiate career, Hodson completed 674 passes on 1,163 attempts for 9,115 total yards (5th All-time in SEC) for a .579 completion percentage, and an impressive 69 touchdowns. Today the Matthews, Louisiana native is a financial consultant in Baton Rouge.

Kevin Faulk, Running Back (1995-1998) 1996, 1997 All-American, LSU's All-Time Leading Rusher, SEC All-Time All-Purpose Yardage Leader (7,000) (Fifth in NCAA history). As primarily a tailback for the Tigers, Faulk rushed for 5.3 yards per carry and 46 touchdowns. The Carencro, Louisiana native finished his career in Baton Rouge second on the all-time SEC rushing list, behind only the legendary Herschel Walker. During his stellar collegiate career for the Bayou Bengals, Kevin Faulk averaged 20.9 carries per game, (856 in 41 total). Another amazing career stat by the prolific Faulk is that he also averaged 111.2 yards rushing per game (4,557 in 41). Faulk was eventually drafted in the second round by the New England Patriots in the 1999 NFL draft. A starter for four straight years for the Tigers, Faulk impressively graduated in three and a half years.

Anthony "Booger" McFarland Defensive Lineman (1995-1998) 1998 All-American. The Winnsboro native was a four-year starter for the Tigers and a two-time All-SEC pick. Possessing unbelievable quickness for a player with his size, McFarland was a terror on the defensive front for the Tigers. A first round draft choice in the 1999 NFL draft, he is currently a defensive tackle for the Tampa Bay Buccaneers.

Josh Reed – A Rayne, Louisiana native, Reed is one of the most decorated players in school history. During his brief gridiron career Reed completely rewrote the LSU and SEC record books for receiving. The 2001 Biletnikoff Award winner and a consensus All-American, Reed proved to be one of the best deep threats the conference ever produced. Despite starting only 15 of 31 games he played in for the Tigers, Reed hauled in 167 passes for 3,001 yards (18.0 yard per catch) and 17 touchdowns, becoming the first player in conference history to gain over 3,000 yards receiving in a career. In all, Reed set a total of 12 school and conference records. His 18 100-yard performances during his LSU career is a school record, and he is joined by Tennessee's Joey Kent (1995-96) as the only player in Southeastern Conference history to gain over 1,000 yards receiving in consecutive seasons. Reed was a first round choice by the Buffalo Bills in the 2002 NFL draft.

Rohan Davey – A Clarendon, Jamaica native, Rohan Davey went to LSU via Miami Lakes, Florida in 1998 and made his mark as one of LSU's all-time signal callers. A natural field general with exceptional leadership skills, Davey was known for his physical brand of play and his uncanny ability to throw on the run. Possessing a large frame, Davey was tough to bring down in the pocket and he had a rifle for an arm. During his senior season Davey used his unique talents to throw for 3347 yards and 18 touchdowns, leading LSU to a 2001 SEC Championship in the process. Davey was a fourth round draft pick by the New England Patriots in 2002.

Michael Clayton – A Baton Rouge native, Clayton is remembered as one of LSU's best all-around athletes. Clayton started 31 games during his three-year career with LSU, leading LSU to two SEC Championships en route. Amazingly, Clayton caught at least one pass in every game he played in wearing an LSU uniform. In

his career, Clayton caught 182 passes for 2,582 yards. The 182 receptions ranks second in school history to Wendell Davis's 183. His 2,582 yards is 4th on the all-time LSU receiving yards list. Clayton ended his college career early by entering the 2004 NFL draft with one year of eligibility remaining.

Matt Mauck – The Jasper, Indiana native spurred the Tigers to a huge upset victory over the 2nd ranked Tennessee Volunteers in the 2001 SEC Championship Game during his non-traditional freshman season. A former professional baseball player, Mauck was 22 when he made an impromptu appearance and earned MVP honors in the 2001 SEC Championship Game. Remembered for his ability to make plays with his feet and for his ability to read defenses, Mauck earned the starting job in 2002. In 2003 he led LSU to its first National Championship in 45 years in a 21-14 victory over Oklahoma in the Sugar Bowl at the New Orleans Superdome. Mauck threw for 2,825 yards and 28 touchdowns during his last year in an LSU uniform. His 18-2 record as a starter is the best winning percentage for an LSU quarterback. Like Clayton, Mauck decided to forego his senior season at LSU to enter the 2004 NFL draft.

Bradie James – A native of West Monroe, Louisiana, James is remembered as a quintessential team leader and a sure tackler. James played in 10 games as a freshman for LSU and started every remaining game of his stellar four-year career, logging an impressive 248 solo tackles and 170 assists (418 total) in the process. After graduating James was drafted in the 4th round by the Dallas Cowboys in the 2003 NFL draft.

Domanick Davis – A dynamic back, Davis finished his quiet career at LSU second in school history and third in league history in all-purpose yards with 5,743 total yards (Kevin Faulk). The pow-

118

erfully athletic Cajun running back and return specialist ranks second in SEC history with 95 career kickoff returns and ninth in punt returns with 94. In all, Davis had 30-100 yard all-purpose games. The Breaux Bridge, Louisiana native was the fourth pick of the fourth round of the 2003 NFL draft. During his rookie season with the Houston Texans Davis rushed for 1031 yards, and in doing so earned runner-up NFL Rookie of the Year honors.

Tradition

John D. McCallum once wrote of football at LSU... "What you find in Baton Rouge is typical of the football frenzy in the South. No city in the country hath greater love for its football team. So deep is the feeling that workers arrange vacations, night shifts, bowling leagues, weddings and even family pregnancies so that they won't conflict with LSU games."

"It's a magical setting," sports author Mike Bynum said. "The excitement, the atmosphere, is unmatched anywhere–and I've been in stadiums from one end of America to the other. They ought to put up a statue to the guy who came up with night football at LSU."

That would be former Tiger athletic director T.P. "Skipper" Heard, who headed the program on the Oct. 3, 1931, evening when LSU played Spring Hill under the lights. It was not a first in college football. Illinois defeated Carlisle in an 1897 game played indoors at the Chicago Coliseum. Nowhere, however, did "after dinner" games become more popular than in Baton Rouge.

Willie Morris, of the *Sporting News*, wrote of the experience of a night game in Tiger Stadium in Baton Rouge: "No scholar of the Dixie gridiron can pass his years in this mortal coil without witnessing a night game in Tiger Stadium in Baton Rouge. The sinking burnt-orange Louisiana sun casts death-like shadows upon this terrain of old tumult, and minutes before kickoff the ceaseless mounting clamor rises in synesthesia, making one feel he is in the presence of some elemental phenomenon of near geological propensity."

Douglas Looney, of *Sports Illustrated* on LSU Football: "It makes a

119

body tingle. These folks go berserk when the band marches on the field. A huge roar is heard for the invocation, for heaven's sake. They not only know the words to the national anthem, they sing them, loudly. And when the Tigers win the toss...there are tears of ecstasy."

Sportswriter John Logue, on the experience of Tiger Stadium in Baton Rouge: "Encircling itself, high and in the air like a fortress abandoned during some particularly bloodied age, towers the most ferocious address in Louisiana. In Tiger Stadium, a game is not merely seen. It is HEARD. The sound of it twists up the steel and concrete enclosure like a particularly sinister tornado. The parts are played out equally in the stands and on the field. Writers in the press box, high over the crowd, find themselves unable to think when the noise stops. If it stops."

History

LSU football began in 1893 under the direction of Dr. Charles E. Coates, a chemistry professor from Baltimore, Maryland. When Coates arrived in Baton Rouge in the early nineties he was surprised that football had not been established. He immediately issued a request for a football team in the fall of 1893. Coates later remarked that "some mighty good-looking prospects" reported. Coates was assisted in his efforts by a young professor of entomology and zoology who had learned the game of Canadian rugby prior to coming to LSU. This young gentleman's name was Harcourt A. Morgan, who went on to become President of the University of Tennessee and a member of the first Board of Directors of the Tennessee Valley Authority. Dr. Coates drove nails into the his players' shoes in order for them to have cleats during their inaugural season. The Tigers went 0-1 that first year, losing to eventual arch rival Tulane. By 1896 the Tiger football schedule had increased to six contests, with LSU winning all of them.

The first night game in Tiger Stadium was played in 1931. Night football increased the attendance at LSU games and allowed tailgating to become a day-long, anticipated event. Legend has it that the Tigers play better in Tiger Stadium at night than they do in the daylight. In the three decades from 1960 to 1990, LSU recorded a nighttime winning percentage in Tiger Stadium of 78.5 percent.

LSU was the very first school to have a squad of female dancers accompany their football team and perform at halftime. The Golden Girls were almost overnight copied by all the universities in the SEC.

Great Bowl Games

1947 Cotton Bowl: LSU-0, Arkansas-0. (Often referred to as the "Ice Bowl")

1959 Sugar Bowl: LSU-7, Clemson-0. LSU wins National Championship.

1966 Cotton Bowl: LSU-14, Arkansas-7. LSU shocks the second-ranked Razorbacks.

1996 Peach Bowl: LSU-10, Clemson-7. LSU clinches 5th 10-win season in history.

1997 Independence Bowl: LSU-27, Notre Dame-9. Tigers avenge regular-season loss to Irish.

2000 Peach Bowl: LSU-28, Georgia Tech-14

2002 Sugar Bowl: LSU-47, Illinois 34

2004 Sugar Bowl: LSU-21, Oklahoma-14 (BCS National Championship)

LSU Alma Mater
By Lloyd Funchess and Harris Downey

Where stately oaks and broad magnolias shade inspiring halls,
There stands our dear old Alma Mater to who us recalls
Fond memories that waken in our hearts a tender glow
And make us happy for the love that we have learned to know,
All praise to thee, our Alma Mater, molder of mankind,
May greater glory, love unending, be forever thine.
Our worth in life will be thy worth, we pray to keep it true,
And may thy spirit live in us, forever LSU.

Hey Fightin' Tigers!

Hey! Fightin' Tigers! Fight all the way!
Hey! Fightin' Tigers! Win the game today!
You've got the know-how, you're doin' fine,
Hang on to the ball as you hit the wall
And smash right through the line.
You've got to go-o-o! For a touchdown, Ru-u-un! up the score!
Make Mike the Tiger stand right up and roar. ROAR!!!!!
So give it all of your might as you fight tonight,
And keep the goal in view—Vic-to-ry for LSU!

Hot Boudin & Cold Cush Cush!

Hot Boudin! Cold cush cush! Come on Tigers! Push! Push! Push!
This short, rather colloquial cheer is a favorite among Cajun Tiger fans. Boudin is a spicy cajun delicacy resembling a sausage that is created by encasing ground pork, rice and seasonings. Cush-cush is fried cornmeal mush served hot with syrup or in milk.

The Boot

LSU and Arkansas play every year for a sectional trophy named "The Boot." "The Boot" is a 24-carat gold trophy in the shape of the states of Arkansas and Louisiana that forms a boot. This new tradition between the two Western Division schools began in 1996 in an attempt to stimulate competition between the two schools. LSU won the Boot in three of its first four years of existence—1996, 97 and 99. Arkansas won it in 1998. The shiny metal trophy always rests on the previous winner's sideline during the game since the victor of the yearly contest always earns ownership of the Boot—as well as bragging rights for the following year.

Chinese Bandits - The term "Chinese Bandits" started when Coach Paul Dietzel recited a line from the old "Terry and The Pirates" comic strip which described Chinese Bandits as the "most vicious people in the world." During their prime, the Chinese Bandits were featured in Chinese masks for a layout in *Life Magazine*. In 1980 the LSU band revived the traditional practice of the Bandit tune being played when the LSU defense stops any opponent's drive.

The Earthquake Game

October 8, 1988, is known simply as the "Night the Tigers Moved the Earth." LSU struggled all night against a tough Auburn team. The visitors from the Plains had held the Tigers scoreless on the night, while Auburn had only managed two field goals. With just 1:41 left to play in the contest, on fourth and nine from the Auburn 11, Tommy Hodson zeroed in with Eddie Fuller in the back of the endzone for a tying touchdown that catapulted LSU to a 7-6 victory. The play caused such an explosion from the rabid crowd of 79,341 that the tremor caused by the subsequent vibrations registered on a nearby campus seismograph in the LSU Geology Department. The seismograph recordings for the week of the game revealed a large track of ink that registered at 9:32 p.m., at the exact moment of the winning touchdown by LSU. In May of 1994, the memorable great moment in Tiger football history was featured in a *Ripley's Believe It Or Not!* segment circulated to newspapers throughout the world.

The Rag

The Rag was the traditional item that was symbolic of victory in the LSU-Tulane rivalry for many years. A flag decorated partly in LSU's colors of purple and gold, and the other partly in the green and white of Tulane, it was customarily held for one full year by the winning school until the next game between the two the following season. The current whereabouts of the storied flag are unknown.

Noteworthy LSU Alumni:

Hubert Humphrey, (deceased) Vice President of the United States (1964-68)

Carlos Roberto Flores, President of Honduras

Lod Cook, Retired Chairman and CEO of ARCO

Max Faget, NASA Engineering & Development Director

Bill Conti, Academy Award Winner, Composer and Conductor for *The Right Stuff*

Rex Reed, New York Author & Critic

Elizabeth Ashley, Actress with *Evening Shade*

Russell Long, Former Senator, Chairman, U.S. Senate Finance Committee

Shaquille O'Neal, NBA Star, Actor, Entertainer

James Carville, Political Consultant, Commentator

John J. Lejeune, WWI Marine Corps Commandant, Camp Lejeune, North Carolina

Gen. Claire Chennault, Founder and Commander of World Renowned "Flying Tigers"

Gen. Troy Middleton, 8th Army Commander, held Bastogne during Battle of the Bulge

D.M. Waghelstein, Operator, USMC Recon, USAF Pararescue, U.S. Special Operations

life in the south

"I'm from Ohio, but if I'd
known when I was two
what it was like down
South, I would have
crawled here on hands
and knees."

~ Frank Sinkwich

Mississippi State University

Amidst a rustic backdrop that includes the gentle, rolling, red-dirt and tall pine-tattered hills of northern Mississippi, rests Mississippi State University, home of the mighty Bulldogs. Mississippi State, in spite of its bucolic setting, has long enjoyed its place as a football school among its more urban SEC counterparts. Possessing a lively fan base, Starkville is a special place for football games where the Bulldog brethren can leave opponent's ears ringing with the near-deafening, continuous clanging of industrial-sized cow bells. In recent years Starkville has enjoyed a rise and fall of football fortune with the arrival and departure of Head Coach Jackie Sherrill. Sherrill's experienced presence in Starkville brought new life to the program and rekindled the hopes of the Bulldog faithful; for lately, during each home contest, Scott Field transforms, to the delight of every Mississippi State football fan, and to the chagrin of every visiting opponent, into the dreaded "Dawg Pound."

Founded: 1878

The university started as the Agricultural and Mechanical College of the State of Mississippi, a national Land-Grant college established after Congress passed the Morrill Act in 1862. The school was created by the Mississippi Legislature on February 28, 1878, to complete "...the mission of providing training in agriculture, horticulture, and the mechanical arts..." By 1932, the school was renamed the Mississippi State College, and later, in 1956, its name was again changed to its present moniker—Mississippi State University. Today, Mississippi State University is the second largest land-grant institution and one of the top 100 division one research facilities in the country.

Location: Starkville

Founded in 1831, the town of Starkville was initially referred to as "Boardtown." Subsequent to its chartering in 1837, the town was renamed for Revolutionary War hero General John Stark. The county seat of Oktibbeha County (pronounced ok-TIB-be-haw), Starkville became the birthplace of Mississippi State University in 1878 with the establishment of its forerunner, Mississippi A&M College. Once known as the "Dairy Center of the South" Starkville's economic composition has evolved over the past several years into a diverse conglomeration of education, industry, service and retail trade. Starkville is located one hour south of Tupelo, Mississippi, the birthplace of "The King of Rock N' Roll," Elvis Presley.

Population: 20,000
Enrollment: 16,236

Nickname: "Bulldogs"

As with many other institutions, Mississippi State teams answered to other nicknames through the years. Mississippi A&M's first football teams were referred to as the "Aggies," and when the college first became Mississippi State College in 1932, the nickname "Maroons," for the club's uniforms, gained acceptance. "Bulldogs" became the official title for State teams in 1961, soon after the school was granted university status. However, references to school athletic teams as "Bulldogs" date back to the early twentieth century, as this moniker was used interchangeably with both "Aggies" and "Maroons," since at least 1905.

Colors: Maroon and White

The origin of the maroon and white dates back to before the turn of the nineteenth century. On November 15, 1895, the first Mississippi State football team was preparing for a road trip the following day to Jackson, Tennessee to play Southern Baptist University (now referred to as Union University). Given that every college was expected to have its own uniform colors, the student body at Mississippi State requested that the team choose a suitable combination. Considering the selection an honor, the team deferred the decision to its captain, W.M. Matthews. Accounts report that Matthews quickly summoned the use of maroon and white as the school's colors, which it has used since.

Mascot: The official mascot of Mississippi State is an American Kennel Club registered English Bulldog, given the inherited title of "Bully."

Use of the bulldog as an official game mascot began in 1935, when Coach Major Ralph Sasse, on 'orders' from his team, traveled to Memphis, Tennessee, to acquire a bulldog. Sasse returned with Ptolemy, a gift of the Edgar Webster family. A litter-mate of Ptolemy became the first mascot called "Bully." Sadly, Bully I was hit by a bus in 1939, ending his short career as MSU mascot. Days of campus mourning ensued, as Bully lay in a glass coffin for all to witness. A half-mile funeral procession accompanied by the Maroon Band and three ROTC battalions went to Scott Field where Bully was buried under the bench at the 50-yard line. The event was such a spectacle that *LIFE Magazine* covered it. Other Bullys have since been buried nearby campus dorms, fraternity houses and also at the football stadium. Furthermore, a student wearing a Bulldog suit, also answering to "Bully" is part of the MSU cheerleading squad, and aids in stirring up school spirit at game and pep rallies.

Stadium: Scott Field

Scott Field - named in honor of Don Magruder Scott, an Olympic sprinter and one of the University's first football stalwarts, the nation's second-oldest football stadium was refurbished and expanded in 1985 and 1986. The 1985-86 construction, which brought the stadium to a capacity of 40,656, was one of three major expansion projects that have occurred at MSU. Prior renovation efforts in 1936 and 1948 brought capacity at Scott Field to 35,000 seats and provided basic concrete grandstand structure.

NOTE: 35 years after the 1948 expansion, the endzone seating structures were removed, lowering the capacity to 32,000 in 1983).

In 1997, a multi-million dollar Sony JumboTron and scoreboard were installed in the north endzone.

Stadium capacity: 40,656

Record crowd: 42,700 (twice) Last-Nov. 1, 1986-Alabama 38, Miss. State 3

First game: On Thanksgiving Day, November 26, 1892, a group of faculty members at Mississippi A&M College met a select group of pupils for a game of the new sport known as 'foot-ball.' Football was brought to MSU by educators and graduates from the eastern colleges. Initially, the game was introduced at MSU and played mainly among the classes of students, who would test their mettle against one another on the gridiron. However, in 1895, MSU joined the Intercollegiate Athletic Association, signaling the beginning of competitive football for the Bulldogs.

During October, 1895, W.M. Mathews organized a true college team and arranged a November 16th game at Southern Baptist University (Now Union University). According to Bob Hartley, Football at Mississippi State made its inaugural debut when Matthews, a student from the State of Texas, organized and coached the Bulldogs during their first season. On November 16th

129

of that same year, the Bulldogs played in Jackson, Tennessee against Southwestern Baptist University (Union University). Disappointingly, the Bulldogs were welcomed to the ranks of college football with a resounding, 21-0 defeat.

The first football game played before the students of Mississippi State was held the following year at the racetrack in Starkville. The game was a rematch of State's first football game against Union. The outcome, however, was no different this time–MSU fell that day by a score of 8-0. An outbreak of yellow fever caused a four year hiatus for football at Mississippi State from 1897 through 1900. However, interest in the sport was rekindled in the fall of 1901 when a Georgetown graduate, Harvey Washington, wrestled control of the football team and coached them to Mississippi State's first successful season on the gridiron. That year, MSU went 2-2-0, defeating Ole Miss (first win) and the Meridian Athletic Club, while losing to both Tulane and Alabama.

First game in stadium: October 1914; MSU-54, Marion Military Institute-0

Band: "Famous Maroon Band"

Directions: Coming from the East or West: Take Hwy 82 to Hwy 12; exit Hwy 12 on College View St. (first exit); turn right (east) on College View St. The stadium is on the left.

Coming from the South: Take Hwy 25 to Hwy 12 eastbound; take Hwy 12 to Russell St.; turn right (east) on Russell St. The stadium is on the left.

Where to go in Starkville:

Starkville Cafe - P.O. Box 1250, Starkville (601) 323-1665. The Starkville Cafe is open 24 hours a day. Specializing in a traditional breakfast menu, Starkville Cafe has been serving good Southern food since 1945.

Rosey Baby - 300 S. Jackson St. Starkville (662) 324-1949

Bulldog Deli - 702 University Drive (601) 324-3354. Located on University Drive in the heart of the Cotton District, conveniently near the university, serves college students and others who crave great tasting "New York Style" sandwiches and iced tea.

Little Dooey - 127 Highway 12 W Starkville, MS 39759 (662) 323-5334 – Find out why the ESPN Gameday crew always eats here. Lord child it's some good barbecue!

Cotton District Grill - 106 Maxwell Street, Starkville, MS In the District (662) 323-6062 – An established local favorite. Good Southern food, drinks and hospitality.

All-Time Record: 464-489-39 (.486)
Bowl Record: Record 12 appearances / 6-6 (.500)
SEC Championships: (1) 1941
SEC Record: 152-289-13 (.344)

MSU Greats:

Coaches:

Allyn McKeen (1939-1948) 65-19-3 (.764) Coach McKeen led the Bulldogs to their first bowl victory ever in 1941, a 14-7 victory over Georgetown in the Orange Bowl. State finished ninth in the final AP poll that year. Subsequent to State's first bowl win, McKeen earned SEC Coach of the Year honors during the 1941 season for leading the Bulldogs to a 4-0-1 league record and their first and only SEC title.

Emory Bellard (1979-1985) 37-42 (.468) A graduate of Southwest Texas State, Coach Ballard is likely best remembered by State fans for leading the Bulldogs to one of its biggest victories in school history–a 6-3 defeat of number-one-ranked Alabama in 1980, a game played in the state's capital of Jackson, Mississippi. State finished 9-3 and ranked 19th nationally in 1980. Under Bellard's

131

direction, State returned in 1981 to go 6-1 versus ranked opponents and climbed to a lofty No. 7 in the national polls, the highest ranking in school history.

Jackie Sherrill (1991-2003) Hired by MSU on December 9, 1990, Sherrill served the Bulldogs well as head coach. A protégé of SEC coaching legend, Paul "Bear" Bryant, Sherrill coached at Washington State (1976), Pittsburgh (1977-1981), and Texas A&M (1982-1988), prior to his arrival in Starkville. Successful coaches that have coached under Sherrill include Jimmy Johnson and Dave Wannstedt. Sherrill is the only head coach at MSU to lead the Bulldogs to three bowl games. Seventeen of the top 25 crowds to ever see the Bulldogs play at Scott Field have congregated during the Sherrill era. On October 1, 1992, Sherrill's Bulldogs handed Steve Spurrier one of his worst, and only SEC losses, before the largest home-opening crowd in Scott Field history (38,886–it has since been shattered) as well as a national TV audience. The 24th-ranked Bulldogs humbled the 13th-ranked Gators by a score of 30-6. Also, on November 16, 1996, MSU defeated then No. 8 Alabama 17-16 in Starkville, for the Bulldog's first-ever victory over the Crimson Tide in Starkville. Sherrill's 1998 team won the SEC Western Division Championship.

In 1999, Sherrill's Bulldogs finished 10-2 after defeating Clemson 17-7 in the Peach Bowl. In 2000 Sherrill led his team to an 8-4 record and a dramatic 43-41 overtime win against his former Texas A&M squad. In 13 seasons at MSU, 7 at Texas A&M, 5 at Pitt, and the lone year at Washington State, Sherrill compiled a 180-120-4 record (.600). At the time of his retirement at the end of the 2003 season, Sherrill was 4th among active division one coaches in wins behind Joe Paterno, Bobby Bowden and Lou Holtz. Sherrill was replaced in December, 2003 by Sylvester Croom, the SEC's first black head coach since the league began in 1933.

Players:

W.D. "Dub" Garrett - A four-time All-Southeastern Conference selection on Mississippi State's offensive line from 1944-47.

David Smith - MSU's All-Time Receiving Leader (catches - 162) from 1968-1970. Played in 29 games for an average of 5.6 catches per game, and a total of 2,168 receiving yards. Smith set Mississippi State's all-time receiving mark on October 17, 1970, with a 215-yard performance (12 catches and two touchdowns) vs. Texas Tech in Jackson.

Walter Packer - MSU's All-Time Career Rushing Yardage Leader (2,820) from 1973-1975. Played in 42 games for a 5.8 yard-per-carry average.

Don Smith - MSU's All-Time Total Offensive Yardage Leader (7,097) from

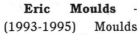

1983-1986. Played in 39 games for a 182.0 yards-per-game average.

Derrick Taite - MSU's All-Time Career Passing Yardage Leader (5,232) from 1993-1996. Played in 38 games for a 137.7 yards-per-game average. As a sophomore, Taite broke the MSU single-game passing mark with 466 yards in a 66-22 thrashing of Tulane.

Eric Moulds - (1993-1995) Moulds was known as an explosive open field runner with reliable hands and excellent concentration, enabling him to make the difficult catches in traffic. Ranks third on school's career receiving list with 118 catches for 2,022 yards. His 17.1 average per catch ranks sixth on the school's all-time list. Moulds started 23 of his 31 career games, and he

holds the school record for the most catches in a game–15 for 183 yards against Tennessee in 1995. Today, Moulds is a standout receiver for the Buffalo Bills organization. During his rookie year in 1996, Moulds caught 20 passes for 279 yards (14.0 yard average) for 2 touchdowns.

Johnie Cooks – An All-America linebacker for the Bulldogs in 1981, Cook starred for State from 1977-1981. A Leland native, Cooks was also a first team All-SEC player in 1980 and 1981, and he was named the Birmingham Touchdown Club SEC Most Valuable Player and United Press International's SEC Defensive Player of the Year. Following his college career the MSU Hall of Fame member spent six years in the NFL with the Baltimore Colts and another three seasons with the New York Giants, winning a Super Bowl with the Giants in 1990. Today, Cooks works as an assistant athletic director at Mississippi State University.

Fred Smoot – A Jackson native, Smoot was a standout silky-smooth cornerback for the Bulldogs that possessed excellent cover skills. Smoot was undoubtedly one of the most colorful characters to ever wear the MSU uniform. A walking quotation book, Smoot provided Bulldog and SEC fans with a steady dose of his witty, insightful commentary on his very own website, "Smootsmack.com." Smoot once said, "3/4 of the world is covered by water and the rest is covered by Smoot." The two-year starter for MSU (99-00) was an All-American JUCO transfer from Hinds Community College. Smoot recorded 10 career interceptions for MSU and he was a second round draft pick of the Washington Redskins during the 2001 NFL draft.

Bowl Victories

Orange Bowl: Miami, Florida January 1, 1941 MSU 14, Georgetown 7

Liberty Bowl: Philadelphia, Pennsylvania December 21, 1963 MSU 16, North Carolina St. 12

Sun Bowl: El Paso, Texas December 28, 1974 MSU 26, North Carolina 24

Hall of Fame Bowl: Birmingham, Alabama MSU 10, Kansas 0
Chick Fil-A Peach Bowl: Atlanta Georgia Dome, December 30, 1999 MSU 17 Clemson 7
2000 Independence Bowl: MSU 43, Texas A&M 41 Overtime (Blizzard Bowl)

Traditions/History:

The most noteworthy symbol of Mississippi State University is the infamous cowbell. Despite years of repeated attempts to banish their use on gamedays, diehard State fans still loudly cheer on the Dogs with the distinctive ringing sound of cowbells. Oddly, this practice continues despite the fact that a 1974 SEC rule outlaws the use of noisemakers at all games.

Mississippi State football got an inauspicious start in 1895 under the tutelage of a student coach. The schedule that uneventful year held a mere two games—one against Southern Baptist and the other against the Memphis Athletic Club. Mississippi State dropped both games against the upstart opponents. However, Mississippi State soon gained a foothold in college football. By 1907, the Bulldogs had posted a 7-2 regular season record.

The Egg Bowl - Mississippi State, and its long-time, in-state, arch-rival, Ole Miss, since Thanksgiving Day in 1927, have played what amounts to the "Egg Bowl" in the Magnolia State. According to William George Barner III, who wrote a book titled *Mississippi Mayhem* chronicling the boisterous beginnings of the Egg Bowl, the rivalry has a great story behind it.

The 1927 inaugural "Golden Egg" game was originally proposed by members of Sigma Iota, an Ole Miss honorary society, in an effort to temper the 1926 post-game exploits of some of the overzealous and unruly fans involved for both sides. The game of 1926 saw a series that had been traditionally dominated by Mississippi State—the Bulldogs had won 18 of the last 23 contests, turn sour for the fans from Starkville.

Ole Miss won a hard-fought, 7-6 ball game that fateful day. After the game, a throng of Ole Miss fans banded together on the west side

135

and rushed triumphantly onto the field toward the object of their destructive desire–the goal posts, while the Mississippi State "Aggie" supporters on that side of the field stood calmly and sang their alma mater. However, on the east side, matters were not as stable, and cooler heads did not prevail, as many of the disgruntled Mississippi State fans brandished cane bottom chairs raised high over their heads and sought quickly after the Rebel revelers hell-bent on tearing down their goal posts. As imaginable, many fights ensued shortly thereafter.

As described in an article by the Commercial Appeal by Ben Hilbun, who later became President of the Starkville campus, "The phantom of victory, that for 13 years eluded Ole Miss, returned to the bearded Berserkers...and they won over A&M, their traditional rivals, 7-6." Ole Miss students fought for the goal posts, he added, "but were restrained." The Mississippian replied that the Aggie chair brigade which defended their goal posts "came to the field with malice afterthought...with the intent of staging a 'free for all'..."

Ole Miss and Mississippi State students, shocked by the injuries to spectators, vowed that it should never happen again. The resulting agreement by the two student bodies was the Golden Egg, a trophy that would cool the heated battle between the two bitter in-state rivals. Because the trophy was shaped in the likeness of the more standard, rounded, ball of the day, it eventually came to be called the "Golden Egg."

That initial meeting of the two schools in 1927 for the "Golden Egg" ended in a 20-12 victory for Ole Miss. However, unlike during the previous year's contest, the game ended with a much-dignified ceremony celebrating the participants and the winners. As agreed upon before the game, the schools sang their alma maters. Ole Miss, the victor, sang first, followed by Mississippi State. After the serenading was complete, the two teams captains, the presidents of the two student bodies, and the leaders of the two schools met on the fifty yard line. There, B.M. Walker, President of Mississippi State, presented the first Golden Egg trophy to Ole Miss Captain Applewhite. Applewhite was reportedly then carried off the field by a "score of students."

Today, the golden Egg remains one of the most treasured prizes of either school. Symbolizing the football supremacy in the State of Mississippi, the trophy is engraved annually with the score of each preceding year's game. Additionally, it rests in a place of great honor at both schools. During years in which there was a tie, the trophy would return to the previous winner's school for the first half of the year, then it would go to the other school for display.

Hail State (Fight Song)
Hail dear 'ole State! Fight for that victory today.
Hit that line and tote that ball,
Cross the goal before you fall! And then we'll yell, yell, yell, yell!
For dear 'ole State we'll yell like H-E-L-L!
Fight for Mis-sis-sip-pi State, Win that game today!

Maroon and White (Alma Mater)
In the heart of Mississippi, Made by none but God's own hands
Stately in her nat'ral splendor Our Alma Mater proudly stands.
State College of Mississippi, Fondest mem'ries cling to thee.
Life shall hoard thy spirit ever, Loyal sons we'll always be.
Chorus: Maroon and White! Maroon and White!
Of thee with joy we sing.
Thy colors bright, our souls delight,
With praise our voices ring.
Tho' our life some pow'r may vanquish,
Loyalty can't be o'er run;
Honors true on thee we lavish, Until the setting of the sun;
Live Maroon and White for ever, Ne'er can evil mar thy fame,
Nothing us from thee can sever, Alma Mater we acclaim.

Noteworthy Mississippi State Alumni:
John Grisham - novelist
John C. Stennis - United States Senator
Hunter Henry - Former CEO, Dow Chemical

G.V. "Sonny" Montgomery - Congressman, (Montgomery G.I. Bill, 1984)

Hartley Peavey - founder of Peavey Electronics

Eugene Butler - founder of *Progressive Farmer Magazine*, forerunner of *Southern Living*

Janet Marie Smith - former president of Turner Sports and Entertainment Development

Brad Watson - author, and 2002 National Book Award finalist

E.B. "Barney" McCool - founder of the Holiday Inn hotel franchise

"Deep inside, we're still
the boys of autumn, that
magic time of the year that
once swept us onto
America's fields."

~ Archie Manning

The University of Mississippi
"Ole Miss"

Distinctively Southern in its flair for good food, beautiful coeds, and hospitality, Oxford holds a special place among its urban counterparts in the SEC. A college town that contains the quiet seclusion of any other typical small Southern town, Oxford is where people from all walks of life come to gain enlightenment and education at the University of Mississippi. Affectionately known by all who know her well as "Ole Miss," the University of Mississippi is the quintessential Southern college experience, and one of the last great vestiges of the Deep South. The tradition of SEC football runs deep at the University of Mississippi. Like so many of its SEC brethren, Ole Miss has too enjoyed its reign at the top of the national polls at the end of a regular season on the gridiron. Legendary Coach Johnny Vaught led Ole Miss to the National Championship in 1960, whetting the insatiable appetite of the Rebel football fanbase like never before. Since that magical time in the days of Rebel lore, Ole Miss has represented the SEC as one of the nation's finer football programs.

Founded:

The University of Mississippi was chartered on February 24, 1844. The university began educating eighty students in Oxford a short four years later in 1848. For twenty three years (1848-1871) Ole Miss was the state of Mississippi's only public higher institution of learning. Mississippi's flagship university during that period, Ole Miss established the fourth state-supported law school in the nation in 1854, and was also one of the first schools in the United States to offer Engineering, also in 1854. Additionally, Ole Miss was one of the first schools in the South to admit women (1882) and the first school to hire a female faculty member (1885).

"Ole Miss" The University of Mississippi gained its famous nickname over a hundred years ago, in 1896, when it was selected in a student contest held to designate the name of the new student yearbook. The term "Ole Miss" was recommended by Miss Elma Meek, a native of Oxford. The name "Ole Miss" eventually became an ingrained aspect of the institution and today remains a treasured aspect of the University's rich and storied history.

Nickname: Rebels

The name "Rebels" as Ole Miss' official athletic moniker first began back in 1936. Submitted by Judge Ben Guider of Vicksburg, it was one of five entries submitted to various southern sportswriters for a final selection from among over two hundred different suggestions. The promotion was sponsored by the student newspaper at the time, "The Mississippian." The sportswriters unanimously chose the nickname of "Rebels" by a vote of 18 to 3. The late Judge William Hemingway of the University Athletic community commemorated the event with the following statement: "If 18 sports writers wish to use Rebels, I shall not rebel, so let it go Ole Miss Rebels."

The late Frank E. Everett, Jr., B.A. 1932, LLB 1934, described the meaning of "Ole Miss" best when he wrote: "There is a valid distinction between The University and Ole Miss even though the separate threads are closely interwoven. The University is buildings, trees and people. Ole Miss is mood, emotion and personality. One is physical, and the other is spiritual. One is tangible, and the other intangible. The University is respected, but Ole Miss is loved. The University gives a diploma and regretfully terminates tenure, but one never graduates from Ole Miss."

Location: Oxford

Nestled among the rolling hills of northern Mississippi thrives the sleepy little town of Oxford. Once home to authors William Faulkner, and John Grisham, the historical ties to this old Southern enclave are as strong as the boughs of the hundred year-old magnolias that drape its rhythmical, undulating landscape.
Population: 10,026

Enrollment: 16,080

Colors: Cardinal and Navy (Red and Blue)

In 1893, when Ole Miss' original football team was preparing for a five game season, Dr. A. Bondurant, organizer and manager coach, later recalled that "The team had much discussion as to the colors that should be adopted, but it was finally suggested by the manager that the union of the crimson of Harvard and the navy blue of Yale would be harmonious, and that it was well to have the spirit of both of these good colleges." And hence, the red and blue were adopted by the university as its official colors.

Mascot name: Colonel Rebel

The likeness of "Colonel Reb" first appeared in the Ole Miss yearbook in 1938, as the leading illustration in the publication referred to as "The Rebel Number."

"Colonel Rebel," represents Ole Miss as the quintessential caricature of the old Southern gentleman. He's a distinguished-looking chap with a bushy white moustache and beard. His ensemble includes a tailed suit with an old-fashioned ribbon tie, flowered lapel, cane and two-gallon hat. Over the years since the inception of his likeness, Colonel Reb has become a near-official insignia for the University of Mississippi.

Stadium: Vaught-Hemingway

Physically located on the southeast section of the Ole Miss campus, historic Vaught-Hemingway is home to the Rebel football team. The Stadium, known in its beginnings simply as Hemingway Stadium, was erected initially in 1915 when students of the University of Mississippi pitched in to help build the grandstand at its present site. The effort to build the stadium was a federally-funded project that lasted 3 years. Stadium capacity after the initial construction was listed as 24,000, an impressive figure for that day and time. In 1950, the stadium was expanded with the addition

of an 80-yard long press box. In 1970, Astroturf was added. 1971 saw the insertion of custom blue fiber glass seating to the west side stands. The east side would receive a similar seating upgrade in 1973. Furthermore, aluminum bench bleachers were added to the end zones in 1980 to bring the stadium's capacity to 41,000.

During the summer of 1984, the Astroturf was removed from the field and was replaced with prescription athletic turf. The summer of 1998 saw another major facelift for Vaught-Hemingway Stadium. A new pressbox was constructed along with new aluminum sideline seating, restrooms and concession stands, in addition to a new club level seating section for 700 people.

Further renovations continued in the summer of 1990 when lights were added to the stadium. Later for the start of the 1997 season, a Sony Jumbotron screen and a scoreboard/message center was added. Construction on the east side of the stadium was completed prior to the 1998 football season, which included a Rebel Club seating section with an enclosed lounge area. This final stadium improvement pushed stadium capacity to over the mark of 50,000.

The stadium's name honors two great University of Mississippi men. Judge William Hemingway (1869-1937), was a professor of law and a longtime chairman of the University's Committee on Athletics. The football stadium bore his name until October 16,

1982, when John Howard Vaught saw his namesake juxtaposed with Hemingway's, and the stadium was officially renamed Vaught-Hemingway Stadium. As head football coach at Ole Miss, Vaught posted an overall record of 190-61-11, and led the Rebels to their only fully-recognized national championship in 1960.

Stadium capacity: 60,580

Band: "Band of the South"

First game: November 11, 1893 - Ole Miss 56, Southwest Baptist University of Jackson, Tennessee 0. Ole Miss's first game was held on campus against Southwest Baptist University of Jackson, Tennessee. The Rebels made quick work of their first-ever gridiron opponent, defeating Southwest 56-0.

Ole Miss began playing football in 1893 by completing a five-game schedule with four wins and one loss, with the first three victories coming by shutout. Dr. Alexander Bondurant, a Latin professor who was a staunch proponent of athletic competition at the collegiate level, organized the first Rebel football squad, and the first athletic association. Bondurant continued to serve at Ole Miss for a number of years as manager of the Rebel football team.

According to James "Bobo" Champion, during the fall of 1893, Ole Miss' first year playing football, the University Magazine wrote the following: "The athletic fever has now taken full possession of the University...and the time is already here when, in order to rank high in college or society, one must join the running crowd and play on the football team."

First game in stadium: October 1, 1915 Arkansas Aggies 10, Ole Miss 0

Directions: Coming from East or West: Take Hwy 6 and get off Rd. Head north until you reach University Ave. Turn left and go over bridge. Entry to campus is also available on Coliseum Drive. Head north until you reach fraternity row. Turn right on fraternity row.

Coming from the North or the South: Take I-55 to Batesville, then take Hwy 6 to either Coliseum Drive or Taylor Road. Also, from the North or South, take Hwy 7 to Hwy 6. Then take Hwy 6 to either Coliseum Drive or Old Taylor Road.

Where to go:
Eating:
Oxford Steak Co.: 302 South 11th St. Oxford, MS (662) 236-6460. A great steak and atmosphere.

Yocona River Inn: 842 Highway 334 Oxford, MS (662) 234-2464. A local favorite.

Ajax Diner: 119 Courthouse Square, Oxford, MS 38655 (662) 232-8880 – Good grub and drinks in a casual atmosphere.

Downtown Grill Restaurant: 110 Courthouse Square, Oxford, MS 38655 (662) 234-2659 – Great food and a great bar. An established local favorite.

Eating and Drinking:
Proud Larry's Restaurant & Spirits: 211 South Lamar Boulevard, Oxford, MS 38655, (601) 236-0500. Enjoy live music and great food at Proud Larry's. Located just south of the Square in Oxford.

City Grocery: 152 Courthouse Square, Oxford, MS (662) 232-8080. A downtown hangout.

All-Time Record: 583-428-35 (.576)
Bowl Appearances: 31
Bowl Record: 19-12 (.613)
SEC Record: 226-204-15 (.525)
SEC Championships: (6) 1947 (9-2), 1955 (10-1), 1962 (10-0), 1954 (9-2), 1960 (10-0-1), 1963 (7-1-2)
National Championships: (3) 1959 (10-1) (SEC Team of the Decade) (Berryman, Billingsley, Dunkel and Sagarin), 1960 (10-0-1)

Football Research, National Championship Foundation and Williamson), 1962 (10-0) (Litkenhous).

Ole Miss Greats:

Ole Miss has 11 former players and coaches in the College Football Hall of Fame

1951 Bruiser Kennard
1965 Charlie Conerly
1973 John Cain
1974 Barney Poole
1979 John Vaught
1984 Doug Kenna
1987 Thad "Pie" Vann
1989 Archie Manning
1991 Parker Hall
1995 Jake Gibbs
1997 Charlie Flowers

Coaches:

Harry Mehre - Mehre, formerly of Notre Dame, coached at Ole Miss from 1938 to 1945, posting an all-time record of 39-26-1. Mehre's tenure at Ole Miss was highlighted by several impressive victories, including notable triumphs over Vanderbilt in 1939 (the school's first ever), LSU in 1938 (first in eleven years), and the first win against Tulane in over 25 years in 1941.

John Vaught- Vaught coached the Rebels from 1947-1970, during which time he led Ole Miss to six SEC titles: the 1959 Dunkel System National Championship, the 1960 Football Writers Association of America, Dunkel System, and Williamson System national championships, the 1962 Litkenhous Ratings National Title, a 190-61-11 record and a position of both regional and  national prominence over the next 24 years. During his 24 year career as head coach at Ole Miss, Vaught led the Rebels to an impressive 18 bowl game appearances, with a 10-8 record in those said games.

The Words of Johnny Vaught

"The worst thing a coach can do is stand pat and think the things that worked yesterday will win tomorrow. Intelligent changes must be made."

"To be a winning team, you must be a hungry team. So remember that every football Saturday is the most important date on the schedule."

"Discipline, with team togetherness, wins football games."

"I consider a tie a loss."

Ole Miss Chancellor Porter L. Fortune once remarked, "Many coaches train boys to become football players. John Vaught trained boys to become men."

Billy Brewer - A player under the great Johnny Vaught, Brewer coached eleven years at Ole Miss, from 1983-1993. Brewer compiled a most respectable 67-56-3 record during that period, making him the second all-time winningest coach in school history behind his former mentor Vaught. Under Brewer's leadership, the Rebels appeared in five bowl games, winning three during that time frame.

David Cutcliffe – On December 2, 1998, after serving 17 years at the University of Tennessee as an assistant coach, David Cutcliffe took over the reins as Ole Miss's 34th head football coach. Cutcliffe, who is known as a keen offensive mind, replaced departing head coach Tommy Tuberville, and has compiled a 39-22 overall record and competed in four bowl games since his hire. During his initial five years with the program Cutcliffe has won at least 7 games in each of his first five years in Oxford, the only coach in school history to accomplish such a feat. Cutcliffe has brought great pride back to Ole Miss and its faithful fan base. The 2003 season produced Cutcliffe's best year as head coach, ending with a share of the SEC Western Division Championship and a bowl win over Oklahoma State in the Cotton Bowl, allowing the Rebels to finish with an impressive 10-3 record.

147

Players:

Kayo Dotley - Fullback, from 1947-1950. Rebels' All-Time leading rusher with 2,654 yards. Dotley rushed the ball 478 times for a 5.55 yard per carry average and 21 touchdowns.

Elisha Archibald "Archie" Manning - (1968-1971) The SEC's most favorite son, Archie Manning is undoubtedly Ole Miss' most

famous college football star. A two-time All-American Quarterback (1969-1970), Manning finished fourth in Heisman voting in 1969 and third in 1970. He was the second overall selection by the New Orleans Saints in the 1971 NFL draft. Manning played for the Saints from 1971 to 1981, for the Houston Oilers from 1982 to 1983 and for the Minnesota Vikings from 1983 to 1984. During his illustrious career at Ole Miss, Manning passed for 31 touchdowns and rushed for another 25. In Birmingham, Alabama, in 1969, in a valiant, losing effort to SEC power Alabama, Manning performed admirably. The Drew redhead account-ed for 540 total yards and three touch-downs, completing 33 passes for 436 yards while rushing for 15 times for another 104.

Manning is remembered by Ole Miss and SEC fans for his unbelievable on-the-field toughness, and his indomitable competitive spirit. In 1971, in a losing Gator Bowl effort, Manning displayed unquestionable courage by playing with a broken left arm with the aid of a makeshift plastic sleeve. Despite his debilitating injury,

Manning still managed 95 yards rushing and 180 yards passing against the Auburn Tigers. Archie's son Peyton was a standout quarterback for the Tennessee Volunteers, and is currently an All-Pro signal-caller for the Indianapolis Colts, while his younger son Eli–also a quarterback, enrolled at Ole Miss prior to the 1999 season.

Ole Miss fans are most familiar with the phrase "Archie Who?" However, the origins of the phrase make for a particularly interesting rebel yarn. As the story goes, University of Tennessee linebacker, Steve Kiner, during an interview was asked: "How do you plan to stop Archie Manning?" The unassuming Volunteer responded, "Archie Who?" Ole Miss went on to defeat the Vols 38-0. The phrase then became part of Ole Miss lore. Subsequently, thousands of "Archie Who?" buttons, pins, and flags were manufactured as Ole Miss fans proudly wore the "Archie Who?" tag.

"Football is the essence of America, but not because of championships or titles. The drive to compete–the guts to play–the will to come from behind–the grace to walk off the field a loser–that's the essence of football."

"Bad teams are creative. They always find a new way to lose."

"One guy can't do it by himself and it's a matter of recognizing this and giving others their share of the credit." ~Archie Manning

Wesley Walls - (1985-1988) Walls began his collegiate career at Ole Miss at defensive end. For his senior season, he was moved to outside linebacker and also added tight end to his duties to serve as a rare two-way contributor for Ole Miss. He excelled in the dual role with 36 receptions for 426 yards and three touchdowns to reap All-America and All-SEC honors in 1988. The engineering major also achieved academic All-SEC honors as a junior. A second-round selection by the San Francisco 49ers in the 1989 NFL draft, Walls played pro ball for the Carolina Panthers.

John Fourcade - A 1979-80 All-SEC quarterback, Fourcade holds the record for the most total offensive yards in a career at 6,713. Fourcade also holds the record for the most plays at 1,275, and the most rushing touchdowns, at 22. Fourcade, after Ole Miss, went on to a professional career in the Canadian Football League with British Columbia in 1982, with Memphis in the now defunct USFL in 1984, and with the New Orleans Saints (NFL) from 1987-1990.

Kent Austin - A quarterback at Ole Miss from 1981-1985, Austin is the All-time leading passer in Ole Miss history with 6,184 total passing yards (566 of 981 for 31 touchdowns). Austin was drafted in the 12th round of the 1985 NFL draft by St. Louis. In 1986, Austin began a lengthy Canadian professional football career with Saskatchewan, where he played from 1987-1991. Austin later played for British Columbia in 1994, Toronto in 1995, and Winnipeg in 1996. He was the 1989 Grey Cup MVP, a CFL Western All-Star and also a CFL All-Canadian All-Star in 1990.

Dou Innocent - (1991-1992, 1994-1995) Innoccent is Ole Miss' second all-time career rushing leader behind Kayo Dottley. Innocent, who played both fullback and running back for the Rebels, rushed for 2322 yards on 494 carries for an average of 4.7 yards per play, with 11 touchdowns. Innocent was acquired by the New York Giants in the 1997 NFL draft.

Kristofer (Kris) Mangum - (1994-1996) A First Team All-American, Mangum caught 74 passes for 729 yards (9.9 yard average) and 4 touchdowns. Against LSU in 1995, Mangum caught 7 passes for 57 yards. The Magee, Mississippi native is the son of John Mangum, a defensive tackle for the Boston Patriots from 1966-1967, and the brother of John Mangum, Jr., a cornerback for the Chicago Bears. Mangum was drafted in the 7th round of the 1997 NFL draft by the Carolina Panthers.

John Avery - A 1996 and 1997 All-SEC Tailback and kick return-er, Avery is the fifth All-Time rusher in Ole Miss history with 1,650 yards on 347 carries for a 4.8 yard per carry average and 12 touchdowns. During the 1997 season, Avery accomplished the longest rushing play from scrimmage in the SEC, a 97-yard jaunt he perfected against the Arkansas Razorbacks on November 6th. Earlier that year, on October 4th against Tennessee, Avery rushed for 74 yards on a single rushing play. Avery was the 29th pick overall in the 1998 NFL draft. During his abbreviated career at Ole Miss, Avery was also a standout kick returner, boasting a blazing sub 4.4 second forty yard dash.

Eli Manning - The New Orleans, Louisiana native, is the final offspring of the SEC's "Favorite Son," Archie Manning, who also starred at quarterback for Ole Miss and head coach Johnny Vaught during the 1960's. A consummate collegiate quarterback, Manning drew favorable comparisons to both his older brother and father throughout his highly publicized tenure in Oxford. Rebuffing LSU, Tennessee and the other SEC schools for his services, the youngest Manning chose his father's alma mater to earn an education and to play football. During his unbelievable SEC career Eli started 36 games and played in 42, throwing for 10,119 yards and 81 touchdowns. Manning is Ole Miss's all-time passing leader and he also ranks fifth all-time among SEC passers. Manning holds 45 different school records and was named the 2003 SEC Offensive Player of the Year by the Associated Press. Manning has the lowest career percentage of interceptions thrown at Ole Miss at 2.55, which is good enough for third all-time in the conference. At the end of the successful 2003 campaign in which Eli led Ole Miss to a 31-28 Cotton Bowl victory over Oklahoma State in January, 2004, he was also named one of 15 scholar-athletes by the National Foundation and College Hall of Fame. The Cotton Bowl victory gave Ole Miss their 10th win of a magical season. In the spring of 2004 Eli was a first round draft choice in the NFL draft by the San Diego Chargers. He was later traded to the New York Giants.

Deuce McCallister - Considered one of Ole Miss's greatest all-around backs, Mcallister ended his Ole Miss playing days with 18 school career, season and single-game records. Blessed with incredible size and speed, Mcallister finished his career with 3,060 rushing yards on 616 rushing attempts for 37 touchdowns, 14 100-yard rush-

151

ing games and 246 total points scored. In addition to his running skills, Mcallister was also a talented punt and kick returner for the Rebels, evidenced by his 4,889 career all-purpose yards. The first player in Rebel history to record three consecutive seasons with at least 1,000 all-purpose yards, Mcallister was a first round draft choice by the New Orleans Saints in the 2001 NFL draft.

Charlie Conerly - The Clarksdale, Mississippi native is remembered as one of the SEC's greatest football players. A standout tailback at Ole Miss during the war-torn years of 1941 and 1942, Conerly spent three years as a Marine during World War II. Upon his return to Oxford after the war in 1946, Conerly became the Rebels' quarterback in the newly formed T formation. Conerly captained and quarterbacked Mississippi to a 9-2-0 record in 1947, when Mississippi won its first SEC Championship and beat Texas Christian 13-9 in the Delta Bowl. Conerly went on to become an NFL star. He joined the New York Giants in 1948 and was named Rookie of the Year. "Chuckin' Charlie" as he was called, retired from the NFL in 1961. As a pro, he completed 1,418 of 2,833 passes for 19,488 yards and 173 touchdowns, impressive passing statistics during an era in football that had not yet embraced fully passing as a means to move the football.

Traditions/History

The Walk of Champions - Two hours before kickoff, the team walks down the sidewalk that goes through The Grove, a 10-acre grassy plot shaded by oak trees at the center of campus. Fans fight for position on both sides of the sidewalk and greet the players with loud cheers.

Roy Lee "Chucky" Mullins Courage Award - This award is presented each spring to Ole Miss' top defensive player, who then has the distinguished honor of wearing Chucky's number 38 the following football season. Mullins died in 1991 as the result of a tragic football related accident. He is remembered for his dedication to the game and for his steadfast courage. Chucky, in the face of overwhelming adversity, once stated, "No matter how bad things seem, never give up..." and "You'll never know how much God means to you, till tragedy hits and friends come through."

Egg Bowl - Ole Miss, and its long-time, in-state, arch-rival, Mississippi State, since Thanksgiving Day in 1927, have played what amounts to the "Egg Bowl" in the Magnolia State. According to William George Barner III, who wrote a book titled "Mississippi Mayhem" chronicling the boisterous beginnings of the Egg Bowl, the rivalry has a great story behind it. The 1927 inaugural "Golden Egg" game was originally proposed by members of Sigma Iota, an Ole Miss honorary society, in an effort to temper the 1926 post-game exploits of some of the overzealous and unruly fans involved for both sides. The game of 1926 saw a series that had been traditionally dominated by Mississippi State—the Bulldogs had won 18 of the last 23 contests—turn sour for the fans from Starkville. Ole Miss won a hard-fought, 7-6 ball game that fateful day. After the game, a throng of Ole Miss fans banded together on the west side and rushed triumphantly onto the field toward the object of their destructive desire—the goalposts—while the Mississippi State "Aggie" supporters on that side of the field stood calmly and sang their alma mater. However, on the east side, matters were not as stable, and cooler heads did not prevail, as many of the disgruntled Mississippi State fans brandished cane bottom chairs raised high over their heads and sought quickly after the Rebel revelers hell-bent on tearing down their goalposts. As imaginable, many fights ensued shortly thereafter.

As described in an article by the Commercial Appeal by Ben Hilbun, who would later become President of the Starkville campus, "The phantom of victory, that for 13 years eluded Ole Miss, returned to the bearded Berserkers...and they won over A&M, their traditional rivals, 7-6." Ole Miss students fought for the goal posts, he added, "but were restrained." The Mississippian replied that the Aggie chair brigade which defended their goal posts "came to the field with malice after-thought...with the intent of staging a 'free for all'..."

Ole Miss and Mississippi State students, shocked by the injuries to spectators, vowed that it should never happen again. The resulting agreement by the two student bodies was the Golden Egg, a trophy that would cool the heated battle between the two bitter in-state rivals.

Because the trophy was shaped in the likeness of the more standard, rounded ball of the day, it eventually came to be called the "Golden Egg."

That initial meeting of the two schools in 1927 for the "Golden Egg" ended in a 20-12 victory for Ole Miss. However, unlike during the previous year's contest, the game ended with a much-dignified ceremony celebrating the participants and the winners. As agreed upon before the game, the schools sang their alma maters. Ole Miss, the victor, sang first, followed by Mississippi State. After the serenading was complete, the two team captains, the presidents of the two student bodies, and the leaders of the two schools met on the fifty yard line. There, B.M. Walker, President of Mississippi State, presented the first Golden Egg trophy to Ole Miss Captain Applewhite. Applewhite was then carried off the field by a "score of students."

Today, the golden Egg remains one of the most treasured prizes of either school. Symbolizing football supremacy in the State of Mississippi, the trophy is engraved annually with the score of each preceding year's game. Additionally, the trophy rests in a place of great honor at both schools. During years in which there was a tie, the trophy would return to the previous winner's school for the first half of the year, then it would go to the other school for display.

"Hotty Toddy"
Are You Ready?
Hell Yes! Damn Right!
Hotty Toddy, Gosh-A-Mighty!
Who In the Hell Are We?
Hey! Flim-Flam, Bim-Bam,
Ole Miss, By Damn!

The "Hott Toddy" cheer at Ole Miss is a unique and cherished part of the history and tradition of the university. This cheer, which makes no reference to anything hot with temperature (such as a toddy), is a corruption of "highty-tighty" an expression of the eighteenth and nineteenth centuries which was used as an exclamation or as a descriptive term like "high-falutin." A mispronunciation of hoity-toity, "highty-tighty" was the original phrase in the football cheer as required by the rhyme with "Gosh-A-Mighty." The date of the origination of the cheer is unknown for certain, but is thought to have started as early as the 1920's.

Great Bowl Games:

Delta Bowl: January 1, 1948 Ole Miss 13, Texas Christian 9
Sugar Bowl: January 1, 1958, Ole Miss 39, Texas 7
Sugar Bowl: January 1, 1960, Ole Miss 21, LSU 0
Sugar Bowl: January 1, 1963, Ole Miss 17, Arkansas 13
Liberty Bowl: December 28, 1965 Ole Miss 13, Auburn 7
Peach Bowl: December 30, 1971, Ole Miss 41, Georgia Tech 18
Motor City Bowl: December 26, 1997 Ole Miss 34, Marshall 31
2002 Independence Bowl: Ole Miss 27, Nebraska 23
2004 Cotton Bowl: Ole Miss 31, Oklahoma State 28

Fight Song:
Forward, Rebels, march to fame,
Hit that line and win this game
We know that you'll fight it through,
For your colors read and blue. Rah, rah, rah.

Rebels you are the Southland's pride,
Take that ball and hit your stride,
Don't stop till the victory's won, for you Ole Miss.
Fight, fight for your Ole Miss.

Alma Mater
Way down South in Mississippi, there's a spot that ever calls
Where among the hills enfolded, Stand Old Alma Mater's halls.
Where the trees lift high their branches,
To the whisp'ring southern breeze. There Ole Miss is calling,
To our hearts fond memories.

With united hearts we praise thee, All our loyalty is thine,
And we hail thee, Alma Mater, May they light forever shine;
May it brighter grow and brighter, And with deep affection true,
Our thoughts shall ever cluster 'round thee, Dear Old Red and Blue.

May thy fame throughout the nation,
Through thy sons and daughters grow,
May they name forever waken, in our hearts a tender glow,
May thy counsel and thy spirit, Ever keep us one in this,
That our own shall be thine honor, now and ever dear Ole Miss.

Words by Mrs. A.W. Kahle, Music by W.F. Kahle

Noteworthy Ole Miss Alumni:
  Mose Allison - jazz and blues pianist
  Haley Barbour - Governor of Mississippi and former chairman of the NRC
  Jim Barksdale - founder and former CEO of Netscape
  Ron Franklin - sports broadcaster
  John Grisham - best-selling novelist (Law School)
  Kate Jackson - actress
  Gerald McRaney - actor (*Promised Land, Simon & Simon, Major Dad*)
  David Molpus - reporter for National Public Radio
  Trent Lott - U.S. Senator
  Thad Cochran - U.S. Senator
  Lt. Gen. James E. Sherrard III - Chief of Air Force Reserves
  Shepard Smith - Fox News anchor
  Larry Speakes - former press secretary to the President of the United States
  Three Miss Americas - **Mary Ann Mobley**, 1959, **Lynda Lee Mead Shea**, 1960, and **Susan Akin-Lynch**, 1986

Growing up in Mississippi I was baptized as a small
boy into the religion of SEC Football; and we
worshiped every Saturday afternoon. Like every kid
on my street I dreamed of playing for great coaches
like Bear Bryant, Johnny Vaught, Shug Jordan, Vince
Dooley and Charlie McClendon. In our biggest dreams
we would become heroes ourselves–the next Archie
Manning or Kenny Stabler. Most of us were good
enough to play high school football. Wearing the
uniform on Friday nights heightened our dreams of
playing the great shrines of SEC Football–between the
hedges in Athens and in Tiger Stadium, the noisiest
place in the world. For childhood friends David Green
and David Pollack, the dream has become a reality.
From the sandlots of their hometown of Snellville,
Georgia to Sanford Stadium in Athens, they have
rekindled the glory of Georgia football. Now the
Bulldogs stand on the threshold of back-to-back conference titles. As small boys in Louisiana, Chad
Lavalais and Michael Clayton could hear the roar of
Tiger Stadium echoing through the bayous on
Saturday nights. Now like their heroes before them,
they too are building a championship legacy. Emotion,
passion, pride, honor, tradition...this is the essence of
SEC Football.

~ John Grisham
Introduction to the 2003 SEC championship game televised by CBS.

SEC Championship Game Quick Facts

Date: First Saturday in December
Site: Georgia Dome; Atlanta, Georgia.
Capacity: 71,500
Time: TBA
Television: CBS Sports
Georgia Dome Contract: Through 2009 game
Highest TV Rating: 10.5 (30 million viewers) - 1994
Largest Crowd: 83,091 (Alabama vs. Florida, Legion Field) - 1992
Top Passer: Danny Wuerffel, Florida (20-35-2, 401 yds, 6 TDs) - 1996
Top Rusher: Justin Vincent, LSU (201 yards) - 2004
Previous Scores/Most Valuable Players:
1992 - Alabama 28, Florida 21 [at Birmingham, Ala.]
(83,091) - DB Antonio Langham (Alabama)
1993 - Florida 28, Alabama 13 [at Birmingham, Ala.]
(76,345) - QB Terry Dean (Florida)
1994 - Florida 24, Alabama 23 [at Atlanta, Ga.]
(74,751) - DT Ellis Johnson (Florida)
1995 - Florida 34, Arkansas 3 [at Atlanta, Ga.]
(71,325) - QB Danny Wuerffel (Florida)
1996 - Florida 45, Alabama 30 [at Atlanta, Ga.]
(74,132) - QB Danny Wuerffel (Florida)
1997 - Tennessee 30, Auburn 29 [at Atlanta, Ga.]
(74,896) - QB Peyton Manning (Tennessee)
1998 - Tennessee 24, Miss. State 14 [at Atlanta, Ga.]
(74,795) - WR Peerless Price (Tennessee)
1999 - Alabama 34, Florida 7 [at Atlanta, Ga.]
(71,500) - WR Freddie Milons (Alabama)
2000 - Florida 28, Auburn 6 [at Atlanta, Ga.]
(73,427) - QB Rex Grossman (Florida)
2001 - LSU 31, Tennessee 20 [at Atlanta, Ga.]
(74,843) - QB Matt Mauck (LSU)
2002 - Georgia 30, Arkansas 3 [at Atlanta, Ga.]
(74,835) - QB David Greene (Georgia)
2003 - LSU 34, Georgia 14 [at Atlanta, Ga.]
(74,843) – RB Justin Vincent (LSU)

Sugar Bowl History, How sweet it is!

While Division I college football remains the only NCAA-sanctioned sport without a playoff, it does possess a unique postseason aspect: the bowl games—and there is perhaps no sweeter venue than the Nokia Sugar Bowl in New Orleans, Louisiana. Always a popular tourist town, New Orleans offers a special bowl game experience for traveling football fans from across the country. With its unparalleled French and Spanish architecture, along with its hip cultural vibe, the Big Easy is one of America's favorite travel destinations. Throw in a college football game with potential national championship ramifications, and it's easy to see why the Sugar Bowl is one of the hottest bowl game tickets around.

The Sugar Bowl was first played in Tulane Stadium on Jan. 1, 1935, regularly featuring the SEC champion in its early years. The SEC champion's participation was later formalized through an agreement with the conference during the 1946 season, and the practice continued through the 1994 season. In 1975, the Sugar Bowl found a permanent home in the brand new Louisiana Superdome, becoming the first (and still the only) major bowl game played indoors.

The Sugar Bowl in 1987 became the first major bowl game to adopt corporate sponsorship, under an agreement with USF&G Financial Services, which continued through 1995. Nokia, a cellular telephone corporation based in Finland, has sponsored the game since 1996. As a member of the Bowl Alliance and Bowl Championship Series (BCS), the Sugar Bowl currently hosts one of the top three post-season contests. On Jan. 3, 2000, the Sugar Bowl hosted the second annual national championship game played under the auspices of the BCS.

While the Sugar Bowl has held mainly an SEC flair over the years, the game has hosted some of the better teams from conferences throughout the country, including the PAC-10, the Big 10, the ACC and the Big East, to name a few. Considered one of the top-tier bowls in college football, the Sugar Bowl is an event that attracts many fans of football and fun.

In January 1, 2002 the LSU Tigers played Illinois in New Orleans and defeated the Big East champs to take their first Sugar Bowl crown since 1968. In 2003, the SEC Champion Georgia Bulldogs met the Florida State Seminoles in a showdown of two of the South's better teams. Georgia prevailed in the contest, giving the school its first Sugar Bowl victory since 1981 (Notre Dame). In 2004, SEC Champion LSU defeated Oklahoma for the BCS National Championship game in the Sugar Bowl.

Regardless of which SEC team represents the conference in the Sugar Bowl, the historic college event always means plenty of New Orleans style football and fun for the fans who are lucky enough to attend.

Tailgating...The Colorful History of America's Biggest Sporting Pastime

By Chris Warner

Tailgating-its mere mention among football fans conjures cool, leaf-blown images of the fall and football season. This widely anticipated weekend engagement is regularly staged against the inviting autumn backdrop of sexy young coeds, ice cold beer and of course, food. Ah yes-tailgating, the veritable game before the game, and for many football fans-the more important one, is today as much a feature of the modern football experience as the forward pass. This burgeoning American cultural phenomenon is ubiquitous, and it can be witnessed prior to kickoff in the parking lot of your favorite pro stadium or on the lazy, sprawling campus of your revered alma mater. Tailgating has grown in recent years into the quintessential culinary side show of the modern sporting era; a veritable Epicurean outdoor feast that regularly precedes the fall ritual of collegiate and pro football games. While modern tailgating has only recently (within the last thirty years) become popular, the practice of enjoying both food and football, has post-Civil War, nineteenth century roots.

Early Times

In the beginning, there was only college football. Professional football did not arrive on the American sporting scene until the 1950's, while the first college football game ironically occurred between Ivy League schools Rutgers and Princeton in New Brunswick as early as 1869. Twelve years later, in 1881, the first collegiate football game south of the Mason-Dixon Line occurred on the bluegrass at Old Stoll Field in Lexington, Kentucky. Even during the earliest days of the sport, food and football went hand in hand. In those days it was customary for the fans of each team to engage in a wild fish and game supper before the contest and then

161

to revisit the leftovers after the game where they relived the on-field exploits of the daring young gridders.

Because of football's brutal nature it was a game at its onset played by only the toughest young men. Players in those days wore little protective equipment like that enjoyed by today's players. It was common instead for the young men to grow their hair long and wear it in a bun to cushion the fierce bodily contact that typified the game. Furthermore, the most common way of bringing down a ball carrier during football's late nineteenth century roots was to simply strike him in the face with a closed fist.

Amidst the painful aftermath of the bloody North-South conflict, college football quickly bore into the core of the American cultural psyche, especially in the South, where the game's mythical connections to the lost cause of the Confederacy of the Civil War were omnipresent. College football games for young men in the South after the Civil War presented an immediate opportunity for them to recapture the pride they had been stripped of in the bitter conflict. Furthermore, playing college football allowed young Southern men to assert themselves well in a tough physical game and thereby again demonstrate their superiority over the North. In short, football, at the time, was a game that brought otherwise highly divergent national institutions like the North and the South together with a common purpose and point of cultural reference. However, football was not only a veritable rite of passage for the players, but also for their adoring fans, who saw winning football and its social trappings-the rudiments of tailgating, as the grand redeemer of a pride earlier lost.

And Then There Was Light

For years after the turn of the century up until the advent of electric lighting and night football during the late 1920s and early 1930s, college football games were played almost exclusively during the day. Towering electric lamps and night football games brought about the practice of hosting all day football parties at fans' homes where they would congregate and leisurely hop from house-to-house as the evening kickoff approached. Night games were a critical social development since they allowed for cooler game time temperatures and for men and women to dress up for the popular pre-game parties. Women commonly wore their best Sunday dresses adorned with team-colored corsages while men frequently donned spiffy coats, ties and the now-forgotten, but once-popular derbies and fedoras.

These festive pre-game jaunts continued unabated for forty years or more until daytime college football on television pre-empted the house parties that were previously the norm. Along with much-needed athletic department revenue, TV coverage also brought with it the dreaded day football games, which entirely precluded the practice of party hopping around town prior to the contest. The alternative to not house partying was simple to the legions of football fans that had been weaned on pre-game football parties: Take the party to the stadium! And that they did, because today tailgating at or near the stadium is a social practice that seems to have found a continual flow of willing fall participants. Predictably, tailgating now occurs regularly prior to night games and day games as college football's fan base-and their propensity to tailgate—only grows with each passing year. Tailgating has become so popular that some football fans enjoy it as much as the game itself-and that's saying something in the football-crazed American heartland!

One often-overlooked or under-studied aspect of tailgating is its name. Simple logic leads one to surmise that the term describes the practice of having an outdoor picnic on the tailgate of a truck or station wagon, and this is largely understood to be true. However, no official etymology of the American word exists, further reinforcing the fledgling status of this growing sporting tradition.

The "Commissioner" of Tailgating

There is perhaps no individual that can better explain the fascinating sociology of American tailgating than the self-proclaimed

"Commissioner of Tailgating," Joe Cahn, of New Orleans, Louisiana. Although his dream job is a tough one, Cahn, over the past seven years has made a comprehensive national pilgrimage in his fully functional recreational vehicle to frequent the hottest tailgating locales the country has to offer. Now in his eighth season on the road, Cahn has amazingly steered his "Joemobile" over 217,000 miles, visited hundreds of venues and tailgated with thousands of hungry football fans. Like a nomad with a purpose, Cahn has burned nearly 35,000 gallons of gasoline during his journey to all 32 NFL stadiums and over 60 college stadiums across the nation. Along the way Joe has delighted his discriminating taste buds with delicacies like barbecue brisket in Dallas, grits in Atlanta, Bratwurst in Green Bay, cheesesteaks in Philly, smoked salmon in Seattle, boiled lobsters in New England, Jambalaya in Cajun country and Pierogi's in Pittsburgh, just to name a few.

Cahn, a tireless promoter of the pastime who also enjoys Dorito's as a corporate sponsor (somebody has to pay his gas bill!), claims that tailgating has taken the place of the State Fair and the forgotten front porch visit in Americana. Cahn, who maintains an internet website dedicated to his cause (tailgating.com), contends that tailgating brings people together better than any other modern outdoor event.

"It (tailgating) is the new community social and the biggest weekly party in the nation! Tailgating is the last great American neighborhood...the Tailgating Neighborhood...where no one locks their doors, everyone is happy to see you and all are together sharing food and football. Tailgating is great because it's family, friends, fun and football! Wouldn't it be great if we could all just tailgate?"

So this fall, when you hitch up your family truckster and prepare your numerous tailgating wares and eats, remember that the modern cultural ritual you are fulfilling on game day finds its humble origins during the tumultuous times following the Civil War. Furthermore, when the unruly throngs of thousands of well-fed screaming football fans inevitably electrify the night air inside arenas across the country with the deafening roar of their bourbon soaked voices, remember that they are unknowingly reliving the glory and pride of their fallen Civil War brethren.

Contact information for Chris Warner:
cewarner@mindspring.com

The "Art" of Tailgating

Inevitably, it's the neat feeling you get when you wake up with a tinge of nervousness on a crisp fall Saturday morning, knowing well, that as the

sands pass through the hourglass, the spectacle is inching ever closer. It's the enjoyment of good southern food and hospitality, the reunion of lasting friendships, and the continual blur of your school's colors that taints the entire affair. It's staying the knotted apprehension of watching your team play a tough opponent...the goosebumps that eventually riddle the surface of your skin as the anticipation subsides and the teams pour out of the locker rooms accompanied by a ubiquitous, deafening roar that grips your inner soul. It's the surreal ambience and the realization that you are part of something much larger.

The pure exhilaration of it all—a cataclysmic catharsis of emotion that reflects the pride and spirit of the fans of the Southeastern Conference. Saturdays during football season in the South are undeniably the weekly main event, and tailgating on game day is as much a part of the entire experience as the game itself; some might even argue that it's bigger.

Tailgating has become a practiced art among SEC football fans everywhere. The period of time prior to a gridiron contest is one in which the entire college community comes together to enjoy themselves. Southerners have long been known for their unquenchable "joie de vivre" (joy of life), and it seems that Saturday afternoons prior to game time have become a rite of food and fun that is largely indicative of the way southerners approach and enjoy life.

Almost like clockwork, prior to every pigskin matchup, SEC fans from near and far congregate–whether they are at the game or not, to partake in the joy of tailgating. Every family and coterie of true football fans seem to have their very own method for cooking up their groceries before game time. Some fans choose to barbecue ribs, chicken and spicy sausage. Some opt for jambalaya or gumbo, if the weather and inclination are right. Still other fans even go as far to hire out catering services to prepare a meal on their behalf for the occasion. Whatever the case may be, tailgating is undoubtedly an integral part of every SEC fan's gameday experience.

Jeffrey Warner is currently the owner of a catering company in Baton Rouge. Hailing from New Iberia, Louisiana, a small, rural enclave of Cajun people within the heart of Acadiana, Jeff attended culinary school in Baton Rouge, Louisiana. After graduating from cooking school, Jeff spent three years on a popular Mississippi River paddlewheeler and then spent another three years in various restaurant management and catering positions. During that time he finely honed his culinary skills and acumen for producing unforgettable dishes. Hungry crowds are always pleased when Jeff "The Chef" is on hand to provide the throng with the likes of his succulent crawfish etouffeé over puffy white rice, or his alligator sauce piquante'—a rich, scarlet gravy with caramelized onions and peppers laden with generous portions of tasty white gator meat, served over white rice. In the past, Jeff has even been known to go to such lengths as to prepare an authentic cochon de lait'—a whole gutted pig smoked to perfection above-ground in a homemade box, augmented by savory portions of creamy, southern-style white beans and rice.

Although Jeff spends many hours in the kitchen every day, he always enjoys preparing food for tailgating parties—graciously giving his time to feed fellow football fans. "Good food always has the effect of bringing people together," says Jeff. "Growing up, my grandmother was a huge influence on me, cooking for our family and friends. I truly enjoy my role in facilitating a good time for all. It's really a lot of fun."

For the enjoyment of your own family and friends on gameday, Jeff has provided twelve of his most favored tailgating recipes. Be sure and try them out the next time you "pass a good time" at your regular tailgate party. One thing's for sure—your tastebuds and your stomach will be happy you did, cher!

Contact Chef Jeff for your tailgate party! (225) 248-9903

Crimson Tide Seafood Gumbo

1 cup flour	1/2 cup parsley (chopped)
1 cup oil	2 lbs. small shrimp
2 lg. onions	1 lb. lump crabmeat
2 lg. Bell peppers	1 lb. of crawfish tails
1 bunch celery	Cajun seasoning to taste
1 lb. of pork tasso	Mashed roasted garlic
1 bunch of green onions	(15 cloves)
1/2 gal water	Cayenne pepper and salt to taste
1 cup of dried shrimp	1 Bay leaf
1 teaspoon Italian seasoning	Louisiana Hot Sauce to taste

In a gumbo pot, on high to medium heat, mix oil and flour to make a chocolate colored roux. Add onions, peppers, celery and garlic and sauté well. Stir in tasso and cook for 2 minutes, and then add water. Stir well and cook for 1 hour, seasoning occasionally to taste. Add parsley and dried shrimp during this procedure as well. Add shrimp after gumbo boils for an hour then cook additional 20 minutes. Then add crawfish tails and lump crabmeat. Cook for additional half-hour. Add green onions, season again and serve!

NOTE: May acquire more flavors by adding additional dried shrimp or small whole gumbo crabs from the parish, and oysters would be great in this recipe also.

Serve over great Louisiana rice and French bread, Enjoy!

18-20 servings

Razorback Jambalaya

2 lbs. of the cheapest hog out there (Dice up pork)	2 lbs. smoked sausage
2 cups of diced pork tasso	4 lbs. Louisiana rice
2 large peppers chopped	2 large onions chopped
1 bunch green onions	1/2 bunch of celery chopped
Cajun seasoning	Lots of minced garlic
3 cans of chicken broth	Hot sauce to taste
1/2 cup of oil	1/2 cup flour
1 cup of parsley	Salt and pepper to taste

NOTE: always add 1/2 parts of water to rice if you are using broth!

In a large black iron skillet begin by browning meat on high heat. After meat is browned remove and set aside. While skillet is still hot add some of your rice and brown very well. After your small amount of rice is browned, add celery, onions, peppers, garlic and a lot of your seasoning. Sauté until onions are tender, then add chicken broth, water, and meat, bring to a boil. After water begins to boil add the rest of the rice, turn the heat to low, cover and stir occasionally. Rice will begin to get fluffy after about 25 or 30 minutes. Season more if you desire while adding parsley and green onions. If rice is still hard add more water and let steam again.

NOTE: Flour in this recipe should be used to brown the meat in the skillet with small amounts added at a time. This will also give you a lot of color for your jambalaya. If desired a darker color just add a little Kitchen Bouquet!

25 servings

Jordan-Hare Shrimp & Okra Stew

1 lb. fresh gulf shrimp   1 onion minced

1 can of diced tom. w/green chilis   1 green pepper chopped

1 bunch of celery chopped   lots of mashed garlic

1 lb. of fresh or frozen chopped okra   1/2 cup flour & 1/2 cup oil

Cajun seasoning   1 cup of shrimp stock or boullion cubes

Hot sauce   1 cup of water

1 cup of dried shrimp   1 teaspoon of nutmeg

In a heavy pot, add flour and oil; stir to make a dark roux. Add onions, peppers, celery and garlic and sauté until tender. Add okra and sauteé over medium temperature to high heat for about 20 minutes. After boiling, add diced tomatoes with green chilis, season occasionally and add shrimp, stock and water, cook while stirring on low heat for one hour. Serve over some of that fluffy Louisiana white or brown rice, Enjoy!

NOTE: Great recipe after that first shrimp boil of the season. Simply use the shrimp that you could not eat!

12 servings

Death Valley Crawfish Etouffeé

3 lbs. Louisiana crawfish tails
1/2 cup of crawfish fat (if available)
1 cup of chopped parsley
2 cups of green onions chopped
3 tablespoons of mashed roasted garlic
Cajun seasoning to taste
1 tablespoon of paprika

2 bell peppers
2 onions
1 bunch of celery
1 cup of flour
1 cup of oil
Salt and hot sauce to taste
Water as needed

Using flour and oil, make a light golden brown roux. Add all of chopped onion, peppers, celery and garlic. Cook until onions are tender. Add crawfish and fat, cook for 20 minutes. Add very little water; slowly add water a little at a time. Your etouffeé should begin to thicken up; it should be very thick, start to add paprika and season to taste. Throw in some of those great chopped green onions and serve over some of that fluffy Louisiana rice. Enjoy!

NOTE: Shrimp, lump crabmeat, or chicken are also great substitutes. Best when served on cold game days with the smell of a win in the air!

12-14 servings

Starkville Shrimp & Corn Soup

2 16 oz. cans of whole
chopped kernel corn
1 cup of oil
1 cup of flour
2 12 oz. cans of chicken broth
2 bell peppers chopped
Cajun hot sauce

2 large onions,
1/2 bunch celery, chopped
2 16 oz. cans of diced Rotel tomatoes
Fresh Shrimp, (save shells to make stock)
1 cup chopped parsley
6 shallots chopped
Cajun seasoning to taste

Start by making a golden colored roux, by heating the flour and roux in a skillet. Make sure you don't burn the roux. Stir frequently on low-medium heat. In a second pot add the chicken broth and shrimp peelings with about 4 quarts of water and boil for 30 minutes. Strain into large pot, add all chopped vegetables, can corn and tomatoes. When soup has reached a boil again lower fire to low and add roux slowly to add color and base to your soup. Add shrimp when soup returns to a low boil, season to taste. Cook soup after shrimp where added for about 40 minutes, just in time to make some great garlic French Bread to accompany this great meal for a great game!

12-14 servings

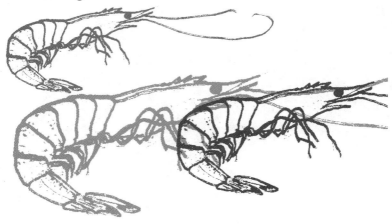

Rebel Red Beans With Pork Sausage & Rice

1 ham bone
1 lb. of dried red beans
1 lb. of smoked pork sausage (hot)
1 lg. onion
1 bunch of celery chopped
1 cup of green onion
Hot sauce
Salt and pepper to taste

Lots of garlic
1/2 c. of chopped parsley
1 bay leaf
1 lg. green pepper
1/2 c. butter (sweet cream)
Cajun seasoning to taste
1 teaspoon of Italian seasoning

Soak your beans overnight. After you bring them to a boil, (this helps them to cream better when you cook them) add a ham bone. It adds real color and flavor that is otherwise impossible to achieve. Sauté on high heat with sausage and ham bones for 5 minutes. In doing so, you will retain all of that great fat that came from the sausage to cook your onions, peppers, celery and garlic. Cook on high heat while adding all beans and remaining ingredients. It is important to note: you must bring beans to a boil to cream them by mashing them to the side of the pot as they cook, and you stir. Once you get the right consistency, you can add some of those great green onions and serve over some of your favorite style of rice. Enjoy!

NOTE: Hot fresh French bread is something that you should not forget for this event!

Remember to cook your beans slow so you can enjoy the fun as well!

12-14 servings

Gainesville Alligator Sauce Piquanté

1 cup of flour	lots of chopped garlic
1 cup of oil	1/2 cup of sugar
1 crushed bay leaf	1 quart of tomato sauce
1 quart of diced tomatoes	3 lbs. of gator tail meat
w/ green chilis	1 large bell pepper chopped
3 cups of celery chopped	1 bunch green onions
2 cups of parsley	2 pints of mushrooms sliced
Cajun seasoning to taste	Hot sauce to taste
1 tablespoon of Italian seasoning	Salt and pepper to taste
Seafood base or cubes (4 oz.)	1 large onion chopped

In large pot, over med. to high heat, begin by adding flour and oil to make a roux. Add vegetables, tomato sauce and diced tomatoes, garlic, sugar, bay leaf, and cook for 2 hours. In a separate pot begin browning the alligator meat with salt and pepper (Only brown meat; do not overcook meat you will finish the cooking in the red sauce). After browning meat set aside and add after sauce has cooked for 2 hours, cook for another hour on med. to low heat after adding meat. Once meat is tender, add mushrooms, parsley, and green onions; simmer for 30- 40 minutes. Serve over fluffy rice and Enjoy!

NOTE: Seafood base is not required, but will add flavor to this great recipe. You may substitute turtle, chicken, rabbit or squirrel to this recipe.

12-14 servings

174

Athens' Redfish Courtboullion

8 lbs. of redfish fillets, cut in 3-in. squares   1/2 bunch celery, chopped

1/2 cup garlic, chopped   4 tablespoons of Worcestershire sauce

1 1/2 cup peanut oil   2 tablespoons of sugar

2 cups of water   2 bunches green onions, chopped

1 cup of flour   4 lemons

1 12 oz. can of tomato paste   Salt, black-red pepper and Cajun

3 large onions chopped   seasoning to taste

2 medium bell peppers, chopped   2 bunches of parsley, chopped

1 12 oz. can of diced Rotel tomatoes   5 bay leaves

Hot sauce to taste   2 packages of dried shrimp

Soak dried shrimp in 1 quart of warm water for 30 minutes prior to inclusion.

In a large pot, combine oil and flour to make a golden colored roux. Stir frequently on a low to medium heat watching not to burn roux. Once you have reached a golden color, begin adding all chopped vegetables and stir until onions are translucent. Slowly add stock with shrimp in it to the pot, bring to soft boil and begin adding tomato paste slowly along with the can of Rotel tomatoes. Add 1 quart water and stir. Lower heat to medium and cook for 30 minutes. Your sauce should turn from dark red to orange red, if not cook a little longer. Add sugar, lemon juice and Worcestershire sauce to pot and begin stirring in redfish cutlets. Add bay leaves, season to taste. Cook on low to medium heat for about 30 to 40 minutes stirring occasionally. Serve over some great fluffy white rice. Enjoy!

25 servings

Cock-A-Boose
Chicken-Andouille Gumbo

1 lb. chicken dark, white, or turkey

Lots of garlic (chopped)

1 lb. andouille sliced

Cajun seasoning

3 large onions

1 cup of flour

2 large bell peppers

1 cup of oil

1 bunch of celery

1 gallon of water

Hot sauce to taste

2 cans of chicken broth

1 bunch green onions

Smoked turkey wings or necks

1 cup parsley

(All vegetables chopped)

Start by cutting up chicken and sausage and basic vegetables. Heat oil in large pot and brown chicken and put aside. With remaining oil from browning chicken make roux, by adding flour slowly, until the color is a deep golden-chocolate brown. Remember to cook roux slowly, and stirring often not to let the roux burn. After roux is made lower heat and add all chopped ingredients including garlic and seasoning, except parsley and green onions. Sauté until onions are tender (should only take a few minutes, because roux should be very hot). Add water and stock, slowly stirring so roux can be distributed evenly; cook on high heat until a soft boil begins. Once boiling soft add chicken and sausage and bring to soft boil again, cook for 1 hour constantly stirring. After cooking for desired time you should lower the heat and begin skimming the fat off the top of the pot. Cook on low heat for 30-40 minutes. Add chopped green onions and parsley for last 30 minutes on low to medium heat. Serve over fluffy white rice and enjoy!

NOTE: Smoked turkey wings give a great flavor to your gumbo and should always be added early so they fall off the bone. A great addition to this recipe would be turkey necks or leftover holiday turkey or chicken. Always serve with good fresh garlic French bread! Also, this recipe is a must to serve for the first cold weather football game!

12-14 servings

Hearty Bayou Wildcat Soup

1 1/2 lbs. beef brisket (cubed)	1/2 cup turnips
1 1/2 lb. soup bone	1/2 cup corn
1/2 head cabbage chopped	1 large onion chopped
1 large pepper chopped	2 cups of celery chopped
1 large can whole tomatoes	1 cup of fresh or frozen beans
1 cup diced carrots	3 quarts of water
1 can chicken broth	Cajun seasoning to taste
Lots of garlic	Hot sauce to taste
Salt and pepper to taste	1/2 cup vermicelli pasta
1 tablespoon Italian seasoning	1 crushed bay leaf

Salt water and broth to taste and put to boil with brisket and soup bone. Let boil for one hour, then add vegetables. Add tomatoes and cook until meat and vegetables are tender. Add more water if needed. Add pasta the last 15 minutes of cooking. Season to taste and serve! Enjoy!

NOTE: You may add red potatoes for thicker soup. You may substitute beef for any other meat you would desire, or leave out for vegetarians.

12-14 servings

Tennessee Spicy Short Ribs

10 lbs. of beef short ribs
2 cups sugar
1/2 cup salt
1/2 cup cayenne pepper
1 gallon barbecue sauce
12 ounces bacon fat
4 large red onions
Louisiana hot sauce

1 cup liquid smoke
1 cup garlic powder
1 cup black pepper
water
1 quart apple juice
4 large bell peppers
Cajun seasoning to taste

Start by filling a large pot more than half with water; add liquid smoke, salt, and apple juice. Bring water to boil and add ribs. Boil until somewhat tender, (45 min to an hour). Let cool and brush bacon fat on ribs.

Make dry rub for ribs, mix garlic powder, black pepper, sugar, and cayenne pepper

After fat on rib cools, start adding dry rub on the ribs generously. This all should be done before you barbecue on site. If you choose to cook ahead, start ahead!

When barbecuing, use wood chips for best results. You should cook ribs on a med-low fire for about 1 1/2 hours, constantly basting with your own barbecue sauce. Your ribs should turn out sweet as candy if you keep a watchful eye. Cut up peppers and onions and add the last 15 minutes, grill and serve as a nice touch to this delicious recipe. Enjoy!

NOTE: A great side dish for this recipe would have to be some of grandmas best Southern potato salad, and fresh Louisiana French Bread!

18-20 servings

Sweet Vandy Brisket

2 beef briskets, 5-6 pounds	1 tablespoon of cayenne pepper
2 tablespoons of salt	1 tablespoon of black pepper
2 tablespoons of garlic powder	1 tablespoon of thyme
Cajun seasoning to taste	

Marinade:

1 cup firmly packed dark, brown sugar	1 cup LA hot sauce
1 cup unsweetened pineapple juice	1/2 cup red wine vinegar
3 T Worcestershire sauce	1/2 cup honey
1/2 cup cane syrup	3 cloves garlic minced
1 1/2 cup minced onion	

Start by seasoning the meat with seasoning mix of salt, peppers, garlic powder and thyme. Place seasoned brisket in a large glass-baking dish.

Mix marinade and pour over brisket. Cover tightly and place in refrigerator for a maximum of 6 days and a minimum of 2 days. Rotate brisket every 12 hours during the chosen time period.

Reserve marinade. Grill over coals and wood chips, until browned completely for 1 hour. Place in large disposable aluminum roasting pan. Pour marinade over the top. Seal pan with foil and cook over coals for an additional 2 hours. Drain marinade off, take brisket and baste with your own barbecue sauce for the last 20 minutes. Should be tender and sweet by the time you serve your friends and family, just watch out because, they gonna fight you for it!

NOTE: Leftovers from this recipe, makes a great brisket sandwich for the kids!

Pecan wood chips are top choice on my list for this recipe!

12-14 servings

"They had grown up in a time during which football had a special place. The game was a powerful source of pride and self-esteem for individuals, families, towns, cities and the entire state. The mythic connections to the lost cause of the Confederacy were part of the reason. It was not simply that football gave the South a way to excel – it was a way to excel in the virtues that Southerners most valued. Few people from Alabama had been exposed to "the North" and fewer still had an understanding of the advantages a strong industrial base, top quality educational establishments and progressive attitudes afforded their rival region. So they didn't really believe that they were disadvantaged. All they knew about the North was that people there looked down upon them and thought of them as bigoted, pellagra-ridden and lazy. What better way to prove otherwise than to kick ass in a hard, physical game."

Tom Stoddard, excerpted from his book,
*Turnaround: The Untold Story of Bear Bryant's
First Season at Alabama*

East

University of Florida

The Sunshine State is known for football, and the University of Florida is one of the main reasons for that particular claim to fame. Florida is the SEC's largest school, and sixth-largest in the country, with over 41,000 students. During the 1990's, the Gators were the SEC's most successful football program, winning over eighty percent of their ball games. Florida's most recent winning streak has been the brain trust of its most favorite football son—former Gator Steve Spurrier, the 1966 Heisman trophy winner and two-time All-American. Named one of the nation's five premier schools for combining academic and athletic achievement, the University of Florida is one of the country's finest modern-day collegiate institutions.

Founded: In 1853, the state-funded East Florida Seminary took over the Kingsbury Academy in Ocala. The seminary moved to Gainesville in the 1860's and later was consolidated with the state's land-grant Florida Agricultural College, then in Lake City. In 1905, by legislative action, the college became a university and was moved to Gainesville. Classes first met with 102 students on the present site on September 26, 1906.

The University of Florida opened its doors to women in 1947 and was integrated in 1958. The University of Florida is a 2,000 acre campus that consists of nearly 900 separate buildings—160 of which contain classrooms. The northeast quadrant of the sprawling campus is an official Historic District—complete with a listing on the National Register of Historic Places. The 34 residence halls on campus have a capacity of nearly 7,000 students. Furthermore, the campus of the University of Florida also possesses the impressive Florida Museum of National History, which ranks among the nation's top 10 natural history museums.

Nickname: Gators - In 1907, Austin Miller, a law student of the University of Virginia at Charlottesville, was visited by his father, Phillip. Phillip Miller was the owner of a drug store back in

Gainesville, Florida, and while he was in Virginia visiting his son, he decided to purchase pennants adorned with the University of Florida on them to resell to student customers back in Florida. When the manager of the shop asked for Florida's emblem, the elder Miller realized that the school did not have one. The younger Austin Miller suggested to his father that the alligator be used since no other school had adopted it and since the alligator was native to the State of Florida. Miller's off the cuff suggestion stuck and the first appearance of the alligator emblem was in Phillip Miller's Gainesville drug store in 1908.

Location: Gainesville

Gainesville was named the nation's most livable city in a 1995 national ranking. Gainesville is not only the home of the Florida Gators, it is also host to some of the most pristine fresh-water springs in the country. Surrounded by lush state parks and other recreational facilities, Gainesville offers visitors a surprising variety of outdoor activities in a moderate climate. If the beaches of the Sunshine State are more your cup of tea, the Gulf of Mexico and Atlantic Ocean are both an hour's drive away from the main campus. Furthermore, the University of Florida's influence is felt throughout the social and cultural life of the city.

Population: 85,000
Enrollment: 48,500
Colors: Orange and Blue
Mascot: Alligator
Mascot name: The Gators have two costumed mascots who roam the sidelines during football games. Albert and Alberta are fan favorites at the University of Florida.

Since 1984, Jan Timmerberg, the Director of Community Relations at the University Athletic Association has been assigned to the job of wearing the gator costume and playing "Albert," a duty she has maintained well over the years. Timmerberg helped innovate the look of Albert in 1986 by dressing the Gator with the now-infamous orange "F" emblazoned on the blue sweater. Timmerberg also came up with the idea for Alberta in 1991. Eight different students collaborate to effectively handle the demanding duties of Albert and Alberta on gameday, where hot and humid Florida temperatures can commonly range in the high 90's.

Stadium: Ben Hill Griffin Stadium

The "Swamp" is the nickname for Ben Hill Griffin Stadium at Florida Field. It is currently the largest stadium in the entire state of Florida. Constructed in 1930, the stadium had an original capacity of 21,769. Initially, the entire stadium was constructed below ground. In 1950, over 11,000 seats were added on the west side and another 7,000 were provided by bleachers on the east side. The addition brought seating capacity to 40,116. Additional bleacher seats were added during the 1950s, bringing capacity to 46,164 by 1960. In December of 1965, construction began on an expansion that would add over 10,000 permanent seats on the east side as well as temporary bleachers moved from the east side to the south endzone, providing a total capacity of 62,800.

The south endzone expansion in 1982 enclosed the south end of the stadium, and brought its capacity to 72,000. Later, the north end horseshoe was turned into a bowl and this raised capacity to 83,000. Ben Hill Griffin is a bowl stadium with some openings, but for the most part it is completely enclosed by seats. Possessing a steep seating angle throughout the stadium, the sound level is deafening. Florida Field also has 46 luxury skyboxes, where alcohol and food are served. In 1991, Coach Steve Spurrier commented, "The swamp is where the Gators live. We feel comfortable there, but we hope our opponents feel tentative. A swamp is hot and sticky and dangerous." *The Atlanta Journal Constitution* has recently proclaimed The Swamp as "the loudest, most obnoxious and notorious piece of real estate in all of college football." In 1996, the *Sporting News College Football Preview*, ranked Florida Field among the nation's loudest stadiums.

Stadium capacity: 83,000
Record crowd: 85,714 Sept. 20, 1997 Florida 33, Tennessee 20

First game: Although the University of Florida was playing football prior to the turn of the century, official records list the school's first game in 1906, a game that the University of Florida won, defeating nearby Gainesville AC by the score of 6-0. Due to the United States' involvement in World War II, the University of Florida did not have a football team in 1943.

First game in stadium: 1930, Florida 33, Alabama 20

   Directions: Coming from the North or South on I-75: Take Exit 76 (Hwy 26/Newberry Rd.). Head East to North-South Drive. Turn right, stadium is on left.

   From North or South on 441: Go to University Avenue and head West (from the south turn left, from the north turn right). Go to North-South Drive. Turn left, stadium is on left.

Where to go:
Eating and Drinking:
   Phil-Nick's "A Good Place To Eat" - 37 N Main St. - (352) 376-8269 – Homemade cooking, Southern style.

185

Gainseville Ale House and Raw Bar: Seafood, Steaks, Chicken, Burgers, Full Bar, Regular Menu Served until 11:30 pm, Patio, Big Screen Tvs, Located on SW Archer Road near I-75. 3950 SW Archer Rd, Gainesville, FL (352)371-0818

David's Real Pit BBQ Restaurant: "The best BBQ in Gainesville." David's also serves breakfast 7 days a week. David's BBQ was voted the Best BBQ and Ribs for 1998 in *Where the Locals Eat* and was also voted the Best Food at the Greater Gainesville Beer Festival. Located at Exit 77 just 2 miles East of I-75 on 39th Avenue (Hwy. 222)

Amelia's Restaurant: 235 S. Main St., (352) 373-1919

All-Time Record: 590-359-40 (.621)
SEC Record: 235-182-15 (.563)
Bowl Appearances: 27
Bowl Record: 31 / 14-17 (.452)
SEC Championships: (5) (1991, 93, 94, 95, 96)
National Championship: 1996
Great Bowl Games:

1953 Gator Bowl: January 1, 1953, Jacksonville, FL   Florida 14, Tulsa 13

1962 Gator Bowl: December 30, 1962, Jacksonville, FL Florida 17, Penn State 7

1967 Orange Bowl: January 1, 1967, Miami, FL Florida 27, Georgia Tech 12

1994 Sugar Bowl: January 1, 1994, New Orleans, LA Florida 41, West Virginia 7

1997 Sugar Bowl: January 2, 1997, New Orleans, LA Florida 52, Florida State 20

Florida wins its first National Championship under Steve Spurrier

1998 Citrus Bowl: January 1, 1998, Orlando, FL Florida 21, Penn State 6

1999 Orange Bowl: January 2, 1999, Miami, FL Florida 31, Syracuse 10

2002 Orange Bowl: Florida 56, Maryland 23

186

Florida Greats:

Coaches:

Ray Graves - A coach whose decade-long tenure represented a resurgent time for the hopes of Gator football fans. During his stay in Gainesville, from 1960 to 1969, Florida won seventy games (70-31-4 .686), and won four of five bowl games. Graves is probably best remembered by Florida fans for his shocking upset of Alabama during his fourth year as head coach. In October of 1963, Graves' Gators went to Tuscaloosa and pulled off the unimaginable upset of Bear Bryant's Crimson Tide–a 10-0 shutout. The sheer magnitude of the win grew exponentially in the following years since Bryant's boys would not lose another game at home in Tuscaloosa until 1982. Perhaps Graves' best squad was his 1969 team that finished 9-1-1 and defeated Tennessee by the score of 14-13 in the Gator Bowl. That particular team had players like Jack Youngblood, Carlos Alvarez, and All-American quarterback John Reaves. Graves is a member of the National Football Foundation and College Football Hall of Fame.

Doug Dickey (58-43-2 .573) came back to Florida from Tennessee to coach the Gators in 1970. During the nine-year tenure of Dickey, Florida attended four bowl games, but unfortunately lost all of them.

Charley Pell (1979-1984) (33-26-3 .549) signaled a turnaround for the Gator program in 1979 by taking over the leadership of the Florida football team. Although his first year was a disastrous 0-10-1, Pell's next four seasons in Gainesville were successful, leading the Gators to four bowl games in four consecutive years.

Pell's tenure was highlighted by protegé stalwarts Wilbur Marshall and Chris Collinsworth, who would both later go on to NFL greatness.

Pell - *"I want players to think as positively as the 85-year old man who married a 25-year old woman and bought a five-bedroom house next to the elementary school."*

Galen Hall (40-18-1 .703) In 1984, Galen Hall followed in the footsteps of Charley Pell as Head Coach of the Gators. Hall's first two

 years in Gainesville produced a record of 18-2-2, although the Gators were ineligible for post-season play due to NCAA sanctions. Emmitt Smith, one of the NFL's most talented running backs of all time, played during the Galen Hall years at Florida. In 1985, Florida defeated Auburn 14-10 at Jordan-Hare Stadium. The SEC win resulted in Florida being ranked number one in the nation in the AP Poll for the first time in school history. Hall coached through game five of the 1989 season and was replaced by Gary Darnell to finish out the remainder of the season.

Steve Spurrier - The winningest coach in Florida history, Steve Spurrier is the modern-day standard bearer for the ultra-competitive SEC. Spurrier returned to his alma mater in 1990 and implemented his seemingly unstoppable Fun N' Gun style of offense, achieving overnight success in the process. Spurrier is the only major college coach in the 20th century to win more than 90 games in his first nine seasons and he is the only SEC coach in history to win 10 or more games in six consecutive seasons (1993-98). He is also one of only three in major conference history to achieve that distinction. Florida appeared in each of the first five SEC Championship games (1992-1996), with wins in four of those games (1993-96). The Gators under Spurrier won a total of five SEC championships during the nineties. Remarkably, Spurrier's teams lost only four games at home. Spurrier's dominance of the league during the 1990's, coupled with his cantankerous demeanor, led many of his SEC admirers and detractors to label him as the "Evil Genius." Spurrier's 1996-97 squad won the National Championship.

Spurrier finished his 14 year career at Florida with an astounding 132-38-2 record. His 112 victories from 1990-2000 at Florida ranks as the best win total for a major college coach in his first 11 years at a school in college history. Spurrier achieved his 100th victory at Florida faster than any other major college coach in the 20th century (10th season, 8th game). His 81-12 record in SEC play ranks as the best winning percentage (.871) in conference history and his 73 league wins in the 1990s is the most in conference history during a decade. Spurrier and Paul Bryant are the only coaches in SEC history to win as many as four consecutive league championships (1993-96). What's so amazing about Spurrier is that he accomplished all that he did with the 85 scholarship limit. Spurrier left Florida at the end of the 2001 season to take a short-lived head coaching position with the Washington Redskins during the 2002 and 2003 NFL seasons. Spurrier's two-year NFL coaching career record was 12-20.

The Words of Steve Spurrier:
"Discover the talent that God has given you. Then, go out and make the most of it."
"But the real tragedy was that 15 hadn't been colored yet." ~Steve Spurrier, Head Coach of the Florida Gators, in 1991, telling fans that a fire at Auburn's football dorm had destroyed 20 books.
"If I'm a good football coach, it's because of my mistakes. I try to learn from them."

Players

Steve Spurrier - A two-time All-American (1965, 1966) and 1966 Heisman Trophy winner at quarterback for the Gators. During his career, he broke every Florida record for game, season, and career in passing and total offense, as well as all of the league records for passing. In 1966, Spurrier led the Gators to a 9-2 mark and an Orange Bowl victory over Georgia Tech. A little known fact regarding Steve Spurrier is that he was the Gator's punter for three seasons, averaging over forty yards per kick. Spurrier kicked field goals for the Gators as well. He was named to the College Football Hall of Fame in 1986.

John Reaves - An All-American performer who was the NCAA passing champion, Reaves played for the Gators from 1969-1971. Reaves finished his stellar career in Gainesville as the SEC's leading total offensive player. An NFL first-round pick in 1972,

Reaves played in the league with the Philadelphia Eagles from 1972 to 1975, with the Cincinnati Bengals from 1975-1978, the Minnesota Vikings (1979), and the Houston Oilers, 1981. Reaves, from 1983-85, also played for the Tampa Bandits, in the now defunct USFL.

Carlos Alvarez - An All-American in 1969, Alvarez was a record-setting receiver for the Gators. An honor student who was an Academic All-American from 1969-1971, and the winner of the Post-Graduate Scholarship in 1971, Alvarez was named to the Academic All-American Hall of Fame in 1989. His 88 receptions during the 1969 season still stand as the University of Florida's single-season record and his 172 career catches still rank first in the annals of Gator football.

Jack Youngblood - A 1970 All-American, Youngblood is considered one of the top defensive ends in Gator history. A member of the All-SEC Team of the Decade in the 1970's, and also the SEC Quarter Century Team (1950-1974), he was known for a rugged style of play. Following college, he was drafted in the first round of the professional draft and became an All-Pro standout for the Los Angeles Rams from 1971 to 1984. During his pro career Youngblood was twice named the NFL Defensive Player of the Year. He was named to the College Football Hall of Fame in 1992.

Chris Collinsworth - A 1980 All-American for the Gators, Collinsworth was a superb multi-talented player who excelled at a number of positions in college (linebacker, receiver, quarterback–he is still tied for the longest touchdown pass in college history–99 yards). During his career at Florida he caught 120 passes for 1937 yards and 14 touchdowns. Collinsworth was a three-time All-SEC selection from 1978 to 1980, and an Academic All-American in 1980. After college, Collinsworth went on to star for the Cincinnati Bengals where he eventually attained All-Pro status and was named NFL Rookie of the Year in 1981. Today, Collinsworth is an NFL color analyst for FOX TV.

Wilbur Marshall - The National Defensive Player of the Year in 1983, Marshall was a first-round draft pick in 1984. He earned All-Pro honors in 1986, 1987 and 1992.

Brad Culpepper - (1988-1991) Recipient of the 1991 Draddy Trophy (presented to the nation's top scholar-athlete), Culpepper was a first-team All-American selection in 1991. He completed his career at Florida with 47 tackles for losses, then the highest total for a defensive lineman in school history. Culpepper was also named the Toyota Leader of the year recipient in 1991 and was a member of the GTE Academic All-American and CFA Scholar-Athlete Teams. Culpepper is currently a starting defensive lineman for the Tampa Bay Buccaneers. Prior to joining the Bucs, Brad starred for the Minnesota Vikings from 1992-93.

Emmitt Smith - A 1989 All-American running back for the Gators. He was the SEC Player of the Year in 1989. Smith completed his junior year with 58 Florida records and 3,928 rushing yards, making him the school's all-time leading rusher. A first team All-SEC selection three years, from 1987 to 1989, he was selected in the first round by the Dallas Cowboys in 1990. Smith was chosen as the 1990 NFL "Rookie of the Year." Smith was the league's leading rusher from 1991 to 1993 and 1995, and was the NFL MVP in 1993.

Danny Wuerffel - A two-time All-American for the Gators during the 1995 and 1996 seasons. Wuerffel was the Heisman Trophy winner in 1996. He is considered by many to be one of the top college quarterbacks ever. Wuerffel's remarkable career culminated in a National Championship for the Gators in 1996, a victory earned over in-state arch rival, Florida State. Wuerffel completed his career at Florida connecting on an amazing 798 of 1170 passes for 10,875 yards (fifth-best in major college history) with 114 TD passes, which is best in SEC history and second best in division one history. Additionally, his pass efficiency rating in 1995 of 178.4 was the highest ever recorded in college football history. After his illustrious Florida Gator career, which culminated with a National Championship Sugar Bowl victory over arch-rival, Florida State, Wuerffel was drafted in the fourth round of the 1997 professional draft by the New Orleans Saints.

Ike Hilliard - All-American Receiver, 1996. For his remarkable exploits on the gridiron while attending the University of Florida, Hilliard gained first-team All-American honors from the American Football Coaches Association, Walter Camp Foundation and Football News. During the 1996 season Hilliard nabbed 47 receptions for 900 yards and 10 touchdowns. He finished his playing days at Florida with 126 catches (7th best in Florida history) for 2,214 total yards (4th best in school history) and 29 touchdowns (2nd best in school history). His touchdown catch ratio of 4.34 (29 TD's/126 receptions) ranked second best in UF history. Hilliard, a native of Patterson, Louisiana, was selected in the first round of the 1997 NFL draft by the New York Giants.

Jevon Kearse - All-American Linebacker, 1998. During his last year as a Florida Gator, Kearse was a consensus First-Team All-SEC selection who was also chosen as the Associated Press SEC Defensive Player of the Year. Kearse, in 1998, was also one of three finalists for the Butkus Award and also one of three finalists for the Bednarik National Defensive Player of the Year award. Possessing amazing speed and a penchant for delivering vicious hits to opposing offensive players, Kearse earned the nickname "The Freak" during his Gator playing days–a moniker he carried with him to the pros, where he signed with the Tennessee Oilers as a first-round pick in the 1999 NFL draft.

Dale Van Sickel – Van Sickel was Florida's first All-American in 1928. A standout two- way player for the Gators, Van Sickel played on the nation's highest scoring team (336 points in nine games). The late Van Sickel was one of Hollywood's premier stunt men for nearly five decades and was twice elected President of the Motion Picture Stunt Men's Association. Unfortunately, he died as the result of injuries in his late 60s.

Larry Smith – In 1968 Smith became only the fifth offensive back in SEC history to earn All-SEC honors three straight years. He became the top career rusher in Gator history with 2,186 on a record 520 carries from 1966-68. Smith was a first round selection with the Los Angeles Rams and also played for the Washington Redskins.

Jabar Gaffney – A consensus All-America selection as a redshirt sophomore in 2001, Gaffney was only the second sophomore wide receiver in Florida history to garner such honors. A finalist for the Biletnikoff Award in 2001, Gaffney was the National Freshman Player of the Year in 2000, and a 2nd round NFL draft selection by the Houston Texans in 2002.

Jacquez Green – A first-team All-America selection in 1997 by the AP and the Walter Camp Football Foundation, Green is one of three finalists in 1997 for the Biletnikoff Award as the nation's top wide receiver. In 1997 he caught 61 passes for 1,024 yards (4th in school history) with nine touchdown catches. A consensus First Team All-SEC selection in 1997, Green completed his Gator career with 113 catches for 2,181 yards and 23 touchdowns. In 1998, Green was a 2nd round draft choice by Tampa Bay.

Rex Grossman – In 2001 Grossman became the first sophomore in Florida history to garner first-team All-America honors. The runner-up in Heisman balloting in 2001, he is only the fifth sophomore to rank in the top two for the nation's top football honor. That same year Grossman was named National Player of the Year by the AP. His 55 combined TD's during the 2000-01 season rank as the most for a player over the combined course of their freshman and sophomore seasons in major college football history.

History and Tradition:

It is customary at home games, between the 3rd and 4th quarter, for all of the Florida fans to sway side to side to the University of Florida fight song "We are the Boys of 'Ole Florida."

Mr. Two Bits: George Edmundson has played his part as "Mr. Two Bits" for over 40 years. During every home game Mr. Edmundson, who is a graduate of the Citadel, wanders around the entire stadium in a goofy yellow shirt and tie, leading cheers for the fans. One of Mr. Edmundson's favorite Florida cheers is Two-Bits, as follows:

"Two-bits, four-bits, six-bits, a dollar...all for the Gators get up and holler!"

Band Name: "Fighting Gators"

One great and longstanding tradition at Florida is the Gator Growl. What began as an orientation service for families and potential students in 1906 has turned into a full-blown reception during the latter part of the twentieth century. The event was originally known as "Dad's Day" in the early years, and it served as the beginning of the pep rally at the University of Florida. As the custom grew, blue and orange beanie-wearing freshmen were forced to carry their weight in firewood to a bonfire constructed for the night before the big Thanksgiving football game. The event later expanded its boundaries by taking on a parade, skits, speakers and singing and dancing. Today, the Gator Growl is a huge campus event, drawing crowds of 75,000 people to join in the fun where the Homecoming Queen and the senior football players are introduced to the crowd.

History:

The University of Florida was the last institution of higher learning in the SEC to begin playing football. In 1906, during its first season on the gridiron, Florida played eight games. The Gators played five with athletic clubs, two with Rollins, and one with Mercer College. By 1910, Florida had embarked on an annual, regular schedule of seven football games versus various colleges, averaging six wins and one loss per season.

School Songs for Florida:

Orange and Blue

So give a cheer for the orange and blue, waving forever,
Forever pride of old Florida, may she droop never,
Let's sing a song for the flag today, cheer for the team at play,
On to the goal we'll fight our way for Florida!

Alma Mater

Florida our Alma Mater, thy glorious name we praise.
All thy loyal sons and daughters a joyous song shall raise.
Where palm and pine are blowing,
Where southern seas are flowing,
Shine forth thy noble gothic walls, thy lovely vine clad halls.
'Neath the orange and blue victorious, our love shall never fail.
There's no other name so glorious, all hail, Florida hail.

Noteworthy UF Alumni:

Faye Dunaway - Actress

Forrest Sawyer - ABC News Anchor

Buddy Ebson - Actor

John Atanasoff - inventor of the electronic digital computer

Tracy Caulkins - Olympic Gold Medal swimmer

Lawton Chiles - former Governor of Florida

Bob Graham - U.S. Senator

Connie Mack - U.S. Senator

Jim McGee - Pulitzer Prize-winning reporter

Hugh Wilson - movie producer and creator of *WKRP in Cincinnati*

"Play...is the
outward expression
of the inward
endeavor to achieve
self-realization."

~John S. Brubacher

Georgia

Football fans from the "Peach Tree State" know well that the University of Georgia is historically one of the SEC's most successful football-playing schools. Georgia Bulldog fans, like so many others in the Southeastern Conference, have enjoyed their share of the national championship experience. The University of Georgia has won the national championship on two separate occasions, ranking it among the SEC's elite football-playing programs. This great winning tradition can be traced to the endearing Southern school's two greatest coaches–Wally Butts and Vince Dooley. Butts brought Georgia its first national championship team in 1942, and Dooley followed his lead with his own national crown 38 years later. Regarding Dooley's championship squad–what modern-day college football fan can forget the 1980 Georgia national championship team? In fact, how could anyone forget the absolute brilliance of Herschel Walker's amazing display of talent en route to receiving college football's highest accolade? Today Georgia fans have more than just the past to be proud of. Recently, under Head Coach Mark Richt, Georgia has made a resounding, noteworthy return to the forefront of competitive football in the Southeastern Conference.

Founded: In January, 1785

Two years after the Revolutionary War ended and four years before George Washington's first inauguration, the Georgia Legislature adopted the charter that created the University of Georgia. In founding the nation's first state university, the legislature also gave birth to the American system of public higher education. The University of Georgia is the fourth-largest research university in the Southeast and ranks 32nd in the nation in that category.

Location: Athens

Known as the "Classic City," it is the home of the University of Georgia and serves as the gateway to the Antebellum Trail. Located in northeast Georgia's rolling hills, Athens is perched about

65 miles east of Atlanta and surrounded by a number of tiny, quaint townships. Northeast Georgia is famous for its natural beauty. Miles of farmland, forests, lakes and rivers surround the Athens area making it a veritable enclave for outdoor enthusiasts. Popular local spots include the Oconee National Forest, Lake Hartwell, Lake Oconee, the State Botanical Garden and the Oconee River, which runs through the town. In addition to its rustic magnetism, Athens is also an incredibly dense mixture of music, restaurants, bars, sports, college students, intellectuals, bands, football weekends, art, and culture. Popular rock bands such as R.E.M., Widespread Panic, and the B-52s made their meteoric starts in Athens.

Population: (Clarke County) 89,361
Enrollment: 32,317
Colors: Red and Black. Official school colors since 1887.
Band: "Georgia Redcoat Band"
Since 1905, Georgia's famous 375 member Redcoat Marching Band has been at the heart of the Georgia Bulldog spirit.

Nickname: "Bulldogs"
Many alumni claim that Georgia acquired the nickname, "Bulldogs," because of the strong ties with Yale whose nickname is also Bulldogs. Georgia's first President, Abraham Baldwin, was a Yale graduate, and the early buildings on campus were designed from blue prints of the same buildings at Yale. Regardless of the obvious connection to Yale, Morgan Blake, a reporter for the Atlanta Journal, wrote on November 3, 1920, about school nicknames, "The Georgia "Bulldogs" would sound good because there is a certain dignity about a bulldog, as well as ferocity." Furthermore, after a 0-0 tie with Virginia in Charlottesville on November 6, 1920, the Atlanta Constitution writer Cliff Wheatley used the name "Bulldogs" in his story five times. The name has been used ever since.
Mascot: English Bulldog
Mascot Name: "Uga"

"Uga" is a bulldog from a long line owned by the Frank W. (Sonny) Seiler family of Savannah, Georgia. Uga I was born on December 2, 1955, beginning the line that still represents the University of Georgia at all football games. A solid white English bulldog, he hailed from Columbus, Georgia, and was initially named "Hood's Ole Dan."

Georgia's current mascot, Uga V, was featured on the cover of *Sports Illustrated* on April 28, 1997 when Uga was honored by the magazine as the best mascot in the country. *SI* spoke highly of Uga in the feature, stating, "If you can't appreciate the swaggering gait and Churchillian physiognomy of Uga V, the Bulldog's bulldog, you must be a cat lover." Uga is so revered in Georgia that he has even visited the Georgia House of Representatives and the Senate Chamber in the State Capitol upon invitation by the Speaker of the House. He even once had his picture taken with Governor Joe Frank Harris while standing on the Governor's desk.

Stadium: Sanford Stadium

Named for Dr. Steadman Vincent Sanford. Joining the faculty of the University of Georgia in 1903, Sanford was one of the most popular men on campus at the University of Georgia during the early years of the twentieth century. Founder of the Henry W. Grady School of Journalism in 1921, Sanford served as University Dean from 1927-32, and held the post of University President and Chancellor until 1935. Sanford was a guiding force behind the construction of Sanford Stadium in 1929 and was termed many times as "the best friend of athletics." Sanford is largely responsible for persuading the Bulldogs of Yale to make their first trip ever south of the Mason-Dixon line to play the dedication game of Sanford Stadium in 1929. The venue is also referred to as "Between the Hedges"–a reference to Sanford Stadium that dates back to the early 1930's. The famous English privet hedges that surround Sanford's playing field were only one foot high when the stadium was dedicated in 1929 and were protected by a wooden fence.

Familiar southern sportswriter Grantland Rice later cleverly observed "that the bulldogs will have their opponent between the hedges." Sanford Stadium has been augmented several times over the years. It was originally built in 1929, for $360,000, when it held 30,000. It saw additions completed in 1949, '64, '67, '81, '84, '91, and 1994 when deluxe luxury skyboxes were installed.

Stadium capacity: 92,058, sixth-largest in the country.

Through a $25 million expansion completed in 2003, Sanford Stadium added a second upper deck on the north side bringing the new capacity to 92,058—the fifth largest on-campus stadium in the country. Sanford Stadium is unique in that it is situated in the middle of campus. It is a reminder of how important Georgia Bulldog football is to the people of the Peach State.

First game: January 30, 1892. Georgia played Mercer College. On February 20th, Georgia and Auburn met at Atlanta's Piedmont Park, marking the inaugural game of what became the South's oldest college rivalry.

First game in stadium: November 12, 1929 Georgia 15, Yale 0 (30,000+ attendance)

First night game in stadium: October 26, 1940 Georgia 7, Kentucky 7

Directions: Coming from Atlanta via I-20 E: Take I-20 to the Conyers Exit (Exit 42 Hwy. 138). Turn left. Continue for approximately 20 miles where highway 138 will merge into Hwy. 78 East. Continue on 78 East for 18 miles and turn right onto Hwy. 316. Continue approximately 4 miles to the Athens Bypass (Loop 10) southbound. Take College Station Road Exit and turn left.

Coming from Augusta via I-20 W: Take I-20 and exit at Hwy. 78 N (west) to Athens. Continue on 78 to Athens. Turn left onto the Athens Bypass (Loop 10) southbound. Take College Station Road exit and turn left.

Coming from Greenville via I-85 S: Take I-85 S to the Carnesville Exit-Hwy. 106. Continue to Athens. The road changes to Danielsville Road, then North Ave., then Thomas St. and the East Campus Road.

Where to go:
Eating and Drinking:
  Athens Brewing Company: 312 East Washington St. 549-0027
  Burntstone Brewhouse: 140 E. Washington St. 613-2918
  Athens Sushi Bar: Utage 440 E. Clayton St. 227-0339
  Gus Garcia's Gulf Coast Grill and Bar: 364 E. Broad St. 543-3097
  Flanagan's: 301 E. Clayton St. 208-9711
  Munchies: 131 E. Broad St. 543-1212
  Wilson's Soul Food: 351 N. Hull St. 353-7289
  Steverino's: 1583 S. Lumpkin St. 353-7777

Live Music: The city that gave birth to R.E.M., the B-52's and Widespread Panic is a club mecca. There are nearly 40 taverns within walking distance of the campus where one can find drinks that are dirt cheap and where the music is always blaring. Other traditional hot spots include the 40 Watt Club (285 W. Washington St.), the High Hat Blues Club (321 E. Clayton St.), the Uptown Lounge (120 E. Washington St.) and Bone Shakers (433 E. Hancock).

All-Time Record: 673-370-54 (.645)

Bowl Appearances: 39

Georgia has been to more different bowl games than any other school–15.

Bowl Record: 21-15-3 (.577)

SEC Record: 261-176-14 (.597)

SEC Championships: 10 (1942, 46t, 48, 59, 66t 68, 76t, 80, 81t, 82) 2002

National Championships: Two Georgia teams have been consensus national champions–1942 and 1980. Three others have been declared national champions by at least one recognized poll at season's end–1927, 1946, and 1968.

Georgia Greats:

Coaches:

Glen "Pop" Warner (1895-96). A Cornell graduate, Warner took a job coaching for the University of Georgia in 1895 for the salary of $34 a week for ten weeks during his first season and for $40 a week during his second season. Warner led the Bulldogs to a 7-4 record in two years and later started the largest and most successful youth football league in the country that is still operating today–Pop Warner Football.

Harry Mehre (1928-1937). A graduate of Notre Dame, Mehr arrived at Georgia upon recommendation of Notre Dame's Knute Rockne. Mehr assumed head coaching duties in 1928 and led Georgia to a 59-34-6 record in his ten years as head coach. Known as a master motivator, Mehre is perhaps known best for his smashing 15-0 defeat of Yale in the 1929 dedication game of Sanford Stadium. Mehre was the only coach in the country at the time to have beaten Yale five straight times at the height of their football existence. Mehre left Athens in 1937 to assume the head coaching position at Ole Miss, where he remained in that capacity for eight more seasons before retiring to a 22-year career as a football analyst for the *Atlanta Journal*.

Wally Butts (1939-1960). A graduate of Mercer, Butts coached the Bulldogs to a 22-year record of 140-86-9, six bowl games, four SEC championships, a consensus national championship in 1942 and another national title recognized by some polls in 1946. Known affectionately by Georgia fans far and wide as "Little Round Man", Butts was one of the greatest football coaches of his era. Butts was known as an advocate of the passing game when passing had not yet gained equal footing with the run as a means for moving the football.

Butts resigned his head coaching position in 1960 so he could become the Athletic Director at Georgia, a post he held until his retirement in 1963. The Butts-Mehre Heritage Hall on the campus of Georgia is named in his honor.

 **Vince Dooley** (1964-1988). Considered to be one of the greatest college coaches of all time. A graduate of Auburn, Dooley coached the Bulldogs for 25 years, leading Georgia to a consensus national championship in 1980 and another national title recognized by one poll in 1968, six SEC championships(1966,68, 76, 80,81,82), and 20 bowl games. His 201 career victories (201-77-10) made him only the ninth coach in Division 1A history to win 200 or more games. Dooley is a seven-time SEC Coach of the year. He was named the National Coach of the Year in 1980. He is also a 1994 inductee to the National College Football Hall of Fame. Dooley served as the Athletic Director at Georgia before retiring in 2004. Dooley was replaced by Damon Evans, the SEC's first black athletic director.

The words of Vince Dooley:

"I don't care where a man comes from or how he spells his name. All I ask is that he be loyal to Georgia, proud of that jersey and try like the devil to win."

"Keep rules to a minimum and enforce the ones you have."

"There are two kinds of discipline: self-discipline and team discipline. You need both."

"You've got to do everything well, but you've got to play defense first."

Jim Donnan – A North Carolina State graduate, Donnan got his head coaching start at Marshall in 1990, after holding the position of offensive coordinator for Oklahoma from 1985-89. Donnan coached Marshall to the Division I-AA championship in 1992 with a 31-28 win over Youngstown St. He took over the reigns at Georgia in 1996 and over five years led the Bulldogs to four straight winning seasons and an overall mark of 40-19 (.677). At the time of his departure from UGA Donnan's career coaching record was an impressive 104-40. Even after being fired from his Athens job, Donnan led his 24th-ranked Bulldogs to a 37-14 victory over Virginia in the 2000 Oahu Bowl. Although Donnan had been let go prior to the bowl game, the Bulldog players campaigned to have him coach them in the Honolulu bowl game. Donnan may have had trouble beating Georgia's traditional rivals, but he never had trouble winning bowl games. Donnan became the first coach in school history to lead Georgia to four straight postseason victories. Today Donnan works as a college football analyst.

Mark Richt – In 2001 Miami graduate Mark Richt was hired as head coach of the Georgia football program to replace embattled coach Jim Donnan. Prior to taking the Georgia job Richt was an offensive coordinator for East Carolina and Florida State University for legendary head coach Bobby Bowden. Richt is known to have a keen offensive mind as well as a recruiting knack, evidenced by the fact that in just three seasons he's won 32 games and lost 8 (.750). Since his hiring Richt has won an SEC Championship (2002), a Sugar Bowl (2003), and a Capital One Bowl (2004).

Players

Frank Sinkwich - 1942 Heisman Trophy recipient. During his senior season, Sinkwich was a unanimous All-American selection at quarterback after setting the SEC total offense record of 2,187 yards (795 yards rushing, 1,392 passing). During that same year, Sinkwich led Georgia to an 11-1 overall record and scored the Bulldogs' only touchdown in a 9-0 win over UCLA in the Rose Bowl.

205

Georgia

Charlie Trippi - Many have said that he is the greatest athlete to ever play at Georgia. Finished second in the Heisman voting in 1946, leading Georgia to a perfect 10-0 record and a victory in the Sugar Bowl. Trippi played alongside Frank Sinkwich in 1942 before World War II abruptly put his college career on hold. He returned from duty in 1945 to play in Georgia's last six ball games and against arch-rival Georgia Tech, he set an SEC record for yards gained passing (323) and total offense (384).

Fran Tarkenton - Georgia's most famous quarterback of all-time (1958-1960). Known as the "Peerless Pilot" by the Georgia fans, the 1960 All-American Quarterback went on to an All-Pro career with the Minnesota Vikings, as well as the New York Giants. During his senior season, Tarkenton threw for 1,189 yards and seven touchdowns for the Bulldogs. After his impressive football career ended, Tarkenton went on to enjoy a successful television career. Tarkenton was once quoted on the topic of leadership: "Leadership must be demonstrated, not announced."

Patrick Dye - One of Georgia's toughest offensive linemen to ever suit up and play the game. Dye was a second team All-SEC guard in 1959 and first team in 1960. Dye played for coach Wallace Butts, leading the way for the "Peerless Pilot," Fran Tarkenton. After a stellar senior season in 1960, Dye played in the annual post-season Blue-Gray game between all-star players from various schools representing the North and the South.

Herschel Walker - Unequivocally Georgia's most dominating offensive player of all time. Herschel's brilliance as a running back transcended the college game. He won the Heisman Trophy in 1982 after placing as runnerup in 1981, and finishing third as a freshman in 1980. A native Georgian from Wrightsville, Walker led Georgia to the 1980 National Championship, three consecutive SEC titles (1980, 81, 82) a three-year record of 33-3, and three consecutive Sugar Bowl

appearances. A three-time consensus All-American, Herschel once
said, "I never get tired of running.
The ball ain't that heavy." In 1980,
as a freshman, Walker once carried
the football 23 times for a stagger-
ing 283 yards–an average of 12.3
yards a clip. Walker finished his
career at Georgia as the SEC's All-
Time leading rusher.

Eric Zier - Georgia's greatest
statistical quarterback. A 1994
All-American, Zier set 67 school,
and 18 SEC individual passing
records. He finished his career with 11,153 passing yards–third most
in NCAA Division I history. Zier once threw for 544 yards against
Southern Miss in 1993. During his career, Zier completed 838 passes
in 1,402 attempts. During one stretch in his college career from 1993-
94, Zier threw for 176 consecutive attempts without an interception.
Zier finished up at Georgia with 7 games in which he threw for over 400
yards, 15 games in which he threw for over 300 yards, and 26 games
in which he threw for over 200.

Garrison Hearst - (1990-92). Hearst led the nation in touchdowns
scored in 1992 with 21, and in scoring (11.5 points per game), finished
second nationally in rushing with 140.6 yards per game (6.8 yards per

carry), and fourth in all-purpose running (173.6
yards per game). A consensus All-American in
1992, to go along with SEC Player of the Year
honors, and the recipient of the Doak Walker
award, Hearst, in an MVP award-winning performance, led Georgia to a stunning 21-14 victory
over Ohio State in the 1993 Florida Citrus Bowl.
For his remarkable senior season in which he
was named SEC Player of the Week four times,

ESPN granted Hearst its proudest "Espy Award" as the nation's outstanding collegiate football player.

Kevin Butler – One of the greatest kickers in college history, Butler connected on 78.6 percent of his attempts at Georgia despite the fact that over twenty percent of them were from over 50 yards. During his final game for the Dawgs Butler nailed field goals from 57, 50 and 34 yards and added an extra point (his 72nd straight). Butler made 5 of 7 from beyond 50 yards as a senior, including a 60-yarder against Clemson and he left UGA with 13 school records, 7 SEC records and 4 national marks, including the highest percentage of field goals made from 50 yards and beyond.

Champ Bailey – The Folkston, Georgia native starred for the Bulldogs from 1996-1998 as a versatile athlete that regularly played on both sides of the ball and special teams. In 1998 Bailey was nominated for the Jim Thorpe Award that goes annually to the nation's top defensive back, and he won the Bronko Nagurski Award which goes to the nation's top defensive player. An All-America First Team player, Bailey  was also a standout track performer for Georgia, setting a Georgia indoor long-jump record of 25 feet 10 inches. A first round draft choice of the Washington Redskins in 1999, Bailey is a three-time pro bowler and has started every game of his early pro career. During his rookie season Bailey set a NFL record for being the youngest player (21) to intercept three passes in a single game.

Jon Stinchcomb - In the footsteps of his older brother, Matt, Jon was also one of Georgia's most decorated players. In addition to All-America recognition, he was a two-time first team Academic All-

American, a semi-finalist for the Rotary Lombardi Award, and he graduated impressively with a 3.75 GPA in Microbiology. An offensive lineman, Stinchcomb helped pave the way for a 2002 offense that led the SEC in scoring (32.6 ppg) and was voted the offensive captain of a team that led the 'Dogs to a 13-1 record, SEC and Nokia Sugar Bowl Championships, and final No. 3 national ranking. Stinchcomb was a second round draft choice in the 2003 NFL draft by the New Orleans Saints.

Richard Seymour – The Gadsden, South Carolina native is one of the most dominating defensive players ever at Georgia, Symour filled the middle of the defensive front for four years through 25 starts. In 1999, he was one of the few defensive linemen in college football that led his team in tackles (74). In his career he recorded 223 tackles, 10 sacks, and 26 tackles-for-loss. Seymour was a semi-finalist for national defensive player of the year as named by Football News. Seymour was a first round draft choice by the New England Patriots in the 2001 NFL draft.

Great Bowl Games: 1981 Sugar Bowl Georgia 17 Notre Dame 10
  1984 Cotton Bowl: Georgia 10 Texas 9
  1989 Gator Bowl: Georgia 34 Michigan State 27
  1993 Florida Citrus: Georgia 21 Ohio State 14
  1998 Peach Bowl: Georgia 35 Virginia 33
  2003 Sugar Bowl: Georgia 26 Florida State 13
  2004 Capital One Bowl: Georgia 34 Purdue 27 (Overtime)

History:

Atlanta developed as a transportation crossroads and became a city in 1845. However, with the start of the Civil War in 1861, Georgia's progress came to a halt. During the war, in 1863, William Tecumseh Sherman's Union forces marched across Georgia, destroying and burning nearly everything in their path. After the Civil War, Georgia's cities prospered and her economy slowly recovered, buoyed by the growth of the manufacturing, banking and railroad industries.

Beginnings of football at Georgia:

In the beginning, it was a 24-year-old University of Georgia Chemistry Professor, Dr. Charles Herty, who introduced the sport of football to his alma mater. During the fall of 1891, Herty introduced the game of "football," a "new style" of rugby developed by Walter Camp, to the Georgia students. During that fall of 1891, Herty brought to the University of Georgia a Walter Camp rulebook and a penchant for the new contest played on a gridiron–a game that he learned while playing it at Johns Hopkins University. Herty was instrumental in laying out the first football field at Georgia, as well as organizing and coaching its first team. Although there were no opponents for the fledgling Georgia squad in that first fall of 1891, the students at nearby Mercer agreed to organize a team and play Georgia following Christmas. The Mercer team was organized and as a result, Georgia played its first football game on January 30, 1892. According to Dr. John F. Stegeman, the game was the first in the Deep South of its kind, a contention he makes at the opposition of the University of Auburn, which also claims the most noteworthy distinction of being the first school to play the game. The final score of the Georgia-Mercer contest was Georgia 50, Mercer 0. Professor Herty's name was memorialized on the home arena of the University of Georgia, "Herty Field" until Sanford Field was constructed in the early 1920's.

The Georgia "G" Helmet

The Georgia football helmet featuring the oval "G" has become a tradition that is know across the country as the logo of the Georgia Bulldogs. The helmet's design originated when Vince Dooley became head coach in 1964. Dooley was impressed with the Green Bay Packers' helmet, which also featured the oval "G" in a different color pattern. Dooley liked the black oval "G" accompanied by a white oval background reting on each side of the bright red helmet. A white stripe was also placed over the top. The design has remained basically the same since, although a smaller black stripe was added inside the white stripe over the top in 1996 by then head coach Jim Donnan.

The Arch:

The historic arch which sits on the edge of north campus was installed in 1864. For years, freshmen were forbidden to walk under the Arch. Violators risked punishment from upperclassmen.

Once rigidly enforced, the tradition of hazing freshmen became passe.' However, many freshmen, learning of the tradition during orientation or from other sources, still choose to honor the century-old tradition.

Silver Britches:

Silver Britches were the brain trust of Coach Wally Butts, who took over as head coach in 1939. The silver pants, complimented by a bright red jersey, made for a striking uniform. Through the years the fans referred to the Bulldogs' silver britches in their chants and on banners, but the phrase really caught on in the early fifties with a cheer, banners, and colorful vests that proclaimed "Go You Silver Britches."

Ringing of the Chapel Bell.

The ringing of the chapel bell after a Georgia victory is a tradition that continues even though freshmen are no longer ordered to perform the chore. In the 1890's the football field was located a stone's throw away from the Chapel and first year students were compelled to ring the bell until midnight in celebration of a Bulldog victory. Today, students, alumni and townspeople still rush to the Chapel to ring the bell after a Georgia gridiron victory.

Georgia's First Game:

"Atlanta will be the scene Saturday of the first interstate intercol-

legiate football game. Both teams have been practicing for weeks."
~Atlanta Journal, February 17, 1892

Alabama Polytechnic and Mechanical School at Auburn defeated Georgia in that game 10-0, marking the beginning of the South's oldest football rivalry.

Fight Song:

Georgia's fights song, *Glory, Glory*, which is sung to the tune of the *Battle Hymn of the Republic* was sung at Georgia games as early as 1890. However, the song in its current form was rearranged by Georgia musician-composer Hugh Hodson in 1915.

Glory

Glory, glory to old Georgia!
Glory, glory to old Georgia!
Glory, glory to old Georgia!

G-E-O-R-G-I-A.

Glory, glory to old Georgia!
Glory, glory to old Georgia!
Glory, glory to old Georgia!

G-E-O-R-G-I-A.

Alma Mater

From the hills of Georgia's northland, Beams thy noble brow,
And the sons of Georgia rising, Pledge with sacred vow.

'Neath the pine tree's stately shadow, Spread thy riches rare,
And thy sons, dear Alma mater, Will thy treasure share.

And thy daughters proudly join thee, Take their rightful place,

Side by side into the future, Equal dreams embrace.

Through the ages, Alma Mater, Men will look to thee;
Thou the fairest of the Southland Georgia's Varsity.

Chorus:
Alma Mater, thee we'll honor, True and loyal be,
Ever crowned with praise and glory, Georgia, hail to thee.

The "Circle of Honor"
The highest tribute to former Bulldog athletes and coaches. This honor was created in 1996 with the induction of Frank Sinkwich, Charley Trippi and other Bulldog greats.

"How 'Bout Them Dogs"
Although this is a slogan that has been employed by Bulldog fans only recently, it is still one that has become a vintage battle cry of the Georgia faithful. The yell started in the mid 1970's when the Bulldogs became known for pulling out unlikely victories in close games. The phrase caught on fully in 1980 when Georgia won its second national championship.

Noteworthy Georgia Alumni:
Zell Miller - United States Senator
Saxby Chambliss - United States Senator
Bill Anderson - country music recording artist
Robert Benham - first African American appointed to Georgia Supreme Court
D.W. Brooks - presidential advisor to seven presidents
Mike Edwards - senior writer, National Geographic
Phil Gramm - United States Senator (Texas)
Lewis Grizzard - author, humorist (deceased)
Dewey Grantham - historian

W. Randall "Randy" Jones - founder of *Worth Magazine*

Julie Moran - former ABC sports reporter, weekend host *Entertainment Tonight*

Philip Lee Williams - author

Stuart Woods - author

Southerners don't think; they *feel*.

~Mark Carleton
LSU Professor (deceased)

Kentucky

When most SEC sports enthusiasts think of the University of Kentucky, they think of the school's longstanding, winning basketball tradition. Although Kentucky has dominated the indoor game on the hardwood developed by Dr. James Naismith, it has also had its shining moments on the gridiron. Past Wildcat greats like Paul "Bear" Bryant, Blanton Collier, George Blanda, Jeff Van Note and Tim Couch are reminders to the Kentucky faithful that basketball is not the only game that the Wildcats have succeeded in during their existence in the Southeastern Conference. In fact, Kentucky has a tradition of famous firsts in college football in the South. Kentucky holds the great distinction of being the first college to play football in the South, as well as the first SEC school to sign a black athlete to play football, Nat Northington, in 1965.

Nickname: "Wildcats"

Founded: Originally designated as a land-grant institution in 1865, the 673 acre campus is located just south of downtown Lexington, Kentucky. The University of Kentucky grew from the vision of one man, John Bowman. In 1865, after gaining financial support through the federal Morrill Land-Grant College Act, along with private donations, Bowman saw the realization of his dream with the inauguration of the state's new Agricultural and Mechanical College. The school was renamed the University of Kentucky in 1916.

Location: Lexington

They mean it when they say that Lexington is thoroughbred country. Some of the finest race horses in the country can be found in and around Kentucky's capital city. Kentucky is known as the "bluegrass state," for the beautiful blue tint that mysteriously shades the Kentucky rolling fields and knolls. Lexington is the second-largest city in the state, and after it was founded in the late

170's it quickly thereafter became a cultural and financial focal point in the Alleghenies. Today, Lexington remains one of Kentucky's most progressive cities, serving as the location for the state's flagship university—the University of Kentucky.

Population: (Lexington-Fayette) 241,749
Enrollment: 35,052
Colors: Blue and White

Kentucky formally adopted blue and white as its official colors in 1892. Students originally decided on blue and yellow prior to the Kentucky-Centre football game on December 19, 1891. The students decided on the hue of blue from the color adorning the tie of future football player Richard C. Stoll, who lettered on the 1893-94 teams. The students replaced the yellow with white the following year.

Mascot: "Wildcats" became synonymous with UK shortly after a 6-2 football victory at Illinois on October 9, 1909. Commandant Carbusier, then head of the military department, told a group of students in a chapel service following the game that the Kentucky football team had "fought like wildcats." The nickname shortly thereafter grew in popularity and was officially adopted by the University.

Stadium: Commonwealth

Prior to the construction of Commonwealth Stadium, the Wildcats played their ball at old Stoll Field/McLean Stadium. Stoll Field/McLean Stadium was home to Kentucky football for 56 years (1916-1972). The seating capacity of the stadium was 37,000 when Kentucky played its final game there in 1972, defeating the Vanderbilt Commodores 14-13 on November 11. Stoll Field was dedicated in honor of the late Judge Richard C. Stoll, who was a most generous alumnus and benefactor. Stoll Field was formally dedicated on October 14, 1916. McLean Stadium was dedicated on

November 1, 1924, in memory of Price Innes McLean, a center on the 1923 UK team who passed away as a result of injuries sustained during the Kentucky-Cincinnati game on November 6, 1923.

Stadium capacity: Originally constructed in 1973, prior to the 1999 season, Commonwealth Stadium held a capacity of 57,800. After the 1998 season, the stadium was expanded to a capacity of 67,606 to the delight of the burgeoning Wildcat faithful.

First game: On April 9, 1881, football in the Southeast made its debut at Old Stoll Field on the University of Kentucky, then known as Kentucky A&M. Kentucky served as host to two visiting teams–Transylvania College and Centre college. Transylvania prevailed in that contest 13 3/4 to 0. *The Lexington Daily Transcript* reported on the event: "An estimated 500 ladies and gentlemen watched the game. The head-on collisions between the players were equal to the explosion of Spanish bulls crashing into one another."

Kentucky A&M was enamored by the game of football. They quickly formed their own squad and issued a challenge to Transylvania for a best-of-three series slated for November 1881. Kentucky won the first game, but lost the second two. By 1895, nine colleges from today's SEC were playing intercollegiate football.

218

First forward pass: The first forward pass was thrown on October 13, 1906, by quarterback Earl Stone during a game against Eminence Athletic Club. Kentucky records do not indicate whether or not the first pass was completed. The newly-formed NCAA had just earlier that same year legalized the forward pass in an effort to open up the game and reduce injuries.

First night game: UK was one of the first schools to play at night. On Oct. 5, 1929, at Stoll Field, Kentucky defeated Maryville 40-0 under the lights. Subsequent to that game, Kentucky only played one home night game per season until 1946.

First game in stadium: September 15, 1973 Kentucky 31, Virginia Tech 26

Directions: Coming from the airport or from Bluegrass Parkway: Head east on Highway 60 (Versailles Rd.). Take a right on Mason Headley Rd. Mason-Headley will change to Waller Avenue, then Cooper Dr. Commonwealth Stadium is at the intersection of Cooper Dr. and University Avenue.

From I-75 South, take exit 110 (Winchester Road) and go west into Lexington. Head south on Highway 4 (New Circle Rd.). Take Alumni Dr. exit and turn right. Stay on Alumni Dr. The stadium will be on the right.

From I-75 North, take exit 115 and turn right onto Newtown Rd. Head 1.8 miles and turn right onto Hwy. 4 (New Circle Rd). Stay on New Circle and exit east on Versailles Rd., toward Lexington. Turn right on Mason-Headley Rd.

Where to go:
Eating:
   Guiseppe's Restaurant Italiano: 4456 Nicholasville Rd (606) 272-4053
   Family Affair Restaurant: 124 North Upper Street (606) 254-1756

Regatta Seafood: Since 1994, serving quality fresh seafood. Located in Lexington Green at the intersection of New Circle Road and Nicholasville Road (606) 273-7875

Eating and Drinking:

A1A Sandbar & Grill: 367 East Main (606) 231-7263

The Rosebud Bar & Grill: 121 N. Mill Street (606) 254-1907

De Sha's Grill & Bar: 101 North Broadway (606) 259-3771

All-Time Record: 532-519-44 (.506)

Bowl Appearances: 10

Bowl Record: 5-5 (.500)

SEC Record: 137-298-12 (.312)

SEC Championships: 2 (1950, 76t)

Kentucky Greats:

Coaches: Paul "Bear" Bryant coached at Kentucky from 1946-53 and led the Wildcats to eight consecutive winning seasons and four bowl games. Bryant led the Wildcats to their greatest victory ever in the 1951 Sugar Bowl. The Wildcats scored early and held on for a 13-7 win over the defending National Championship Oklahoma squad. Prior to the game, the Sooners had won 31 straight games. Bryant is considered the most successful coach in Kentucky history. In eight short years he amassed a record of 60-23-5 (.710). The sixty wins are the most by any Kentucky coach.

Blanton Collier followed in the large footsteps of Paul Bryant, coaching Kentucky foes for eight seasons from 1954 to 1962 (41-36-3). Collier found immediate success at Kentucky by leading the Wildcats to a 7-3 mark during his first campaign as the school's head coach. For that accomplishment he was named SEC Coach of the Year by the Nashville Banner. After serving in the Navy in World War II, Collier coached the Cleveland Browns in 1946 as an assistant coach under Paul Brown. After leaving the Browns to Coach Kentucky, Collier ironically later migrated back to the

Browns organization where he coached them to an impressive 76-34-2 record, which included an NFL title in 1964. Kentuckians best remember Collier for posting an impressive 5-2-1 record against its most hated nemesis, Tennessee. Collier's 1959 Coaching Staff is certainly one of the most capable staffs ever assembled. The young apprentices of Collier that year were: Ed Rutledge, Howard Schnellenberger, Ermal Allen, Don Shula, John North, Bob Cummings, and Bill Arnsparger.

Howard Schnellenberger, who played two years under Paul Bryant and two under Blanton Collier, earned four varsity letters as an offensive and defensive lineman at Kentucky. In 1955, he was a first team All-American for the Wildcats. Schnellenberger started his coaching career as an assistant at Kentucky (1959-60) under Head Coach Blanton Collier, his former mentor. From there, Schnellenberger went on to coach at Alabama from 1961-1965 under his other former Kentucky mentor, Paul Bryant. Schnellenberger also coached professional football under George Allen with the Dolphins from 1970-72; and from 1975-79. For two years (1973-74) he served as Head Coach of the Baltimore Colts. In 1983, he led the Miami Hurricanes to a national championship. Later, the experienced and well-traveled Schnellenberger would become head coach at Louisville and Oklahoma.

Jerry Claiborne coached at Kentucky from 1982-89 (41-36-3) (.531). After lettering three years (1946-49) as a player and serving two seasons as an assistant coach at Kentucky, Claiborne returned to his alma mater in 1982 to lead the team. He was successful in leading the Wildcats to two bowls and four non-losing seasons. Claiborne's 1989 team captured the 1989 CFA Academic Achievement Award.

Legendary Coach **Don Shula** (NFL's most winningest coach) was an assistant (Offensive backs) at Kentucky during the 1959 season. Bill Arnsparger (1954-61) and Chuck Knox (1961-62) also served as assistants at Kentucky.

221

Hal Mumme - Mumme took the Kentucky head coaching job in 1997. During his first year, Mumme led the Wildcats to a respectable 5-6 record. Mumme then followed that season with back-to-back winning seasons at Kentucky, making him an immediate sensation with the Wildcat faithful. Mumme coached at Iowa Wesleyan college (1989-1991) and Valdosta State (1992-96) prior to taking the job at Kentucky.

Players:

George Blanda - (1945-48) Quarterback, punter and kicker. In 1947, Blanda helped lead the Wildcats to their first bowl game, and he is the leading scorer in NFL history. Blanda is also a member of the NFL Hall of Fame in Canton, Ohio.

Bob Gain - (1947-50) Tackle/Place Kicker. Gain was a two-time (1949 & 50) first-team All-American and 1950 Outland Trophy winner, serving as the first from the SEC to win the prestigious award. Gain was a three-time All-SEC selection. Kentucky was 33-10-2 during Gain's playing days under Coach Bryant. Gain was a first-round draft choice by the Green Bay Packers in 1951.

Nat Northington - Northington, a native of Louisville, was the first black football player to sign with a Southeastern Conference school in December of 1965. In Lexington, in 1967 he also became the first black player to play in an SEC game where two SEC teams met head-to-head (Ole Miss).

Derrick Ramsey - (1975-77) Quarterback. A 1977 First Team All-SEC, and Third Team All-American, Ramsey was named Outstanding SEC Quarterback subsequent to his senior year by the Birmingham Touchdown Club. Ramsey guided the Wildcats to consecutive 9-3 and 10-1 seasons as a junior and a senior, including a 21-0 victory over North Carolina in the 1976 Peach Bowl. Ramsey played as a tight end for three different teams over a ten year career in the NFL.

Jim Kovach - (1974,75,76,78) Linebacker. Kentucky's All-Time tackles leader with 521, Kovach totaled an amazing 164 during the 1978 football season. A four-year letterman, Kovach was a consensus first-team All-American in 1978. Also an Academic All-American, Kovach played for seven seasons in the NFL. He was a fourth round choice by the New Orleans Saints in the 1979 NFL draft.

Art Still - (1974-77) Defensive End. A four-year letterman and 1977 First Team All-American for the Wildcats. Still broke the Kentucky record for tackles behind the line with 22 in 1977. Still was selected in the first round of the NFL draft the following year and played for 12 years in the NFL. Still ended his college career with an impressive 327 total tackles.

Jeff Van Note - (1966-68) Defensive End. A three year letterman, Van Note was UK MVP in 1968. Originally recruited as a fullback for the Cats, Van Note ended his career as a standout SEC defensive player. Van Note was named the Wildcats' most valuable player in 1968. Van Note later went on to the NFL where he played in six Pro Bowls during his 18 year career. Van Note was an 11th round draft choice for the Atlanta Falcons in 1969. Interestingly, Van Note played center for his 18 years with the Falcons, being named All-Pro in 1982. Today, Van Note is a radio analyst for UK football games.

Craig Yeast - (1995-98) Wide Receiver. Earned unanimous first-team All-SEC honors while setting Kentucky season records with 85 catches, 1311 yards and 14 TDs. during his senior year he went over the 100-yard receiving mark in seven games and led the team in scoring (90). Yeast averaged 29.3 yards on 14 kickoff returns, including a 100-yarder (tie for school record) for a TD vs. Florida in 1998.

Tim Couch – (1996-1998) Quarterback. Couch was an All-American at Kentucky as a junior and a senior under Head Coach Hal Mumme. Couch led the Wildcats to a winning season and a bowl appearance in 1998. Couch was the first pick of the 1999 NFL draft. He holds all of the University of Kentucky's passing records. Couch finished his abbreviated college career (went pro after his junior year) as one of college football's most successful quarterbacks. Despite playing in only 24 games as a starter, Couch shattered Kentucky's career passing records, completing 795 of 1184 attempts for 8835 yards and 74 touchdowns...His 8160 yards in total offense eclipsed the old Kentucky all-time mark of 5456 yards by Bill Ransdell (1983-86). An All-America first-team choice by the Football Writers Association & Walter Camp, Couch also notched second-team honors from *Football News & Associated Press* and third-team accolades from *The Sporting News*. Couch was also a unanimous All-Southeastern Conference first-team

selection. Couch placed fourth in voting for the Heisman Memorial Trophy, pacing the nation with 400 completions (on 553 attempts) while ranking second in pass completion percentage (72.3), yards (4,275) & touchdowns (36). He ranks fourth in the NCAA Division 1-A ranks with 4,151 yards in total offense. Amazingly, he threw for at least 300 yards with one touchdown in every game he played. Couch is a native of Hyden, Kentucky.

Derek Abney – Named a First Team All-American by The Associated Press, Football Writers Association of America, Walter Camp Football Foundation, *The Sporting News*, ESPN.com, CBSSportsLine.com, CNNSI.com, and CollegeFootballNews.com (2002, 2003), Abney was also an All-SEC performer in 2001 and 2002. The Mosinee, Wisconsin native redshirted his first year at Kentucky but started every game thereafter as a receiver and return man. During his impressive college career Abney established numerous Kentucky, SEC and NCAA records for his incredible punt and kick return skills. Possessing an uncommon fearlessness coupled with great speed and the uncanny ability to quickly change direction, Abney was an electric kick returner for the Wildcats, and arguably their best ever at the position. Kentucky records held by Abney include: Most total kick return TDs in a career—8, tying an NCAA record; Most all-purpose yards in a career (5,856); Most yards per all-purpose play (14.7); Most kickoff return yards in a career (2,313); Most kickoff returns in a career (96).

Jared Lorenzen – The Fort Thomas, Kentucky native is remembered as one of the biggest athletes to ever play the quarterback position. The massive, 6-4 260 pound signal caller, who was often referred to by opponents as "The Pillsbury Throw Boy" and "J-Load," finished his career in Lexington with more total yards than former Kentucky and NFL standout, Tim Couch. Lorenzen weighed over 13 pounds at  birth and was always a big kid, evidenced by the fact that his mother had to repeatedly bring his birth certificate to pee wee games to prove his age to the referees. An anomaly of many sorts, Lorenzen is most remembered by SEC fans for possessing a game that easily matched his unusually large athletic frame. During his standout career in Lexington Lorenzen set numerous school records. Wildcat records held by Lorenzen include: Most total offensive plays in a career (1,793), which is also an SEC record; Most total pass attempts in a career (1,514), which is also an SEC record; Most completions in a career (862); Most passing yards in a career (10,354); and Most touchdown passes in a career (78).

Great Bowl Games:
   1947 Great Lakes Bowl: Kentucky 24, Villanova 14
   1951 Sugar Bowl Kentucky: 13, Oklahoma 7
   1952 Cotton Bowl Kentucky: 20, TCU 7
   1976 Peach Bowl Kentucky: 21, N. Carolina 0
   1983 Hall of Fame Bowl: Kentucky 20, Wisconsin 19

History:
   The University of Kentucky was the first SEC school to introduce football, which it did in 1881. During that first year Kentucky Agricultural and Mechanical College (later the University of Kentucky) played Kentucky University (later Transylvania) and won, 2 goals to 1. During World War II in 1943, Kentucky did not play football.

The "Immortals"
   Known simply as "The Immortals," the 1898 University of Kentucky football team remains today the only undefeated, untied, and unscored upon team in school history. During that magical season the Wildcats went a perfect 7-0-0, squashing their seven opponents by a scoring margin of 180-0. The closest of the games was a victory of 6-0 over Centre College. Roscoe Severs was the team captain that fabled year under Coach W.R. Bass.

"The Year"

Quite possibly the greatest year in sports for the University of Kentucky, it transpired in Lexington during the 1977-78 academic year. The 1977 football team went 10-1 and finished in the top 5 with huge victories over North Carolina (10-7), West Virginia (28-13), Penn State (24-20), LSU (33-13), Georgia (33-0), Florida (14-7) and Tennessee (21-17). On the basketball court, the Joe B. Hall-led Wildcats sealed the institution's fifth NCAA title by defeating Duke, 94-88 in St. Louis.

A new tradition: Starting in 1997, before each home football game, in recognition of the team's Air Raid Attack, an air raid siren blares over the stadium sound system while each player of the offensive or defensive unit is introduced.

The **"Bourbon Barrel"** is the trophy presented to the winner of the Kentucky-Indiana football game. The two teams first met as early as 1893. However, the series is relatively young in comparison, having only played 28 games; although the contest has gained increasing attention in recent years. The trophy is actually a half-barrel and lists all the scores of the 28-game series. A blue stripe is painted in the background for a Kentucky win and a red stripe for an Indiana victory. Conversely, the **"Beer Barrel"** is the trophy that is given to the winner of the annual Kentucky-Tennessee game. Currently the third-longest series in the SEC, (trails only the Auburn-Georgia series (102 consecutive games) and the Mississippi-Mississippi State series (95).

Alumni Game: Coach Hal Mumme began a new tradition by instituting an alumni game as part of the Blue-White Spring Football Game festivities. The alumni open the spring game by playing one quarter of touch football. A unique twist is that the score counts as part of the varsity game.

Homecoming at Kentucky: Homecoming games at UK are highlighted by the Homecoming Queen and her court being presented in horse-drawn carriages, giving the event a distinct Kentucky flavor.

British Pub: Prince Charles of Wales witnessed Kentucky play Georgia in Athens on Oct. 22, 1977. All-American Art Still and company blanked the Bulldogs on that day 33-0. At halftime Prince Charles was greeted by the 6-6 Still. Prince Charles told Still, "You're a tall one aren't you?"

Kentucky Fight Song

On on, U of K, we are right for the fight today,
Hold that ball and hit that line;
Ev'ry wildcat star will shine;
We'll fight, fight, fight, for the blue and white
As we roll to that goal, Varsity,
And we'll kick, pass and run, 'til the battle is won,
 And we'll bring home the victory.

UK Alma Mater

Hail Kentucky, Alma Mater!
Loyal sons and daughters sing;
Sound her praise with voice united;
To the breeze her colors fling;
To the blue and white be true;
Badge triumphant age on age;
Blue, the sky that o'er us bends; White,
Kentucky's stainless page.

Noteworthy Kentucky Alumni:
Ashley Judd - actress

Pat Riley - NBA coach

Ernest Fletcher - U.S. House of Representative from Kentucky (1998 to present)

William Kirwan - Former Ohio State President; current Chancellor of Maryland System

Harry Monroe Caudill - Author, lawyer, historian, activist, legislator

Thomas Clark - Former Secretary, Organization of American Historians

228

"Winning isn't everything. It's the only thing."

~Vanderbilt Coach Red Sanders

University of South Carolina

Whether it be the legend of Heisman Trophy winner George Rogers, the allure of the one-of-a-kind Cock-A-Boose Railroad, or the elevated grandeur of the University of South Carolina's Williams-Brice Stadium, the reasons to be a die-hard "Fighting Gamecock" fan are various and sundry, to say the least. The University of South Carolina is a relative newcomer to the ranks of the SEC. They were added to the mix of SEC East schools by way of the ACC in 1990. This timely addition, coupled with the simultaneous induction of Arkansas in the SEC West, has served to round out the total number of SEC schools to its current capacity of twelve member institutions. The Palmetto State's football fans are known to be among the country's most loyal football enthusiasts, evidenced by the fact that regular attendance for the Gamecocks' home games in Columbia are consistently among the league's highest annual totals.

Founded: Chartered in 1801 as South Carolina College

The University of South Carolina was the first state university to be supported annually by state funding. The pre-Civil War USC campus included Longstreet Theatre and the buildings in the vicinity known today as the Horseshoe, with the exception of McKissick Museum. During the Civil War, the campus was forced closed and utilized by the Confederacy as a hospital. By the time William Tecumseh Sherman reached Columbia in 1865, the hospital contained Union soldiers as well.

Since its humble beginnings at the original campus just blocks from the South Carolina State House in Columbia, the university has expanded to include eight separate campuses throughout the state. The modern Columbia campus, the state's flagship institution, sprawls out from the historic Horseshoe, the original site of its predecessor, the South Carolina College campus. With its buildings restored to their natural nineteenth century ambiance, the Horseshoe is the university's heart and soul, while the rest of the 242 acre campus offers a stark architectural contrast of styles.

Location: Columbia

As South Carolina's capital city, Columbia serves as the focal point of the state. Nearby Hilton Head Island is a famous resort area that has in the past served as host to a number of championship sporting events. Darlington Raceway, one of NASCAR's most storied race tracks, and home of the TransSouth 500, is located just an hour away. USC's teeming downtown campus is home to thousands of college students who keep this historical city hopping. Just a two-hour ride in either direction (west or east) out of town leads to the Blue Ridge Mountains or to the sandy beaches of the Atlantic Ocean.

Population: 110,840

Enrollment: 23,700

Colors: Maroon (Garnet) and Black

The two colors were adopted at the turn of the nineteenth century as the official colors of the athletic teams of the University of South Carolina. The colors are dominant of the gamecock, the school's official mascot.

Mascot: Gamecock

The University of South Carolina is the only major college athletic program in the country that uses "Fighting Gamecocks" as its official nickname and mascot. In the 1890's during the early, formative years of football at the University of South Carolina, the team was commonly, yet informally referred to by friend and foe alike as "Game Cocks." It was not until 1903, when the student newspaper on campus, "The State," shortened the moniker to one word–Gamecock, and the athletic teams of South Carolina have been referred to as such ever since. A gamecock is a feisty, fighting rooster "known for its spirit, its courage and its capacity to fight to the very end." Cockfighting, although illegal in certain states, was a popular sport back in the nineteenth century, and it remains so today. The State of South Carolina has long been known for its penchant for breeding and training fighting gamecocks. A famed

231

guerrilla fighter in the Revolutionary War, General Thomas Sumter, was known affectionately as the "Fighting Gamecock."

Mascot name: "Cocky"
The official mascot of the University of South Carolina is "Cocky." The garnet and black plumage-adorned fan favorite can be seen regularly on the sidelines of South Carolina ball games. Introduced in 1980 as his father's (Big Spur) replacement, Cocky won number one mascot honors in 1986 and 1994.

Stadium: Williams-Brice Stadium
Recently expanded to seat more than 80,000 spectators (80,250), Williams-Brice Stadium is on of the premier venues in which to witness a college football game. An aggressive south end zone expansion project in 1996, along with the construction of the ever-popular luxury and executive boxes, has made Williams-Brice one of the largest stadiums in the country. Originally constructed in 1934 by the Works Progress Administration (WPA), Williams-Brice Stadium held 17,600. The facility has undergone a number of changes through the years, with the largest prior to the early eighties coming during the years of 1971-1972. A special request by the estate of Mrs. Martha Williams-Brice helped boost the capacity from 43,000 to over 54,000.

Mrs. Brice's husband, Mr. Thomas H. Brice, was a Gamecock football letterman from 1922-1924, and her family managed the Williams Furniture Company in nearby Sumter. Mrs. Brice left a considerable fortune amassed from her furniture business to her nephews, Thomas W. and Phillip Edwards (much of which they have passed on to the university), and included a bequest for the stadium expansion project.

The name of the stadium was officially changed from Carolina Stadium to Williams-Brice Stadium in dedication ceremonies during the September 9, 1972, home opener with Virginia. For nearly fifteen years, the football field at Williams-Brice Stadium has been sodded with Bermuda grass. Prior to that time, the field was an artificial turf. Through the years, other improvements to the facility have been made in the form of new locker rooms, a weight room expansion; as well as new meeting areas and training rooms.

Stadium capacity: 80,250

Record crowd: 83,700 November 22, 1997 Clemson 47, South Carolina 21

First game: December 24, 1893 vs. Furman at Charleston, SC lost 44-0.

First victory: November 8, 1895 vs. Furman at Columbia (14-10).

First game in stadium: October 6, 1934 South Carolina 22 Virginia Military Institute 6

Directions: Coming from the airport: Take Aviation Way to Hwy 302. Take a left and head 4 miles to Knox Abbot Drive. Merge onto Knox Abbott and go 3 miles to Assembly St. Take a right on Assembly. The Visitor's Center is located one mile on the right.

Coming from I-20 and I-26 (east bound): Take Columbia exit and continue onto Elmwood Avenue. Continue for 1.5 miles and turn right onto Assembly Street. Follow Assembly approximately 4 miles. Visitor's Center is on the left.

Coming from I-26 (west bound): Take I-77 exit and go 4 miles. Take Shop Rd. exit. Continue past one light and merge onto George Rogers Boulevard/Assembly St. The Visitor's Center is on your left at the fifth light.

Where to go:
Eating:

Birds On A Wire: 2631 Devine St. - Golden rotisserie chicken, "down home" veggies, pasta and salads. Bird's on a Wire is the brain child of a couple of USC students! Try their menu including the "redneck cuisine". Rotisserie Chicken, pork and other fine Southern delicacies served. Assorted micros, domestics and wines available. Lunch & dinner, 254-2035.

Blue Marlin Seafood: 1200 Lincoln Street. VOTED BEST SEAFOOD...Low Country specialties include shrimp and grits and crab cakes...fresh grilled fish and fried shrimp platters. $9.95 to $13.95. Lunch & dinner. Major credit cards, 799-3838.

Villa Tronco: 1213 Blanding St., Uptown - 256-7677. Columbia's oldest and finest Italian restaurant. Serving Columbia for over 50 years in an historic firehouse.

Richard's: 1109 Lincoln at Gervais. Located 4 blocks from the Carolina Coliseum in Columbia's historic Vista, Richard's features fine Southern cuisine. Dinner is served Monday - Saturday. Valet parking is available. Phone 212-7217 for reservations. During the week, stop by for lunch between 11-2.

Yesterday's Restaurant & Tavern: 2030 Devine St. Casual Atmosphere, varied menu. Serving specialties from across America for 20 years. In 5 Points. Lunch, dinner & late-night. 799-0196.

Nightlife

Columbia Brewing Company: 931 Senate Street. Voted BEST LOCAL BEER! Columbia Brewing company offers the best in pizza, wings, sandwiches & appetizers. Specializing in handcrafted beer. Lunch, dinner & late-night. Major credit cards. 254-BREW (2739)

Jillian's: 800 Gervais Street - Dining at its wildest!

Out of Bounds Sports Bar & Grille: 201 Columbia Mall Road, (803) 736-4466.

Dug Out Bar & Grille: 1807 Decker Blvd #'s 1 & 2,(803) 782-9623.

Bailey's Sports Grille: 115 Afton Ct., (803) 407-3004.

Congaree Bar & Grill: 5444 Bluff Rd. Columbia (803) 695-5050.

Corner Pocket Bar & Billiards: 489 Piney Grove Rd. Columbia (803) 731-0403.

Five Points Area: During the night, football fans can enjoy elegant dining and quaint sidewalk cafes, clubs and live bands. During the day the area becomes a unique shopping village with a tree-lined street and many specialty shops and galleries.

All-Time Record: 498-502-44 (.498)

Bowl Appearances: 11

Bowl Record: 3-8 (.273)

SEC Record: 34-51-1 (.400)

SEC Championships: None (Entered into the league in 1990 with Arkansas) South Carolina was formerly a member of the Atlantic Coast Conference, where they won a league championship under head coach Paul Dietzel in 1969.

Great Bowl Games: January 2, 1995 (Carquest Bowl) vs. West Virginia (24-21) at Ft. Lauderdale, Florida

South Carolina Greats

Coaches: Paul Dietzel - A native of Mansfield, Ohio, Paul Dietzel served as Athletic Director and Head Coach at South Carolina from 1966-1974. He successfully led the Gamecocks to their first and only conference championship, a 1969 Atlantic Coast Conference Title and subsequent berth in the Peach Bowl in Georgia. For his efforts, Coach Dietzel was awarded ACC Coach of the Year honors. Dietzel compiled a 42-53-1 record while at South

Carolina. Dietzel is best known for his 1958 National Championship season at LSU, a feat that he accomplished at the surprisingly young age of 34. After Dietzel left LSU, he spent four seasons at the United States Military Academy, before finally settling in at South Carolina in 1966.

Joe Morrison - A native of Lima, Ohio, Morrison was the 1984 National Coach of the Year. Morrison served as Head Coach at South Carolina from 1983-1988. Morrison amassed a 39-28-2 record during his six seasons with the Gamecocks. Morrison led the Gamecocks to three bowl games (1984 Gator Bowl, 1987 Gator and the 1988 Liberty). His 1985 team posted a school-best 10-2 record. Morrison was also named the All-South Independent Coach of the Year in 1984. Nicknamed as "Old Dependable" for his reliable all-around ability, Morrison enjoyed an outstanding 14-year career in the NFL with the New York Giants. Following Morrison's retirement from the game in 1972, the seven-time team captain was granted the ultimate honor as a player when his number forty was forever retired by the Giants organization. Sadly, Morrison fell victim to a sudden heart attack in February of 1989.

Lou Holtz – Lou Holtz is one of the most successful college football coaches in American history. The Follansbee, West Virginia native attended Kent State University prior to making a name for himself in coaching first with William & Mary, then North Carolina State, the University of Arkansas, Notre Dame and finally at South Carolina. A veteran of 32 years of experience, Holtz surprised many when he took over the reins of a hapless Gamecock program in 1999 only to go winless (0-11) during his first gridiron campaign in Columbia. However, the undaunted Holtz motivated his squad to an amazing turnaround in 2000 when they won 8 games and defeated Ohio State 24-7 in the Outback Bowl. The 2000 season was impressive because prior to that the Gamecocks and their fan base had endured an unimaginable 21-game losing streak. In 2001 Holtz repeated his magic by leading the Gamecocks to a 9-3 record and a thrilling 31-28 comeback victory again against Ohio State in the

Outback Bowl. The two-year run by Holtz was unprecedented in Carolina Gamecock football history since it was the first time a South Carolina team finished in the top 20 two seasons in a row (19th in 2000 and 13th in 2001.) Holtz is the only coach in NCAA history to lead six different schools to bowl games and he is also the only coach to ever guide four different programs to final Top 20 rankings.

Players

Steve Wadiak - A four-year letterman from 1948-1951, and All-American running back in 1951, Wadiak was named All-Southern in 1950 and 1951. Wadiak played in the 1951 Blue-Gray Classic and the 1952 Senior Bowl. He holds the school record for the longest run from scrimmage (96 yards versus George Washington in 1950). Wadiak ranks 3rd on the all-time career rushing list at South Carolina with 2,878 yards. His number 37 has been retired by the South Carolina Athletic Department.

Tommy Suggs - A native of Lamar, South Carolina, Suggs was a standout quarterback who set numerous South Carolina passing records during his career. He led the Gamecocks to the 1969 Atlantic Coast Conference Championship and subsequent Peach Bowl berth. Throwing for more than 200 yards or more on eight occasions during his stellar career, Suggs altogether completed 355 of 672 passes for 4,916 yards and 34 touchdowns. Named South Carolina football's Most Valuable Player in 1970, Suggs shares the Gamecock record for the most touchdowns ever scored in a game–5. Suggs was also named as the 1970 Blue-Gray game's Most Valuable Player. As a quarterback, Suggs never lost to Clemson during his time in Columbia. For the past twenty years, Suggs has served as the color analyst on the Gamecock Football radio network.

Dan Reeves - Reeves lettered in football for the Gamecocks in 1962, 1963 and 1964. He played quarterback under head coach Marvin Bass. Reeves served as head coach of the Denver Broncos from 1981-1993, and the New York Giants from 1993-1996. He is currently the head coach of the Atlanta Falcons. Reeves played as a running back for the Dallas Cowboys from 1965-1972, and later served as an assistant coach with the Cowboys for a short stint. Dan's brother, Don "Butch" Reeves was also a gamecock—lettering three years in football at South Carolina.

George Rogers - A native of Deluth, Georgia, Rogers was the recipient of the 1980 Heisman Trophy. Rogers was a consensus All-America selection his senior year. He led the country in rushing that year with 1,894 yards. Rogers holds many South Carolina records, including most career rushing yards (5,204); most yards rushing in a single season (1,894); and he is tied with Harold Green for most career touchdowns (33). The stout Rogers rushed for 100 or more yards in 27 of his 46 games at South Carolina. Rogers rushed for over 200 yards in a single game on three separate occasions during his South Carolina career. His single game high total was a 237-yard performance against Wake Forest on November 18, 1978. Rogers is the only player to ever have his jersey (#38) retired while he was still playing as a Gamecock. Rogers was the first pick chosen in the 1981 NFL Draft. He later won Rookie of the Year honors for the New Orleans Saints. Rogers also played for the 1988 Super Bowl Champion Washington Redskins. Rogers was elected to the College Football Hall of Fame in 1997.

Rick Sanford - (1975-78) A native of Rock Hill, South Carolina, Sanford was an All-American defensive back in 1978. Sanford finished his career with nine interceptions, including four his senior year. Sanford went on to play for six years in the NFL with the New England Patriots, and one year with the Seattle Seahawks. Sanford was inducted into the South Carolina Athletic Hall of Fame in 1998. Sanford played for Coach Jim Carlen. He wore number 25 for the Gamecocks.

James Seawright - A native of Simpsonville, South Carolina, Seawright was named first team All-American in 1984 as a linebacker. Seawright is remembered well as the leader of the 1984 "fire ant" defense at South Carolina. During his brilliant 1984 season, Seawright tallied 133 total tackles. He finished his Gamecock career with an impressive 369 tackles. Once, during a game against North Carolina State in 1984, he made 29 tackles. Seawright wore number 45 for the Gamecocks.

Steve Taneyhill - Quarterback Steve Taneyhill made his mark at South Carolina as much for his flashy style as for his enormous football talent. He led the Gamecocks to five of six victories his freshman year. More importantly, he notched the team's only win over Tennessee since joining the Southeastern Conference in 1992. Taneyhill accomplished all of this after earning the starting job midway through his rookie season.  Fans loved his unconventionally long hair, as well as his brazen attitude. Because of the image, Taneyhill was always a favorite among autograph seeking Gamecock fans. Taneyhill led the Gamecocks to their only bowl victory, a 24-21 win over West Virginia in the 1995 Carquest Bowl. He holds several South Carolina records, including 473 yards passing in a game and 62 career touchdown passes.

Sterling Sharpe - Sharpe, a native of Glenville, Georgia, was an All-American Wide Receiver in 1987. He ranks as the top receiver in Gamecock history. Sharpe holds nearly all of South Carolina's receiving records, including career marks for receptions (169) receiving yardage (2,497) and single season records for most receptions (74), receiving yardage (1,106) and TD receptions (10). Sharpe caught at least one ball in 34 consecutive contests. He was the seventh player chosen overall in the 1988 NFL draft, by the Green Bay Packers. An All-Pro with the Packers, Sharpe retired as the Packer's All-time career receptions leader. Today he's a studio analyst for ESPN's Game Day program. Sharpe wore number two for the Gamecocks.

Kalimba Edwards – An East Point, Georgia native, Edwards was both an All-SEC and All-America performer during his playing days at South Carolina. A physically imposing player at 6-5 260 pounds, Edwards was a semi-finalist for the 2001 Butkus Award, and he totaled 208 tackles with 20 tackles for loss and 15 sacks during his prolific four-year career in Columbia. Edwards wore #55 during his playing days at Carolina and was drafted by the Detroit Lions in the 2002 NFL draft.

Duce Staley – A transfer from Itawamba, MS Junior College and Columbia native, Staley is remembered as one of South Carolina's most impressive running backs. Staley was one of college football's best all-around running backs in 1996 when he was ranked 13th in the country with 1,116 rushing yards en route to earning first-team All-SEC honors. Staley finished his two-year college career ranked 13th on Carolina's all-time rushing list with 1,852 yards and 17 TDs on 345 carries. A versatile back, the Duce reeled in 59 passes for 489 yards and 2 TDs and returned 26 kickoffs for 566 yards while at South Carolina. After his Carolina playing days ended Staley was drafted by the Philadelphia Eagles where he has proved to be one of the league's toughest and most prolific runners.

Traditions:

The theme song from "2001–A Space Odyssey" blares over the p.a. system at Williams-Brice Stadium. In synchronization with the music, the Gamecocks take the field. The "2001" theme is linked to the school's 200th birthday in the year 2001.

History:

South Carolina fielded its first football team in 1892, and for the first three seasons no head coach was designated. The all-time won-lost-tie records include those three seasons. No football was played in 1893, and in 1906 the trustees abolished the sport for one season.

Cockaboose Railroad: A unique South Carolina Tailgating Twist

South Carolina can boast of a most unique Southern tailgating tradition. This treasure of treasures–among even the most serious tailgater, is a veritable party on wheels. The Cockaboose Railroad consists of 22 lavishly-restored stationary cabooses lined up on a small sect of track just south of Williams-Brice Stadium. Each of these cabooses contain modern tailgating amenities such as running water, cable television, air conditioning and heating, as well as plenty of comfortable home furnishings. Many of the cabooses are wired with closed-circuit television so that fans can elegantly watch Gamecock away games if the trip is not feasible.

Gamecock Fight Song

Hey, Let's give a cheer, Carolina is here,
The Fighting Gamecocks lead the way.
Who gives a care, If the going gets tough,
And when it is rough, that's when the 'Cocks get going.
Hail to our colors of garnet and Black,
In Carolina pride have we.
So, Go Gamecocks Go - FIGHT!
Drive for the goal - FIGHT!
USC will win today - GO COCKS!
So, let's give a cheer, Carolina is here.
The Fighting Gamecocks All The Way!

About the Fight Song

The tune is from the musical "How Now, Dow Jones" and the original song is titled "Step to the Rear" (composed by Elmer Bernstein with original lyrics by Carolyn Leigh). The sheet music is copyrighted to Carwin Music, Incorporated in 1967. The music was chosen as a USC Fight Song by former football coach and Athletic Director, Paul Deitzel. Mr. Deitzel also wrote the lyrics to this USC Fight Song.

Bowl Games:
2001 Outback Bowl: South Carolina 24 Ohio State 7
2002 Outback Bowl: South Carolina 31 Ohio State 28

Alma Mater

We hail thee, Carolina, and sing thy high praise
With loyal devotion, remembering the days
When proudly we sought thee, thy children to be:
Here's a health, Carolina, forever to thee!
Since pilgrims of learning, we entered thy walls
And found dearest comrades in thy classic halls
We've honored and loved thee as sons faithfully;
Here's a health, Carolina, forever to thee!
Generations of sons have rejoiced to proclaim
Thy watchword of service, thy beauty and fame;
For ages to come shall their rallying cry be:
Here's a health, Carolina, forever to thee!
Fair shrine of high honor and truth, thou shalt still
Blaze forth as a beacon, thy mission fulfill,
And crowned by all hearts in a new jubilee:
Here's a health, Carolina, forever to thee!

About the Alma Mater

"The alma mater was written in 1911 by George A. Wauchope, an English professor at USC, and set to the music of Robert Burns' "Flow Gently, Sweet Afton." It was written as a result of the need for this type of school song. A March 1911 issue of the _Gamecock_ reported that a year or two earlier the faculty, "realizing we should have a soul stirring alma mater," offered a prize of $50, but not much had been done. Several songs, including "A Health to Carolina," were written after this and other articles asked for an alma mater. All of these songs that were submitted were placed in a songbook and sung at chapel.

Although it was several years before the song written by Dr. Wauchope became known as the Alma Mater of the University, it was apparently was the most popular one as soon as it came out. Over the years the custom has arisen of raising the right hand, with fingers cupped, when the phrase "Here's A Health, Carolina" occurs, as if offering a toast. To many alumni, the "toast" is synonymous with events on the athletic field."

Excerpted from: *Remembering the Days: An Illustrated History of the University of South Carolina*, 1982.

Notable South Carolina Alumni:

Leeza Gibbons - TV host, "Entertainment Tonight"

"Hootie & the Blowfish," Darius Rucker, Mark Bryan, James Sonefeld, & Dean Felber

Charles Jones, Jr. - journalist

Floyd D. Spence - U.S. House of Representatives

Brigadier General Charles M. Duke, Jr. - USAF retired

William Price Fox - author, screenwriter, columnist

football "There soon developed a great spectator interest. Crowds of students and friends began following the teams. Identifying themselves with the contestants, they enjoyed an afternoon of jubilation or great agony, depending on the fortunes of their favorite team. Older men and women became as excited as the students. Players carried their coaches off the field when they won, and many of them were observed weeping when they lost. By the mid-1890s sportswriters were having a field day. They had a game which stretched their abilities to describe, and they had an audience which was calling for more. Football was becoming more than a college sport; it was becoming the talk and interest of the town."

~Nathan W. Dougherty,
author of *Educators and Athletes*, 1976, describing the
development of the game of football in the South

University of Tennessee

Shortly up the Tennessee River from Chattanooga stands Knoxville, Tennessee, home of the University of Tennessee. Knoxville is the heart of the Volunteer State, and the people of this football hotbed–Vol fans–are some of the most devoted football enthusiasts among the Southeastern Conference Schools. Claiming a tradition that is perhaps rivaled only by that of the University of Alabama, Tennessee is one of the SEC's most successful football programs. Tennessee's gridiron legacy has been built firmly on the shoulders of coaching virtuoso and patriot, General Robert Neyland. More recently, Phil Fulmer has made his own mark on the SEC, and the national record books, following in the heavy footsteps of his great military predecessor. Overall, the University of Tennessee has won 12 SEC Championships, and has claimed two national titles since the SEC's inception in 1933.

Nickname: "Volunteers"

Known as "The Volunteer State," the State of Tennessee garnered its nickname in the early days of the nineteenth century when General Andrew Jackson mustered large armies from his home state to fight the Indians and later the British at the Battle of New Orleans. The name "Volunteers" became even more popular subsequent to the Mexican-American War when Governor Aaron V. Brown issued a call for 2,800 men to tangle with Santa Ana and over 30,000 volunteered. The dragon uniform donned by Tennessee regulars during that conflict can still be seen adorning the color guard at UT athletic events.

Founded: 1794

The University of Tennessee is the state's largest and oldest university, as well as one of the preeminent public academic institutions of higher learning in the United States. A full land grant institution and a comprehensive research university, the University of Tennessee, which can trace its beginnings to the inception of

245

Blount College in 1794, celebrated its two-hundredth birthday in 1994.

Location: Knoxville

Situated in the center of the East Tennessee Valley, Knoxville serves as the urban pathway to the Smoky Mountains. Surrounded by what is referred to as "The Great Lakes of the South," Knoxville is a teeming metropolitan area with a population of over 600,000, making it easily one of the largest cities among the Southeastern Conference. In early spring, a 50-mile trail of blooming dogwoods beautifully transforms the city into a sea of pink and white.

Population: (City limits) 165,540
Enrollment: 25,058

Colors: Orange and White

The colors of orange and white were selected by Charles Moore, a member of the first football team in 1891. They were later adopted by a vote of the student body. The colors were those of the common American daisy which grew in profusion on The Hill, although Tennessee players did not appear in the now-famous orange jerseys until the season opener in 1922. Coach M.B. Banks led the Vols over Emory and Henry in that game by a score of 50-0.

Mascot: "Smokey"

After a student poll revealed a desire to select a live mascot for the University, the UT Pep Club held a contest in 1953 to select a coon hound, a native breed of the state, as the mascot to represent the school. Announcements of the contest in local newspapers read, "This can't be an ordinary hound. He must be a 'Hound Dawg' in the best sense of the word." The late Rev. W.C. Brooks entered his prize-winning blue tick coon hound, Smokey, in the contest. At halftime of a game in 1953, the dogs were lined up on the old cheerleaders' ramp at Neyland Stadium. Each dog was introduced over the loudspeaker and the student body cheered for their favorite. Smokey was the last hound introduced. When his name was called out, he barked. The students cheered and Smokey threw his head back and howled again. This kept going and soon the whole stadium was in a roar and UT had found its mascot. Rev. Brooks supplied UT with the line of canines until his death in 1986 when his wife Mrs. Mildred Brooks and family friends took over the canine caretaking role.

The dogs have lived exciting lives. Smokey II was dognapped by Kentucky students in 1955 and survived a confrontation with the Baylor bear at the 1956 Sugar Bowl. Smokey VI, who suffered from heat exhaustion in 140 degree temperatures at the 1991 UCLA game, was listed on the Vols injury report until he returned later in the season. Smokey III (1965-77) was the winningest dog with a 105-39-5 record and two SEC championships. Smokey VI, who passed away in 1991, has the highest winning percentage with a mark of .722 and three SEC championships.

One of the most beloved figures in the state, Smokey is famous for leading the Big Orange out of the giant "T" prior to each home game. The present Smokey, now in his second season, is the eighth in the line of blue ticks and is appropriately called Smokey VIII.

Band: "Pride of the Southland"
The University of Tennessee band was organized immediately after the Civil War when the University was reopened. Since that time, the enrollment in the band program has grown to more than three hundred students (in all bands) from all colleges of the University. The band program is divided into several different units. The most famous of these units is the marching band, "The Pride of the Southland Band," which appears at all home football games and three out-of-town games annually.

Stadium: Neyland Stadium.
Neyland Stadium, Shields-Watkins Field saw its beginning in 1919. Colonel W.S. Shields, President of Knoxville's City National

Bank and a Trustee of the University, provided the initial capital to prepare and equip the field. When the field was completed in March 1921, it was thus called Shields-Watkins field, in honor of the donor and his wife, Alice. The stadium, aside from the field it grew to enclose, came to bear its own distinguished name: Neyland Stadium. It was named for the man most responsible for the growth and development of Tennessee Football. General Robert R. Neyland served as Head Coach from 1926 to 1952. After retiring from coaching, General Neyland served as Athletic Director at Tennessee until his death in 1962. Neyland served as the guiding force behind additions to the stadium's capacity, and is the one most responsible for the winning tradition that Volunteer fans have learned to expect through the years.

Neyland Stadium is the second largest football-playing venue in the country, behind Michigan Stadium. Since 1921, it has been expanded 14 times. The last addition came in 1996, in the form of 11,000 North Upper Deck seats. Due to Neyland Stadium's massive

capacity, Tennessee has ranked in the top three in average attendance for the past 24 seasons. Neyland Stadium also holds the Tom
Elam Press Box which contains seven different levels of luxurious
skyboxes and suites.

Stadium Capacity: 106,538 (average)

In 1996, the stadium set a national college football record for
the most people to ever attend a college football game with
107,608. Neyland Stadium ranks second behind Michigan Stadium
of the University of Michigan in Ann Arbor, which holds 107,701.
Tennessee went to 110,000 in 2000 with the addition of numerous
luxury sky boxes. During game day, Neyland Stadium becomes the
3rd largest city in Tennessee.

Volunteer Navy:

In 1962, former Volunteer broadcaster George Mooney found a
quicker and more exciting way to get to Neyland Stadium other than
fighting the notorious Knoxville traffic–via the Tennessee River!
While other Vol fans employed more traditional modes of transportation, Mooney navigated his way to Tennessee football games by boat.
Mooney cruised his little runabout down river to the stadium and
spawned what would later become known as "The Volunteer Navy."
Today, approximately 200 boats of all shapes and sizes make up this
extremely unique, giant floating tailgate party, also known as the
"Floatilla." In the United States, only the University of Washington
has a stadium adjacent to a water body like does Tennessee.

Checkerboard Endzones:

A trademark of the Tennessee program since the 1960s, the practice was reinstated in 1989. The colorful and popular end zones were
a part of Tennessee Football until 1968 when the natural sod was dug
out and artificial turf was put in its place. Grass has since returned
to Shields-Watkins Field.

Record crowd: 107,608 - September 21, 1996 Florida 35, Tennessee 29

First game: November, 1891 Sewanee 24 Volunteers 0

First game in stadium: September 21, 1921 Tennessee 27, Emory & Henry 0

Directions: Coming from the airport, head north on US 129 leaving airport. Following the Tennessee River Bridge, exit on U.S 11/70 (Cumberland Avenue). Turn right at the bottom of the ramp and then right again at the second light onto Volunteer Boulevard. Follow this route to stadium.

From I-40 East (Nashville): Exit at US 129 South. Take 129 South to US 11/70 exit (Cumberland Avenue). Turn left off of ramp and turn right at third light onto Volunteer Boulevard. Follow this route to stadium.

From I-40 West (Asheville): Exit to the left at James White Parkway. Follow the Parkway to Neyland Drive (Highway 153) to stadium area on right hand side.

From I-75 South (Lexington): Exit onto I-275 South. Follow I-275 to I-40 East. Exit I-40 East to the left at James White Parkway. Follow James White Parkway to Neyland Dr. (stadium on right hand side).

Where to go in Knoxville:

Tennessee Riverboat Company: A 325 passenger authentic Southern paddlewheeler equipped with 2 bars and an elegant restaurant open for lunch and dinner. Great for pregame parties. 300 Neyland Drive, Knoxville 37902, (423) 525-7827, 1-800-509-2628

Regas: Choose from a variety of fine dining favorites. Menu includes beef, seafood, chicken, veal, soup, salad and homemade breads. A Knoxville favorite since 1919. 318 North Gay Street, Knoxville, (423) 637-9805

Calhoun's On The River: Great atmosphere on the river close to the stadium. Full menu. 400 Neyland Drive, 865-673-3355.

Charlie Pepper's: on the Strip Bar/Restaurant, a popular haunt.

716 20th Street 865-524-8669.

Patrick Sullivan's Steakhouse and Saloon: 100 N. Central Street 865-637-4255.

Copper Cellar (Cumberland Grill): Bar/Restaurant, another local favorite. 1807 Cumberland Ave. 865-673-3411.

Riverside Tavern: Bar/Restaurant, located at 950 Volunteer Landing Lane 865-673-0303.

All-Time Record: 736-303-53 (.708)
Bowl Appearances: Tennessee ranks second behind Alabama in bowl appearances with 44and third with victories at 21.
Bowl Record: 44 / 23-21 (.523)
SEC Record: 287-152-19 (.653)
SEC Championships: 13 (1938, 39t, 40, 46t, 51t, 56, 67, 69, 85, 89t, 90, 97, 98)
National Championships: (2) 1951, 1998

Tennessee Greats

Coaches:

Z.G. Clevenger - (1911-1915) (26-15-2). A former Indiana player, Clevenger coached the 1914 Tennessee Volunteer football team to the SIAA Championship game in which they defeated a previously undefeated Vanderbilt team, a feat no other Volunteer coach accomplished until the Neyland era. Clevenger's 1914 team went 9-0 en route to the title of SIAA Champions.

John Bender - (1916-1920). A former 1905 Nebraska player who went to Tennessee via Kansas State. Bender immediately installed a short punt scheme at Tennessee and was largely successful as head coach. However, his tenure there was interrupted by World War I in 1917-18. Bender returned to Knoxville in 1920 to post a 7-2 record. Bender's final record at Tennessee was a very respectable 18-5-4.

M.B. Banks - (1921-1925). Banks came to Tennessee during the initial year of the Southern Conference. A former player for

Syracuse University, and a former coach at Duke University, Banks was successful at employing various and sundry offenses for the Volunteers, although his most favored mode of attack was the universal winged-T. Banks became too sick to continue his duties in 1925, finishing with a record of 27-15-3.

General Robert Reese Neyland - (1926-1934) (1936-1940) (1946-1952) (173-31-12) Undoubtedly Tennessee's biggest football legend. Altogether, Neyland coached twenty one years in three separate stints at Tennessee. Twice Neyland left his position as head football coach to serve his country in active military duty. His first nine year jaunt as head coach of the Vols produced a startling 76-
7-5 record, in the meanwhile enjoying undefeated runs of 33 and 28 games as well as winning 14 straight games. During this exceptional time, Neyland used the vaunted single wing to capture SEC championships in 1927 and 1932.

Overall, his football teams won an impressive 173 games and during one span of seven years, they lost a mere two games. Among other amazing accomplishments, Neyland's volunteers held opponents scoreless for 71 consecutive quarters (That's nearly two complete seasons). Furthermore, they battled through eight seasons without recording a regular season loss. Neyland left his beloved Volunteers, and in the volunteer spirit, served his country in the Panama Canal Zone in 1934. During his year-long absence in 1935, Neyland's head coaching duties were assumed by W.H. Britton. Britton coached the Vols to a 4-5 record until Neyland's return from active duty in 1936. Upon his confident return to the states from active duty in 1936, Neyland quickly retooled his football machine in Knoxville by replenishing his team with young talent. The fruits of Neyland's recruiting labors were a jubilant three years of perfect football in Tennessee, from 1938-1940. Impressively, Neyland's

1939 team remains the last team in NCAA history to be unscored upon during regular season play.

In 1941, Neyland again returned to active military duty by serving in World War II. John Barnhill served as an admirable replacement during Neyland's five year hiatus. Neyland returned again in 1956, officially retired from military service. This fact allowed him to concentrate his talented efforts solely on claiming a national championship. After his triumphant return in 1946, Neyland led the Vols to 3 straight major bowl appearances and the 1951 National Championship.

Declining health forced Neyland to retire to the position of athletic director, a post he held until his passing in 1962. In 1956, for his remarkable coaching achievements, and for his many contributions to the collegiate game of football, Neyland was inducted to the College Football Hall of Fame.

The Words of General Robert Neyland:

"The lessons learned upon the football field are carried usefully on to the field of life."

"A football team is like an army. Your men must be in good physical condition. They must have technical ability, and they must have high morale."

"To defeat a weak opponent is not the problem: The problem is to win when he is as good or better than you."

John Barnhill - (1941-45). A valued associate of Douglas McArthur, Coach Robert Neyland volunteered for duty during World War II and served in the Panama Canal fighting zone. In Neyland's absence, Barnhill assumed the position of head coach for the Vols. A former Volunteer, Barnhill posted a most solid record of 32-5-2 during his short tenure as football coach. However, during 1943, no football was played at Tennessee due to the war effort.

Bowden Wyatt - (1952-1962) (49-29-4). A former legend on the Tennessee playing fields, Wyatt returned to his alma mater after claiming coaching championships at Wyoming and Arkansas. In just his second season with the Vols he was awarded National Coach of the Year honors for leading Tennessee to the SEC Championship. Coach Wyatt is a member of the National College Football Hall of Fame as both a player (1972) and coach (1997).

Doug Dickey - (1964-1969) (46-15-4). Originally hired from the staff at the University of Arkansas Razorbacks, Dickey was tapped to rebuild a stagnant Tennessee program. Dickey successfully reversed the Vols football fortunes by guiding the Orange to SEC titles in both 1967 and 1969. The former gator signal-caller eventually returned to his alma mater in Gainesville (1954) following the 1969 season. Today, Dickey is the Athletic Director at the University of Tennessee.

Bill Battle - (1970-1976) (59-22-2). Touted as the youngest head coach in the nation when he assumed the position of head coach for the Vols at the ripe young age of 28. With a poise uncharacteristic of someone his age, Battle confidently led the Orange to five straight bowl games. Three of Battle's teams finished in the top 10 nationally. Interestingly, Battle presided as head coach of the Volunteers during Tennessee's first-ever night game at Neyland Stadium–a contest Tennessee won over the Nittany Lions of Penn State 28 to 21, on September 23, 1972.

Johnny Majors - (1977-92) (116-62-8). A former Volunteer All-America tailback during the 1950s, Majors returned to his alma mater to coach after he led the Pittsburgh Panthers to a national championship in 1976. Three of Majors' squads won SEC championships. His 1985 team went 9-1-2, with a crushing defeat of Miami by a score of 35 to 7 in the Sugar Bowl in New Orleans. His 1989 team finished 11-1-0 with a Cotton Bowl victory over Arkansas in Dallas, by the score of 31 to 27. Majors' 1990 team won 9, lost 2, and tied 2 with a close victory over Virginia in the Sugar Bowl by the score of 23 to 22.

"No head coach can be better than his staff. Show me a winning team, and I'll show you a good group of assistant coaches."–Johnny Majors

Phillip Fulmer - (1992-present) (record). After serving as an assistant coach at UT for 13 seasons, the former Tennessee Vol offensive lineman was named head coach. Fulmer won the 1998 SEC and National Championships and was named National Coach of the Year for his efforts. Fulmer's 1997 team led by quarterback Peyton Manning went 11-2-0 and was crowned SEC Champions by virtue of their 30-29 championship victory over Auburn in the SEC Championship Game. Phillip Fulmer Way is a street on the Tennessee campus.

Players

Francis E. (Hank) Lauricella - Tailback 1949-1951. Lauricella, hailing from the New Orleans suburb of Harahan, Louisiana, was an All-American in 1951, the same year he finished as runnerup for the Heisman Trophy. After graduation, Lauricella returned to his home state of Louisiana where he was elected to the state's legislature as a senator. Lauricella was elected into the College Football Hall of Fame in 1981.

John (Johnny) T. Majors - A tailback at Tennessee from 1954-56. An All-American in 1956, Majors was also the runnerup to the Heisman Trophy winner. Majors later coached at Tennessee, where he was the 1976 Coach of the Year. Majors is originally from Huntland, Tennessee. Majors, who was born on May 21, 1955, is a member of the College Football Hall of Fame.

Bob Johnson - Johnson was a two-time All-American center for the Vols from 1965-67. In July of 1997 Johnson was named to the GTE Academic All-American All-Time Team for his earned B+ grade point average in Industrial Engineering while at UT. Johnson played at Tennessee under Volunteer Great Doug Dickey and went on to a 12 year career in the National Football League.

Reggie White - A Consensus All-American Defensive Tackle in 1983. White was voted the SEC's most outstanding player that same year by the Atlanta and Birmingham Touchdown Clubs. White is such a legend at the University of Tennessee that, during the school's centennial season of football in 1991, he was nominated to the Volunteers' all-time team. Nicknamed the "Minister of Defense" for his gridiron greatness, he was also one of four finalists for the Lombardi Award, given annually to the nation's outstanding

college lineman, during his final season in Knoxville. White went on to an All-Pro career with the Philadelphia Eagles and the Green Bay Packers. He was selected by the Philadelphia Eagles in the first round (fourth pick overall) of the 1984 NFL Supplemental Draft. Reggie White was born on December 19, 1961, in Chattanooga, Tennessee. *"Not mean enough? Not tough enough? I'd like to line up across from some of the people who say that and show them just how mean and tough I can be!" – Reggie White*

Leonard Little - (1995-97) A 1997 Team Co-Captain, as well as AP, Football News, Walter Camp All-American who was the SEC's Defensive Player of the Year. Little and Manning helped lead the Volunteers to the SEC Championship–a goal they attained by virtue of a victory over the Auburn Tigers in the Georgia Dome, by the slim margin of 30-29.

Peyton Manning - Tennessee's greatest quarterback. Peyton holds nearly every statistical passing record for the Vols. Revered by Tennessee fans far and wide for his unselfish decision to complete his playing eligibility at the University of Tennessee instead of

opting for millions of professional dollars, Peyton Manning turned out to be just what the Volunteers needed in 1997. A Consensus All-American, Davey O'Brien National Quarterback Award and Sullivan Award winner that year, Peyton won nearly every post-season accolade possible for a player–except for the highly coveted Heisman Trophy, in which he finished second in the balloting.

Originally from New Orleans, Peyton is the son of former Ole Miss great, Archie Manning, who played for the New Orleans Saints. In addition to his exploits on the gridiron, Peyton was an outstanding student at Tennessee as well. The younger Manning received numerous Academic awards during his career, including the National Football Foundation Scholar Athlete Award and the NASDAQ Scholar Athlete Award. Manning left Tennessee the holder of numerous Tennessee and SEC records. Peyton ran and threw for 11,020 yards during his four-year career in Knoxville (1994-97) which remain both school and league records. Peyton Manning Pass, named in Manning's honor, is a Tennessee campus street.

Tee Martin - Quarterback (1996-1999) Guided Tennessee to the 1998 national football championship. As a junior succeeding Peyton Manning, Martin led the Vols to a 13-0 record and a national championship triumph over Florida State. "Tee Martin Drive" is a new street on the Tennessee campus. During his last season in Knoxville, Martin made All-Southeastern Conference as the Vols went 9-3, eventually losing to Nebraska in a return trip to the Fiesta Bowl.

Travis Stephens – The Clarksville, TN running back was a 2001 All-American, as named by the Football Writers, CNN, Sporting News and the Associated Press. Although he was used mainly as a backup

Tennessee

to guys like Jamal Lewis and Travis Henry, Stephens was nevertheless a 2001 All-SEC player at Tennessee, racking up 1,464 yards on the season and thereby establishing a single-season rushing record for the Vols. Stephens finished his remarkable career (1997-2001) in Knoxville with 2,386 total yards rushing, which ranks sixth all-time at the school. During the 2001 season Stephens carried the ball 291 times (TN record) and led the SEC with a 122 yards per game average.

John Henderson – A Nashville, TN native, Henderson is considered one of the most dominant defensive linemen to ever wear the Volunteer orange. A natural at the defensive line position, Henderson was blessed with a rare combination of raw power and quickness to complement a sturdy 6-7 frame. One of the most decorated players in Tennessee history, Henderson was an All-American and the Outland Trophy winner in 2000, a consensus 1st Team All-America in 2001 and a first round draft pick by the Jacksonville Jaguars in the 2002 NFL draft.

Alex Walls – A native of Bristol, Virginia, Walls was a four-year starter as place kicker for the Vols from 1999-2002. An All-SEC and All-American performer, Walls was a Lou Groza Award Finalist in 2000, scoring 93 points on 18 of 20 field goals and 39 extra points without a miss. In 2001, Walls tied a career long with a 51-yard field goal in the SEC Championship game in Atlanta, which was also a SEC Championship game record. Walls scored 292 points in his career at Tennessee as he connected on 53 of 68 field goals (77.9%) and 133 of 137 extra point attempts. His 53 field goals rank third on the all-time Volunteer list. Walls is currently a kicker for the Seattle Seahawks organization.

History:

The University of Tennessee began playing football in 1891. The one game the Volunteers played that year was against Sewanee. Players and fans of Tennessee traveled to Chattanooga by train to take part in and witness the contest. In 1892, Tennessee began a regular football schedule that consisted of games with Maryville, Vanderbilt twice, and Sewanee twice. The very first game between Vanderbilt and Tennessee was the first played on Dudley Field in

258

Nashville, which later was called Curry Field when Dudley Stadium was built in 1922.

The Formation "T"

Since 1964, the team has entered the stadium through a giant "T" formed on the field by the "Pride of the Southland" Marching Band. Bob Neyland's "63" team began this tradition which continued under Doug Dickey's command and subsequent repositioning of the "T". It continues today in it's present form, from north to south. It is sometimes formed at away games but does lose some of its pizazz without the 107,000 fans.

In 76 seasons, the UT Vols are 373-88-17 at home, for a winning percentage of .772. Tennessee has had 67 winning seasons in 76 years at Shields-Watkins Field, including 33 undefeated years at home.

Great Bowl Games:

1971 Sugar Bowl: January 1, 1971 Tennessee 34, Air Force 13

1986 Sugar Bowl: January 1, 1986 Tennessee 35, Miami 7

1990 Cotton Bowl: January 1, 1990 Tennessee 31, Arkansas 27

1991 Sugar Bowl: January 1, 1991 Tennessee 23, Virginia 22

1999 Fiesta Bowl: January 4, 1999 Tennessee 23, Florida State 6. (Phillip Fulmer led Tennessee to its second National Championship)

2002 Citrus Bowl: Tennessee 45 Michigan 17

The Helmet "T"

The famed letter "T" debuted on Tennessee's helmets in the fall of 1964 as Doug Dickey assumed the head coaching reins. Prior to 1964 the helmets had been white with an orange stripe down the middle. There have, however, been two exceptions. In coach Bowden Wyatt's final season in 1962, the Vols had orange numerals on the sides of their helmets. In 1963 coach Jim McDonald stuck with the numbers on the helmets, but changed the numerals' color to black. When Johnny Majors was named head coach in 1977, he had the "T" slightly redesigned and the orange stripe widened.

Nathan W. Dougherty is considered by many to be the founding father of UT Athletics. Dougherty, an associate professor of Civil

Engineering, was named interim chairman of the University's Athletics Council in 1917 and held this "temporary" position for the next 39 years. During this time, he designed Shields-Watkins Field, helped create the Southeastern Conference, and hired a football coach whose own name would become synonymous with UT football – Robert Reese Neyland.

"The Vol Walk"

The team takes this stroll from Gibbs Hall to the field prior to every home game at Neyland Stadium.

According to the *Tennessee Media Guide*, Tennessee Tradition is defined as:

"...the wave of orange across the 102,854-seat Neyland Stadium...It's tailgating in the parking lots and hearing John Ward's pregame show at the base of the Hill near Alumni Gym...It's hearing public address announcer Bobby Denton say, "Please pay these prices and please pay no more."

"Rocky Top"
Copyright 1967 by House of Bryant Publications
P.O. Box 120608, Nashville, TN 37212

Wish that I was on old Rockytop Down in the Tennessee hills.
Ain't no smoggy smoke on Rockytop Ain't no telephone bills.
Once I had a girl on Rockytop Half bear, the other half cat,
Wild as a mink, but sweet as soda-pop I still dream about that.

Chorus: Rockytop, you'll always be Home sweet home to me.
Good old Rockytop, Rockytop, Tennessee. Rockytop, Tennessee.

Once two strangers climbed old Rockytop
Lookin' for a moonshine still.

Strangers ain't come down from Rockytop, Reckon they never will.
Corn won't grow at all on Rockytop – Dirt's too rocky by far.
That's why all the folks on Rockytop Get their corn from a jar.
Repeat Chorus

I've had years of cooped up city life, Trapped like a dog in a pen.
All I know is it's a pity life Can't be simple again.
Repeat Chorus

Alma Mater
On a hallowed hill in Tennessee Like a beacon shining bright
The stately walls of old UT Rise glorious to the site
So here's to you, old Tennessee Our alma mater true
We pledge in love and harmony Our loyalty to you
What torches kindled at that flame Have passed from hand to hand
What hearts cemented in that name Blind land to stranger land.
O, ever as we strive to rise
On life's unresting stream Dear Alma Mater, may our eyes
Be lifted to that gleam.

Noteworthy UT Alumni:
   Howard Baker Jr., U.S. - ambassador to Japan, former Senate majority leader
   James Buchanan - Nobel Prize winner in economics
   Deana Carter - country music artist
   John Cullum - Tony Award winning actor
   Cormac McCarthy - novelist
   Ali Hassein Abu Ragheb - Prime Minister of Jordan
   Mark Dean - IBM fellow, invented plug-in technology for computers
   Paul Finebaum - Alabama radio commentator, columnist

sec football

"Southern football will remain the most significant social ritual of autumn, an event which has a great deal to do with more than football alone. College football has been, and will be, as much a part of the fabric of Southern society as fried chicken and political rhetoric, grits and evangelical religion, thoroughbred horses, beautiful women, and sourmash whiskey. On any given Saturday in the fall, millions of happy fans will create traffic jams on the highways leading to their alma maters, carrying with them tailgate lunches and fiercely felt hopes and fears, reliving the exploits of the Doak Walkers or Charlie Justices or Herschel Walkers, visiting with sons and daughters who have shared the universal catharsis of college football–the older generation's gift to the coming generation."

~L.W.
Oxford, Mississippi

Vanderbilt University

Through the years Vanderbilt University has established itself as one of the SEC's most prominent academic institutions. Although it is known throughout the country and the world for its success in the classroom, Vanderbilt has enjoyed its share of success on the gridiron as well. During the formative years of the Southeastern Conference, Vanderbilt was one of the nation's most feared football-playing schools. The legend and lore of those early great old gold and black squads led by Head Coach Dan McGugin serve as an ephemeral reminder of the proud Commodore tradition and the rightful place it firmly holds in the annals of SEC football.

Vanderbilt University, with an impressive 83% graduation rate among its enrolled athletes, boasts the highest graduation rate of student athletes of all of the SEC member schools. In light of this, Vanderbilt is undoubtedly the academic leader of the Southeastern Conference. At Vanderbilt University, student athletes receive the best of both worlds–they compete in one of the finest athletic conferences in the country and in some of the nation's most challenging classrooms as well.

Nickname: Commodores

Founded: 1873

Vanderbilt University was founded in 1873 when successful steamboater and railroad baron Commodore Cornelius Vanderbilt gave a million dollars to erect an institution of learning that would, in his words, "contribute to strengthening the ties that should exist between all sections of our common country." A year earlier in 1872, a charter for the constitution of a "Central University" had been set forth in Nashville, but a lack of monetary resources stymied the effort. Commodore Vanderbilt's more than generous donation allowed for the establishment of the school that today still bears his name. At the time of its inception, the city of Nashville had 40,000 residents. The 316 acre campus rested partly within an existing cornfield and the stone wall enveloping the campus served to keep neighboring cows off the school's grounds. Vanderbilt University first opened for classes in October 1875 with an enrollment of 192 students. In 1966, the Peabody campus was named a registered National Historic Landmark.

Location: Nashville, Tennessee

Possessing a metropolitan population of close to one million people, Nashville can stake its claim as the largest urban hometown of any SEC member institution. Despite its strength in numbers, Nashville still retains a small-town feel to those who know it well. Positioned midway between the north and south boundaries of the United States, Nashville is the capital city of Tennessee as well as the cultural and entertainment mecca of the Mid-South. Popularly known as "Music City USA" and home to the Grand Ole Opry, Nashville is a city whose music preferences vary from country to rock n' roll to gospel. Located just two miles from the center of the downtown entertainment, is the thriving urban campus of Vanderbilt University.

Population: 487,969
Enrollment: 6,235
Colors: Old Gold and Black

Some at Vandy say the original colors were actually Orange and Black, given to the university by Judge W.L. Granbery of Princeton. Others say Livingfield More offered the colors of his eastern prep school. When questioned by a writer in the early 1940's, most members of the 1890 team could not recall why they suddenly appeared in Gold and Black. It is also believed that the student body may have formally voted on the school's colors of Old Gold and Black in the mid teens.

Mascot name: Commodores

The name "Commodore" comes from university founder Cornelius Vanderbilt's affinity for steamboats.

Stadium: Vanderbilt Stadium, Dudley Field.

Dr. William L. Dudley was the Dean of the Vanderbilt Medical College from 1895 to 1914. Dr. Dudley helped found the Southern Intercollegiate Athletic Association, which later became the SEC and the ACC. In 1906, he was also instrumental in the inception of the NCAA. He is remembered as the "Father of Clean Athletics." Dudley Field at Vanderbilt stadium is named after him.

Stadium capacity: 41,488
Band: "Vanderbilt Marching Band"
Record crowd: 41,523 Sept. 5, 1996 Notre Dame 14 Vanderbilt 7
First game: 1890 - Vanderbilt defeated Nashville, on the Vanderbilt campus, 40-0.
First game in stadium: September 12, 1981 Vanderbilt 23, Maryland 17

Directions: Coming from the South, Take I-65 North to Exit 2098 (Broadway-West End). Then turn left and go west on Broadway. Broadway splits. Keep right to enter West End Ave.

265

Continue past University and turn left on Natchez Trace. Take the first right and make a sharp right onto 28th Ave.

Coming from the North: Take I-65 South to I-265 to Exit 209B (Broadway-West End). Go right and then west on Broadway. Then follow the above "Coming from the South" directions.

Coming from the East: Take I-40 West to Exit 209B (Broadway-West End). Turn left on Broadway heading west. Then follow the above "Coming from the South" directions.

Coming from the West: Take I-40 East to Exit 209B (Broadway-West End). Turn right and go west on Broadway. Then follow the above "Coming from the South" directions.

Coming from Chattanooga: Take I-24 West until it merges with I-40 West. Continue on I-40 until Exit 209B (Broadway-West End). Turn right and go west on Broadway. Then follow the above "Coming from the South" directions.

Where to go in Nashville:
Eating and Drinking:
Cock o' the Walk: 2624 Music Valley Drive (615/889-1930). Fantastic, reasonably priced catfish in soothing atmosphere.

The Loveless Cafe: Country cooking at its best. Rte 5 off Hwy. 100, 8 miles south of town (615/646-9700). A quaint motel cafe. Breakfasts are best here where hunks of salty ham with gravy, eggs, toast and fluffy biscuits smothered with homemade jam are the staples. The Loveless, is quite simply one of the best country restaurants in the South.

Pancake Pantry: 1796 21st Ave (615/383-9333). One of Nashville's most popular breakfast spots, near Music Row in the likeable Hillsboro Village district. Open daily 6am-5pm.

Sammy B's: 26 Music Square East (615/256-6000). A smart-feeling music industry hangout, serving reasonably priced appetizing lunch platters.

Stock Yard: A Steakhouse on Second Ave & Stockyard Blvd (615/255-6464). A spacious venue serving huge steaks to the stars.

Owned by Buddy Killen, president of Tree International, country music's largest publisher.

Grand Ole Opry (Opryland): Historic auditorium. 2808 Opryland Drive, Nashville, TN 37214 (615/889-3060). Four thousand-plus-seat theater, staging old-timers like Charlie Louvin, perennials like Dolly Parton, and today's chart-toppers. Reservations recommended.

Country Music Hall of Fame: Museum 4 Music Square East. Personal possessions of the stars, video clips and music; admission includes trolley tour of Music Row and RCA's historic Studio B.

Opryland: A Theme park Nine miles northeast of downtown on Briley Parkway, just off the I-40 E loop (summer daily usually 9am-9pm; March-May & Oct Sat & Sun only, hours vary; 615/889-6700). Twenty-plus rides, paddlesteamer trips, plus live music.

Grand Ole Opry Museum: A Museum located conveniently outside the main gates of Opryland, open the same hours as the main attraction. Spectacular overview of major music stars of the past and present. Admission is free.

All-Time Record: 530-502-50 (.513)
All-Time SEC Record: 107-330-18 (.248)
Bowl Appearances: 1955 Gator Bowl (8-3-0) Vanderbilt 25, Auburn 13
  1974 Peach Bowl: (7-3-2) Vanderbilt 6, Texas Tech 6
  1982 Hall of Fame Bowl: (8-4-0) Vanderbilt 28 Air Force 36
Bowl Record: 1-1-1

Vanderbilt Greats

Coaches:
  Dan McGugin (1904-1917, 1919-1934) 197-55-19 All-time record. A member of the College Football Hall of Fame, Legendary Vanderbilt Coach Dan McGugin, whose teams during his thirty-year reign of the Commodores won 197 games, including four undefeated seasons, was one of the greatest college coaches of his time.

McGugin left football temporarily in 1918 to serve his country in World War I. He ranks fourth all-time in NCAA Division I History for most years coached at one school. In his first year as Vanderbilt's head coach, McGugin posted a flawless 9-0-0 record. His three other undefeated campaigns were in 1919, 1921, and 1922. His 1906 and 1911 teams were consensus National Champions. In addition, McGugin won 10 conference titles as head coach at Vanderbilt.

McGugin ranks 18th in all-time NCAA Division I head coaching victories and ranks 4th all-time in NCAA Division I for most years coached at one school. McCugin compiled a flawless 30-0 record (24 shutouts) in season opening games in his coaching career, outscoring opponents 1,302 to 49 in those contests. Amazingly, he compiled a 34-0-1 record versus Southern opposition between 1904-1909.  During his career, McGugin was 18-8-4 versus their in-state arch-nemesis, Tennessee. McGugin once remarked to his players, "Don't live on the fading memories of your forefathers. Go out and make your own records, and leave some memories for others to live by."

Dan McGugin personified the "Golden Era" of Vanderbilt football (1890-1934), which were the Commodores' most successful football-playing years. In 1924, McGugin prepared his team to play the mighty Minnesota Gophers in Minneapolis. The Gophers, at the time, were a team to be reckoned with, having handed Illinois' Red Grange his first collegiate loss the week prior. McGugin, a master motivator, inspired his team that day with the following immortal words:

"Men, those people in the stands out there haven't heard of Southern football. When they think about the South, they think –they think about pain, suffering and death. Many people have no idea of what Southern manhood is all about. Today we can show them. When your mothers looked on you sleeping your cradles twenty years ago, they wondered when the time would come when you could bring honor to the South. That time has arrived!"

The Commodores, subsequent to McGugin's moving motivational speech, handily defeated the heavily-favored Golden Gophers that fateful day in a lopsided, 16-0 shutout.

"Play for your own self-respect and the respect of your teammates." ~Dan McGugin

"How you fight is how you will be remembered."~Dan McGugin

"You are about to be put through an ordeal which will show the stuff that's in you. What a glorious chance you have!" ~Coach Dan McGugin in 1921, addressing his undefeated Vanderbilt squad.

The Vandy Gold website pays fitting homage to the great Dan McGugin with the following eulogy:

"...They have been waiting a long time, most of them. Finally, "Coach" has come home. Beloved, loyal, unselfish and considerate Coach McGugin. The same smile. Those Irish eyes of blue, so big and kindly. A lock of brown hair standing up in the breeze. Those same short steps...

There is plenty of time in that better land of no defeats. Each day they will sit in the circle where the sun is always warm and the grass ever green. And when each Commodore comes out of the battle of life, just a bit weary, "Coach" will stand up, pat him on the back and welcome him to the squad that never dies."

Red Sanders (1943-48) Although he is given credit as being head coach during the war-torn years from 1943-1945, Sanders was on active duty in the military for World War II. Sanders led the Commodores to a most respectable overall record of 36-22-2 (10-9-1 in SEC play) in Nashville. Sanders, ever the competitor, once stated, "The only thing worse than finishing second is to be lying on the desert alone with your back broken. Either way, nobody ever finds out about you."

"Winning isn't everything, it's the only thing." – 1953 saying that is often attributed to Coach Sanders, according to Bartlett's Familiar Quotations, sixteenth edition (1992).

Players

Owsley Manier–1906 Third Team All-American. As the Commodore's top rushing weapon at fullback, Manier was the first Commodore to ever receive All-America accolades of any kind. In 1906, in the opener against Kentucky, Manier rushed for three touchdowns as Vanderbilt gained 630 yards in a 28-0 win. Two games later, Manier scored five times as Vanderbilt thrashed Alabama by the unbelievable margin of 78-0. Still later that season, in the 37-6 win over Georgia Tech in Atlanta, Manier again ran for five scores. Vanderbilt's 1906 Manier-led squad lost only to the potent Michigan Wolverines by the score of 10-4, and scored 278 points while allowing a paltry 16.

Irby Rice Curry–Captain of the 1916 Vanderbilt Commodores, "Rabbit" Curry, as he was affectionately known, scored two touchdowns in the fourth quarter of the 1915 game with Sewanee to lead the Commodores to a climactic, come-from-behind victory and a 9-1 season. Curry was named Third Team All-American in 1916 and was also an All-Southern selection in both 1915 and 1916. He quarterbacked the 1916 Commodores to a 7-1-1 record and to one

of the biggest victories in school history–an 86-0 thrashing of the University of Southwestern Louisiana (now the University of Louisiana at Lafayette). Tragically, Irby Rice "Rabbit" Curry was killed in action serving his country during World War I over France on August 10, 1918.

Jess Neely (Played at Vanderbilt from 1920-1922) (207-176-19) 40 years as a coach at

Southwestern Tennessee from 1924-1927, Clemson from 1931-1939, and Rice from 1940-1966. A member of the College Football Hall of Fame, Neely ranks 12th in all-time head coaching victories. The Captain of the 1922 Vanderbilt Southern Conference Championship team, Neely was 20-3-3 as a Vanderbilt player and was a perfect 3-0 against the Volunteers. Neely was named Vanderbilt Athletic Director Emeritus in 1967. Neely had the honor of tossing the coin at the rededication of Vanderbilt stadium in 1981.

Bob Werckle - 1951 All-American Offensive/Defensive Tackle. Werckle was well known throughout the South for his blocking and tackling skills. Early in his career, he battled culture shock, since he was originally from Brooklyn, New York. As a team captain in 1951, he recalled, "I felt like a Yankee and a stranger when I first came here, but I guess I've been reconstructed. Vanderbilt is the greatest thing that ever happened to me."

George Deiderich - All-American Guard in 1958. Deiderich garnered First Team All-America honors by AP, the nation's coaches, and the Football Writers Association of America. He was a two-time All-SEC selection. Deiderich played both offensive and defensive line for the Commodores, with defense being his specialty. In addition to his exploits in football, Deiderich was also a standout track athlete. He set a then Vanderbilt record in the 120 yard high hurdles with a time of 14.46 seconds. Furthermore, he also scored in four other varsity events for the Vanderbilt track team–the shot put, discus, long jump, and low hurdles. In 1960, Deiderich was drafted by the CFL's Montreal Alouettes, where he played for two seasons. He was known by his teammates as Lu-Lu.

Bob Asher - 1969 All-American Offensive Tackle. A native of Falls Church,Virginia, Asher received numerous awards in his senior season. He was named First team All-American by the Associated Press also played in the College All-Star Game, the Senior Bowl, the North-South Shrine Game and the Canadian-American Bowl. Asher started every game of his three year career at Vandy, serving as an impenetrable pass blocker. In 1970, he was drafted by the Dallas Cowboys and played on the team that won the Super Bowl in 1971. Asher completed his professional football career in Chicago, whee he started for the Bears from 1972-1975. In 1995, Asher was honored as a "Living Legend of SEC Football" at the SEC Championship game in Atlanta.

After football, Asher earned an MBA from the University of Chicago and then went on to a successful investment banking career in the windy city.

Chuck Scott - (1981-1984) Tight End. An All-American at tight end in 1983, Scott nabbed 70 passes to tie an NCAA record for receptions at his position. A first-team All-SEC player in 1983 (tight end) and 1984 (flanker), Scott holds the Vanderbilt record for most touchdown receptions in a career with 20. Most impressively, Scott was an All-SEC Academic selection in 1983 and 1984. Scott is a member of the 1982 Vanderbilt Hall of Fame Team. After his college career, Scott was drafted by the Los Angeles Rams.

Chris Gaines - 1987 All-American Linebacker. A homegrown product of Nashville's DuPont High, Gaines was selected as a First Team Kodak All-American. During his senior season for the Commodores, Gaines set an SEC single-season record for tackles with an unbelievable 214. Tennessean sports columnist Larry Woody once described Gaines as "...sort of a Rambo on a leash." In the annual post-season Blue-Gray game, Gaines led the Gray to a

12-10 victory and was named Most Valuable Player for tallying 18 tackles. Against Tulane that year he registered 37 tackles. He was selected in the fifth round of the 1987 NFL draft by the Phoenix Cardinals and also had brief NFL jaunts with the Miami Dolphins and Tampa Bay Bucs before heading to Canada to play for the With the Argonauts Gaines would set the Argo's single-season record for tackles with 117 in 1990, and he also led the team in special teams tackles in addition to six interceptions. In 1991, he helped lead Toronto to the Grey Cup Championship. Gaines eventually returned to Nashville as the Commodores' strength and conditioning coach in 1995, and was later promoted to linebackers coach in 1997.

Bill Marinangel - 1996 All-American Punter. Marinangel was named First Team All-America by the Sporting News in 1996. That same year, Marinangel won the NCAA punting championship with an average of 46.6 yards. Subsequent to the completion of the regular season, he was tabbed to play in the annual Blue-Gray all-star game. Marinangel is perhaps best remembered for one heroic play in his senior year. During the season's second game, against Alabama in Tuscaloosa, Marinangel surprised everyone-including the Tide's special teams unit, as he took the snap from center and proceeded to scamper 81 yards for an improbable touchdown. The run from scrimmage was the longest in the SEC in 1996.

Jamie Duncan - All-American Linebacker, 1997. Duncan was one of the most dominating linebackers in Commodore history. Duncan was an outstanding defender of both the run and the pass, and he possessed an uncanny knack of causing turnovers and making big plays. At the end of the 1997 season, Duncan was named a First-Team All-American by the Football Writers Association of America. Duncan finished his stellar career in Nashville with 425 tackles and was also named SEC Defensive Player of the Year by the Mobile Press Register. Duncan was chosen by the Tampa Bay Buccaneers in 1997 in the NFL draft (84th overall).

Jimmy Williams – A Baton Rouge, Louisiana native, Williams was a standout defensive back and return man for the Commodores from 1997-2000. A four-year starter Williams was a versatile athlete that played both cornerback and tailback for Vandy. During his outstanding stint at Vanderbilt Williams finished with 403 punt return yards and 1,677 kickoff return yards, ranking him 7th and 3rd respectively in Commodore football history in each category. Furthermore, Williams finished 7th on the Commodore interception list with 10 picks during his college career. Williams received degree in human and organizational studies and speaks three languages--English, French and Japanese. Originally drafted by the Bills in the 6th round of the 2001 NFL draft, Williams signed shortly thereafter with the San Francisco 49ers.

Jamie Winborn – A three-year starter at Vanderbilt, the Wetumpka, Alabama native finished his college career with 377 tackles (236 solo), 16.5 sacks (105 yards) and 45 tackles for loss (198 yards). Winborn was an All-America Dream Team selection by Sports Xchange as junior and he was selected as a Second-Team All-America by Football News and was a first-team All-SEC pick as sophomore. Moreover, in 1998, after a redshirt year in 1997, Winborn was tabbed as a Freshman All-America by Sporting News and Football News. Winborn left Vandy for the pros in 2001 when he was drafted in the second round by the San Francisco 49ers.

History

Vanderbilt began playing football on Thanksgiving Day, November 27, 1890. The Commodores played the University of Nashville, which later became the George Peabody College for Teachers. According to Fred Russell, the following is an account of what Elliot R. Jones, coach and captain of the first Commodore team from 1890-1892, had to say about the beginning of Vanderbilt football.

In November, 1890, a letter was received from the University of Nashville challenging Vandy to a football game on the holiday of Thanksgiving Day. Upon receipt of the communication, the President of the Athletic Association for the Commodores, Dr. William Dudley, called forthwith a meeting of the Executive Committee. The matter was considered a serious one by the committee–so serious that a mass meeting of the student body was called. A considerable turnout resulted. A rather impressive 150 students assembled at four o'clock the next day in the campus gymnasium, which was only two weeks before Thanksgiving Day. The students voted to accept the challenge of the University of Nashville and the game was played. Vanderbilt prevailed in the rout by a score of 40-0.

In 1893, 1894, 1897, 1904 and 1905 Vanderbilt was crowned the Southern Intercollegiate Athletic Association Champions.

In 1906, the Atlanta Journal wrote of the Vanderbilt Commodore football program:

"Vanderbilt is the best team in the South and one of the best in the nation. No Southern team, recruited by any means, has classed with it. This team was secured by honest athletic methods. No inducements are held out for athletes to go to Vanderbilt. The team has been built up by methods above criticism and it proves one thing, that honesty pays in college athletics as well as elsewhere."

Vanderbilt won national championships in 1906 and 1911 under the old Billingsley System Ratings. Vanderbilt, an eleven-time champion of the Southern InterCollegiate Association, also won the Southern Conference Championship, in 1922 and 1923.

Tradition:
The nautical theme spawned by the University's founder, Cornelius Vanderbilt, continues with the sounding of a large ship's horn mounted on the pressbox at high points in the game.

The Vanderbilt Commodore Mission Statement

"As an integral part of a private research University and a charter member of the Southeastern Conference, we are committed to setting and achieving standards of excellence in education and athletics by developing the full potential of our student-athletes and staff. Individually and together, we are accountable for placing the highest value on people, integrity and winning."

Alma Mater
(Text by Robert F. Vaughn, 1907)
On the city's western border
Reared against the sky
Proudly stands our Alma Mater
As the years roll by.

Forward ever be thy watchword, Conquer and Prevail.
Hail to thee our Alma Mater, Vanderbilt, All Hail!

Cherished by thy sons and daughters,
Mem'ries sweet shall throng
Round our hearts, O Alma Mater,
As we sing our song.

Dynamite
(Fight song written by Francis Craig in 1924)
Dynamite, Dynamite When Vandy starts to fight

Down the field with blood to yield
If need be, save the shield.

If vict'rys won when battle's done
Then Vandy's name will rise in fame.

But, win or lose, The Fates will choose,
And Vandy's game will be the same.

Dynamite, Dynamite,
When Vandy starts to fight!

Noteworthy Vanderbilt Alumni:
  Bettie Page - model
  James Patterson - novelist, (Kiss the Girls, Along Came A Spider)
  John Ingram - President of Ingram Distribution Holdings
  Roseanne Cash - songwriter/entertainer
  Marshall Chapman - entertainer
  James Dickey - novelist and poet, author of Deliverance (deceased)
  Grantland Rice - considered the greatest sportswriter of the twentieth century
  Amy Grant - entertainer
  Dinah Shore - entertainer
  Lamar Alexander - Tennessee Governor, US Senator, U.S. Secretary of Education
  Skip Bayless - syndicated newspaper columnist
  John Bloom - humorist, journalist, and actor
  Roy Blount - author and humorist

"Successful coaches are few and far between. It's a wonder they command salaries without limit."

~John Heisman

References

Barber, Phil and Didinger, Ray. *Football America: Celebrating Our National Passion.* 1996, Turner Publishing. Atlanta, Georgia.

Briggs, Jennifer. *Strive To Excel The Will and Wisdom of Vince Lombardi.* 1997 Rutledge Hill Press, Nashville, Tennessee.

Brubacher, John S. *A History of the Problems of Education* (N.Y.: McGraw, 1947).

Danzig, Allison. *The History of American Football*, 1956. Prentice-Hall.

Dougherty, Nathan W. *Educators and Athletes*, 1976. University of Tennessee Athletic Department (Nathan was known by Volunteer fans as "Mr. Volunteer", serving for 35 years as the Faculty Chairman of Athletics).

Finney, Peter. *The Fighting Tigers: Seventy-five Years of LSU Football.* Baton Rouge: Louisiana State University Press, 1968.

Freeman, Criswell. *The Wisdom of Southern Football*, 1995. Walnut Grove Press.

Gambit Baton Rouge Weekly. May 20, 1999. Volume 1 No. 13.

Gruenfelder, M.H. *A History of the Origin and Development of the Southeastern Conference* (B.S. thesis, University of Illinois).

Henry, Orville. *A Story of Arkansas Football*, 1996. University of Arkansas Press.

Irwin, Joseph and Michael. *Cathedrals of College Football.* 1998. Alliance Press.

McCallum, John D. *Southeastern Conference Football*, 1980.

Official Southeastern Conference Football Handbook, 1998 . Bellsouth Advertising and Publishing Company.

Russell, Fred. *Fifty years of Vanderbilt Football.* Nashville, 1938.

Sellers, James B. *History of the University of Alabama.* University of Alabama Press, 1953.

Stegeman, *The Ghosts of Herty Field* (Athens: University of Georgia press, 1966).

Sugar, Burt Randolph. *The SEC: A Pictorial History of Southeastern Conference Football*, 1979.

SEC   SOUTHEASTERN CONFERENCE

Year	Champion(s)
1933	Alabama (5-0-1)
1934	Tulane (8-0) & Alabama (7-0)
1935	LSU (5-0)
1936	LSU (6-0)
1937	Alabama (6-0)
1938	Tennessee (7-0)
1939	Tennessee (6-0), Georgia Tech (6-0) & Tulane (5-0)
1940	Tennessee (5-0)
1941	Mississippi State (4-0-1)
1942	Georgia (6-1)
1943	Georgia Tech (3-0)
1944	Georgia Tech (4-0)
1945	Alabama (6-0)
1946	Georgia (5-0) & Tennessee (5-0)
1947	Mississippi (6-1)
1948	Georgia (6-0)
1949	Tulane (5-1)
1950	Kentucky (5-1)
1951	Georgia Tech (7-0) & Tennessee (5-0)
1952	Georgia Tech (6-0)
1953	Alabama (4-0-3)
1954	Mississippi (5-1)
1955	Mississippi (5-1)
1956	Tennessee (6-0)
1957	Auburn (7-0)
1958	LSU (6-0)
1959	Georgia (7-0)
1960	Mississippi (5-0-1)
1961	Alabama (7-0) & LSU (6-0)
1962	Mississippi (6-0)
1963	Mississippi (5-0-1)
1964	Alabama (8-0)
1965	Alabama (6-1-1)
1966	Alabama (6-0) & Georgia (6-0)
1967	Tennessee (6-0)
1968	Georgia (5-0-1)
1969	Tennessee (5-1)
1970	LSU (5-0)

1971	Alabama (7-0)
1972	Alabama (7-1)
1973	Alabama (8-0)
1974	Alabama (6-0)
1975	Alabama (6-0)
1976	Georgia (5-1) & Kentucky (5-1)
1977	Alabama (7-0) & Kentucky (6-0)
1978	Alabama (6-0)
1979	Alabama (6-0)
1980	Georgia (6-0)
1981	Georgia (6-0) & Alabama (6-0)
1982	Georgia (6-0)
1983	Auburn (6-0)
1984	Florida (5-0-1)*
1985	Florida (5-1)† & Tennessee (5-1)
1986	LSU (5-1)
1987	Auburn (5-0-1)
1988	Auburn (6-1)& LSU (6-1)
1989	Alabama (6-1), Tennessee (6-1) & Auburn (6-1)
1990	Florida (6-1)† & Tennessee (5-1-1)
1991	Florida (7-0)

Championship Game

Year

1992	Alabama 28, Florida 21
1993	Florida 28, Alabama 23
1994	Florida 24, Alabama 23
1995	Florida 34, Arkansas 3
1996	Florida 45, Alabama 30
1997	Tennessee 30, Auburn 29
1998	Tennessee 24, Mississippi State 14
1999	Alabama 34, Florida 7
2000	Florida 28, Auburn 6
2001	LSU 31, Tennessee 20
2002	Georgia 30, Arkansas 3
2003	LSU 34, Georgia 13

All Time Final AP Football Poll

Rank	Team	Points	Top 20	Top 10	Top 5	1st	2nd
1.	Michigan	704	50	36	15	2	2
2.	Notre Dame	684.5	46	34	22	8	5
3.	Oklahoma	662.5	43	31	26	6	4
4.	ALABAMA	619	43	31	18	6	2
5.	Nebraska	615	41	30	13	4	2
6.	Ohio State	602	42	25	16	4	6
7.	TENNESSEE	520	38	23	13	2	4
8.	Texas	498.5	35	21	6	2	1
9.	Southern Cal	481	37	21	13	4	4
10.	Penn State	461	36	21	13	2	3
11.	Miami (Florida)	415	25	15	10	5	4
12.	Florida State	399	22	15	15	2	2
13.	UCLA	342	29	16	9	0	1
14.	GEORGIA	338	25	15	8	1	1
15.	LSU	334	27	16	6	1	2
16.	AUBURN	332	28	14	6	1	0
17.	FLORIDA	319	21	13	8	1	1
18.	ARKANSAS	282	25	13	3	0	1
19.	Michigan State	266	20	13	7	1	4
20.	Texas A&M	264	22	11	2	1	0
21.	Washington	260	20	10	5	0	2
22.	Georgia Tech	227.5	20	10	5	0	2
23.	OLE MISS	223.5	18	10	4	0	2
24.	Colorado	218	18	8	5	1	0
25.	Pittsburgh	206	17	10	6	2	1

SEC Football Coaches All-Time Wins

SEC COACH	TEAM(S)	SEC					NCAA-OVERALL				
		W	L	T	PCT.	#1	W	L	T	PCT.	#1
1 Bear Bryant	Kentucky, 1946-53, Alabama 1958-82	159	46	9	79%	1, 13	323	85	17	78%	6
2 Johnny Vaught	Mississippi, 1947-70	106				6	190	61	12	75%	0
3 Vince Dooley	Georgia, 1964-88	105				6	201	77	10	72%	1
4 Shug Jordan	Auburn, 1951-75	98				1	175	83			1
5 Steve Spurrier	Florida, 1989-2001	82	18	0	82%	6	142	40	2	78%	1
6 Phillip Fulmer	Tennessee, 1992-2003	74	19	0	80%	2	113	27	0	81%	1
7 Wally Butts	Georgia, 1939-60	67				4					1
8 Robert Neyland	Tennessee, 1926-34,36-40,46-52	62	15	5	79%	5	173	31	12	83%	2
9 Charlie McClendon	Louisiana State, 1962-1979	62				1	137	59	7	69%	0
10 Frank Thomas	Alabama, 1931-46	59				4					

National Champions Since 1933

1933	Michigan (CF, NC, HF, Di)	8-0-0	Harry Kipke
	Ohio State (Du)	7-1-0	Sam Williman
	Southern Cal (Wi)	10-1-1	Howard Jones
1934	Minnesota	8-0-0	Bernie Bierman
	Alabama (Du, Wi)	9-0-0	Frank Thomas
1935	Minnesota (CF, NC, HF, Li)	8-0-0	Bernie Bierman
	Southern Methodist (Di)	12-1-0	Matty Bell
	Princeton (Du)	9-0-0	Fritz Crisler
	Louisiana St. (Wi)	9-2-0	Bernie Moore
1936	Minnesota	7-1-0	Bernie Bierman
	Louisiana St. (Wi)	9-1-1	Bernie Moore
1937	Pittsburgh	9-0-1	Jock Sutherland
	California (Du)	10-0-1	Stub Allison
1938	TCU	11-0-0	Dutch Meyer
	Notre Dame (Di)	8-1-0	Elmer Layden
	Tennessee (Li)	11-0-0	Robert Neyland
1939	Texas AM	11-0-0	Homer Norton
	Cornell (Li)	8-0-0	Carl Snavely
1940	Minnesota	8-0-0	Bernie Bierman
	Tennessee (Du, Wi)	10-0-0	Robert Neyland
1941	Minnesota	8-0-0	Bernie Bierman
	Texas (Wi)	8-1-1	Dana X. Bible
1942	Ohio St.	9-1-0	Paul Brown
	Georgia (Li, Wi)	11-1-0	Wally Butts
1943	Notre Dame	9-1-0	Frank Leahy
1944	Army	9-0-0	Red Blaik
1945	Army	9-0-0	Red Blaik
1946	Notre Dame	8-0-1	Frank Leahy
	Georgia (Wi)	11-0-0	Wally Butts
1947	Notre Dame	9-0-0	Frank Leahy
	Michigan (Du, Li, Wi)	10-0-0	Fritz Crisler
1948	Michigan	9-0-0	Bennie Oosterbaan
	Notre Dame (Wi)	9-0-1	Frank Leahy
1949	Notre Dame	10-0-0	Frank Leahy
1950	Oklahoma	10-1-0	Bud Wilkinson

	Tennessee (Du, Li)	11-1-0	Robert Neyland
1951	Tennessee	10-0-0	Robert Neyland
	Maryland (Du)	10-0-0	Jim Tatum
1952	Michigan St. (AP, UP)	9-0-0	Biggie Munn
	Georgia Tech (IN)	12-0-0	Bobby Dodd
1953	Maryland	10-1-0	Jim Tatum
1954	Ohio St. (AP, IN)	10-0-0	Woody Hayes
	UCLA (UP, FW)	9-0-0	Red Sanders
1955	Oklahoma	11-0-0	Bud Wilkinson
1956	Oklahoma	10-0-0	Bud Wilkinson
1957	Auburn (AP)	10-0-0	Shug Jordan
	Ohio St. (UP, FW, IN)	9-1-0	Woody Hayes
1958	LSU (AP, UP)	11-0-0	Paul Dietzel
	Iowa (FW)	8-1-1	Forest Evashevski
1959	Syracuse	11-0-0	Ben Schwartzwalder
1960	Minnesota (AP, UP, NF)	8-2-0	Murray Warmath
	Mississippi (FW)	10-0-1	Johnny Vaught
1961	Alabama (AP, UP, NF)	11-0-0	Bear Bryant
	Ohio St. (FW)	8-0-1	Woody Hayes
1962	Southern California	11-0-0	John McKay
1963	Texas	11-0-0	Darrell Royal
1964	Alabama (AP, UP),	10-1-0	Bear Bryant
	Arkansas (FW)	11-0-0	Frank Broyles
	Notre Dame (NF)	9-1-0	Ara Parseghian
1965	Alabama (AP, FW-T)	9-1-1	Bear Bryant
	Michigan St. (UP, NF, FW-T)	10-1-0	Duffy Daugherty
1966	Notre Dame	9-0-1	Ara Parseghian
	(AP, UP, FW, NF-T)		
	Michigan St. (NF-T)	9-0-1	Duffy Daugherty
1967	Southern California	10-1-0	John McKay
1968	Ohio St.	10-0-0	Woody Hayes
1969	Texas	11-0-0	Darrell Royal
1970	Nebraska (AP, FW)	11-0-1	Bob Devaney
	Texas (UP, NF-T),	10-1-0	Darrell Royal
	Ohio St. (NF-T)	9-1-0	Woody Hayes
1971	Nebraska	13-0-0	Bob Devaney
1972	Southern California	12-0-0	John McKay

1973	Notre Dame (AP, FW, NF)	11-0-0	Ara Parseghian
	Alabama (UP)	11-1-0	Bear Bryant
1974	Oklahoma (AP)	11-0-0	Barry Switzer
	Southern California (UP, FW, NF)	10-1-1	John McKay
1975	Oklahoma	11-1-0	Barry Switzer
1976	Pittsburgh	12-0-0	Johnny Majors
1977	Notre Dame	11-1-0	Dan Devine
1978	Alabama (AP, FW, NF)	11-1-0	Bear Bryant
	Southern California (UP)	12-1-0	John Robinson
1979	Alabama	12-0-0	Bear Bryant
1980	Georgia	12-0-0	Vince Dooley
1981	Clemson	12-0-0	Danny Ford
1982	Penn St.	11-1-0	Joe Paterno
1983	Miami (FL)	11-1-0	H. Schnellenberger
1984	BYU	13-0-0	LaVell Edwards
1985	Oklahoma	11-1-0	Barry Switzer
1986	Penn St.	12-0-0	Joe Paterno
1987	Miami (FL)	12-0-0	Jimmy Johnson
1988	Notre Dame	12-0-0	Lou Holtz
1989	Miami (FL)	11-1-0	Dennis Erickson
1990	Colorado (AP, FW, NF)	11-1-1	Bill McCartney
	Georgia Tech (UP)	11-0-1	Bobby Ross
1991	Miami (FL) (AP)	12-0-0	Dennis Erickson
	Washington (USA, FW, NF)	12-0-0	Don James
1992	Alabama	13-0-0	Gene Stallings
1993	Florida St.	12-1-0	Bobby Bowden
1994	Nebraska	13-0-0	Tom Osborne
1995	Nebraska	12-0-0	Tom Osborne
1996	Florida	12-1	Steve Spurrier
1997	Michigan (AP, FW, NF)	12-0	Lloyd Carr
	Nebraska (ESPN/USA)	13-0	Tom Osborne
1998	Tennessee	13-0	Phillip Fulmer
1989	Miami (FL)	11-1-0	Dennis Erickson
1999	Florida St.	12-0	Bobby Bowden

2000	Oklahoma	13-0	Bob Stoops
2001	Miami (FL)	12-0	Larry Croker
2002	Ohio St.	14-0	Jim Tressel
2003	Southern Cal. (AP)	12-1	Pete Carroll
	Louisiana St. (ESPN/USA)	13-1	Nick Saban

Σ AF = American Football Coaches Association

Σ AP = Asssociated Press

Σ CF = College Football Researchers Association

Σ Di = Dickenson

Σ Du = Dunkel

Σ FW = Football Writers Association of America

Σ HF = Helms Athletic Foundation

Σ IN = International News Service

Σ Li = Litkenhous

Σ NC = National Championship Foundation

Σ NF = National Football Foundation

Σ UP = United Press/UP International

Σ Wi = Williamson

National Champs since 1933.

Compliments HickokSports.com

Sugar Bowl
Seafood Jambalaya

by Chef Jeff Warner

Shrimp 70/90 Count 1 lb.
Peeled & Deveined
Louisiana Crabmeat 1 lb.
Smoked Sausage 1 lb.
(cut in half moon)
Garlic Chopped 1C
Green Pepper, Diced 2Cs
Celery, Diced 1C
Bay Leaves 2-3
Long Grain Rice (parboiled) 3Cs
Salt To Taste

Louisiana Crawfish Tails 1 lb.

Vegetable Oil 4T
Green Onions 1C

Parsley Chopped 1C
Yellow Onions, Diced 2Cs
Diced Tomatoes, Rotel 1 Can
Dried Thyme 2t
Water (or Seafood Stock 2X) 6Cs
Cajun Seasoning To Taste (Tony's)

Prepare seafood, clean shrimp, pick crabmeat, strain crawfish tails–keeping fat. Sauté sausage and oil for about 3-4 minutes. Add parsley, onions, bell pepper, celery and garlic, cook until vegetables are tender. Add diced can tomatoes & seafood (except crabmeat). Cook until shrimp is pink. Add seasoning and rice, stirring constantly. Add stock or water, bring to a boil, turn low cook for 25-30 minutes or until rice is fluffy. Last fold in crabmeat and check to add aeasoning. Garnish with green onions. Enjoy! Yields 15-20 portions.

*And remember, if you're planning on visiting Baton Rouge to watch your favorite team play and would like Chef Jeff Warner to come out and cater your tailgate party at Tiger Stadium, give him a call at (225) 248-9903. Your taste buds will be glad you did!

sport

"The drama of sport is a big part of the drama of life and the scope of that drama is endless."

~Grantland Rice